CASTORLAND

French Refugees
in the Western Adirondacks
1793 - 1814

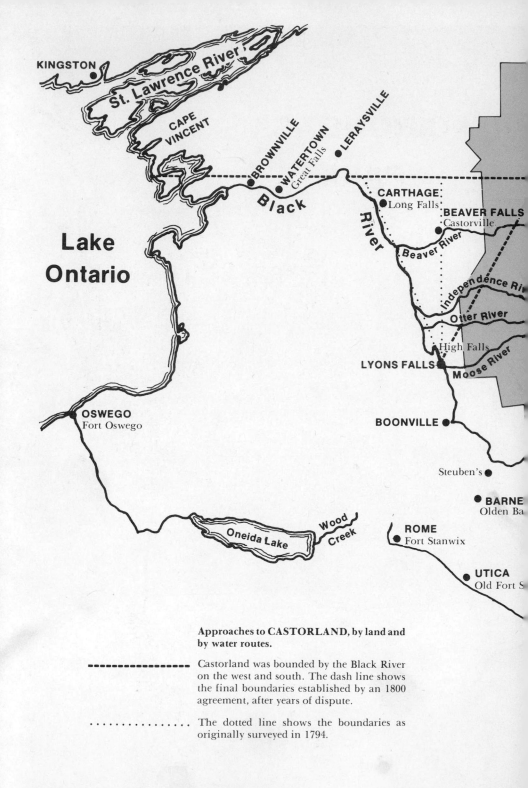

KINGSTON

St. Lawrence River

CAPE VINCENT

Lake Ontario

BROWNVILLE

WATERTOWN
Great Falls

LERAYSVILLE

Black

River

CARTHAGE
Long Falls

BEAVER FALLS
Castorville

Beaver River

Independence Ri

Otter River

High Falls

LYONS FALLS

Moose River

OSWEGO
Fort Oswego

BOONVILLE

Steuben's

BARNE
Olden Ba

Wood Creek

Oneida Lake

ROME
Fort Stanwix

UTICA
Old Fort S

Approaches to CASTORLAND, by land and by water routes.

▬▬▬▬▬▬▬▬▬ Castorland was bounded by the Black River on the west and south. The dash line shows the final boundaries established by an 1800 agreement, after years of dispute.

· · · · · · · · · · · The dotted line shows the boundaries as originally surveyed in 1794.

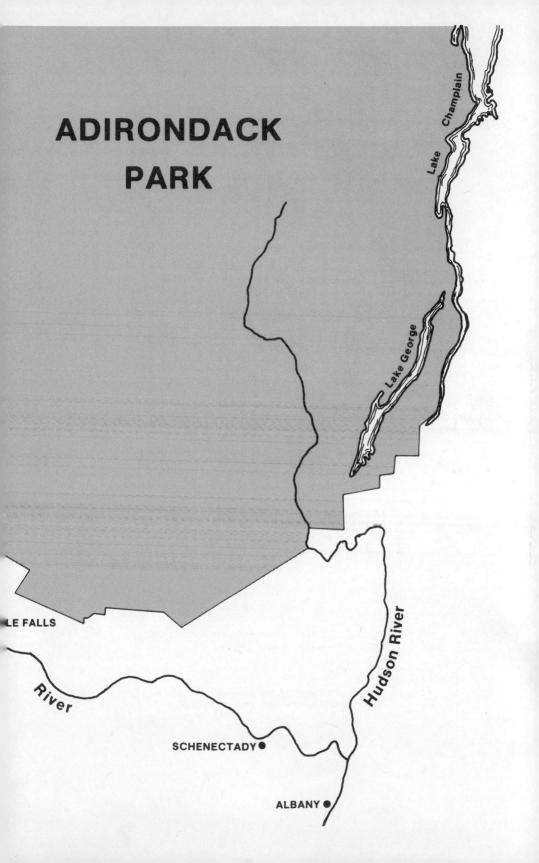

ADIRONDACK
PARK

Lake Champlain

Lake George

LE FALLS

River

Hudson River

SCHENECTADY ●

ALBANY ●

Plans for the First Castorland Establishment were two log cabins, joined by a covered gallery, overlooking the Black River and facing the High Falls (now Lyons Falls).

Sketch is from the original Castorland Manuscript.

CASTORLAND

French Refugees
in the Western Adirondacks
1793 - 1814

By

Edith Pilcher

HARBOR HILL BOOKS
Harrison, New York
1985

Library of Congress Cataloging in Publication Data

Pilcher, Edith, 1928–
    Castorland : French refugees in the western
Adirondacks, 1793–1814.

    Bibliography: p.
    Includes index.
    1. Castorland (N.Y.)—History.   2. French—New York
(State)—Castorland—History. I. Title.
F129.C3P54 1985   974.7'59   85-5456
ISBN 0-916346-55-2

Harbor Hill Books, P.O. Box 407, Harrison, N.Y. 10528

Dr. Franklin B. Hough (1822-1885)

Teacher, Physician, Geologist, Botanist, Historian, Meteorologist, Archeologist, Statistician, Forester and Conservationist: his broad scholarship was so diversified that it transcends easy classification.

This book is dedicated to the memory of Dr. Hough. His unpublished translation of the *Journal of Castorland* and many of his other books and notes provided the main basis for this work. Many of his accomplishments in the historical field have been relatively neglected; it was his hope and is also mine that the true history of Castorland should finally become known and should attract the interest and attention which it so deserves.

Above portrait: Painted by Michael De Santis in 1935. It was presented to Union College, Hough's Alma Mater, in celebration of the 50th Anniversary of the New York State Forest Preserve. (Courtesy of the Union College Portrait Collection)

TABLE OF CONTENTS

Appendices: Several of the following items have been previously published, but are dispersed among different books; three have not been printed before now. Bringing these source materials together under one cover will be useful to those strongly interested in the subject.

LIST OF ILLUSTRATIONS

Maps

Pages and Sketches from Journal of Castorland

Other Illustrations

(Current photos, unless otherwise noted, are by V.E. Pilcher.)

INTRODUCTION

Obscurity and error shroud one of the most romantic, adventurous and heart-breaking episodes in American history — the attempt by French aristocrats to establish a Utopian settlement during the 1790s in the harsh, unmapped wilderness of northern New York.

Castorland, as the settlement was called, was planned as a haven for desperate French émigrés, fleeing their homeland to escape the Reign of Terror. The founders of the colony undertook their task with high hopes, immense enthusiasm and great resourcefulness. Unfortunately, the story of their courageous efforts is practically unknown, although their final failure is common knowledge.

A haze of conflicting and misleading information surrounds the history of this colony's early years because its first and major historian, Dr. Franklin B. Hough, wrote his comprehensive histories of Lewis and Jefferson Counties[1] prior to the discovery of the *Journal of Castorland*. Dr. Hough's works are held in such high repute that they are still the basic regional references. They were first published in 1854 and 1860.

In 1862 the *Journal of Castorland* was discovered by mere chance! The finder was William Appleton, a young Bostonian, who was celebrating his graduation from Harvard by taking a European tour.[2] While in Paris he was browsing among open book stalls along the Seine and came across the *Journal* among materials discarded to be sold for their rag content.[3] Recognizing that the manuscript had some historical value, Appleton bought it for a small sum and, upon his return home the following year, donated it to the Massachusetts Historical Society, where it still remains today.

Written in French, the *Journal* comprises a day-by-day record of the first four years of the Castorland settlement, covering the period from June, 1793 to April, 1797. It is a thick volume of 706 pages, in addition to printed copies of a Prospectus and Constitution, which precede the main text, and an Appendix. Despite preservation efforts, age has taken a toll on the manuscript. The leather binding is now partially disintegrated, and the text is fading. In recent years its contents have been microfilmed to insure their survival.

In 1864, when Dr. Hough learned of the *Journal's* existence, he arranged for a copy to be made for him, so that he could translate and publish it.[4] It must have taken at least a year for the handwritten copy to be completed. Probably it was prepared by Dr. John Appleton who served as Assistant Librarian for the Massachusetts Historical Society at that time. According to his biographical memoir in the *Proceedings of the Society*,[5] Appleton specialized in copying old manuscripts, and was particularly noted for his drawing skills.

The copy is a very fine reproduction of the original: text, sketches, charts, etc. The only major difference is one of page size. Whereas the original was written on lightly-ruled fine quality parchment, approximately 8½ by 11 inches, the copy was written into a legal-size, leatherbound ledger. It comprises 576 pages, in addition to the prefaces.

Both French editions are extraordinarily neat, in fine, highly legible script, with all references carefully footnoted at the bottoms of the pages. Illustrative sketches are reproduced exactly, except that those in the original *Journal* are lightly colored with ink washes, while the copies are only in black and white.

As soon as Dr. Hough received his copy, he set to work translating it into English — a monumental task which occupied three years. His enthusiasm was so great that he was delivering lectures on the subject in Albany and in Lowville long before he had completed the translation.[6]

His English translation is an untidy and unbound collection of legal-size pages, handwritten in a scrawl which is often difficult to decipher. It contains 505 numbered pages, with many additional sheets and small scraps of paper interspersed, containing insertions for footnotes. The entire manuscript totals well over 800 pages.

Hough intended to have this translation printed, and must have been working on it until shortly before his death in 1885. He makes reference to this intention in his revised *History of Lewis County*[7] which was published in 1883. In that volume he had originally intended to include a full, new chapter on Castorland, but later contented himself with a short Appendix on the subject, stating his intention to publish a separate and more complete book:

> "...If printed entire, with accompanying materials, it would make a volume of about the size of this, and we earnestly hope to see it some day in print..."[8]

He described the *Journal*:

> "...as extraordinary in historical interest as its rescue from oblivion has been remarkable."[9]

Unfortunately, it has nearly returned to oblivion! In both his 1860 and his 1883 histories, Hough deleted information he had found to be incorrect, as he added additional facts. However, he failed to direct attention to these changes — a significant departure from his usual practice of careful and extensive footnoting. Therefore, the earlier errors are not obvious unless a reader consults all three volumes and painstakingly notes the discrepancies. The low visibility of his corrections is further compounded by the fact that his earliest editions, rather than the updated 1883 account, have become the standard regional references. They have recently been reprinted and are widely available, while the latter volume is quite scarce and seldom consulted.

Many later writers have based their accounts of the settlement upon Hough's earlier books, thus compounding and perpetuating his errors. Those authors who did know about and consult the *Journal* did not mention this anomaly, although several have summarized the history of Castorland more correctly.

An accurate, detailed history of Castorland has never been published up to this time. The *Journal* is the sole authoritative account of its earliest years, and it tells a fascinating story. It has all the thrills, romance, humor and pathos of a true adventure yarn. It presents a vivid picture of the hardships experienced in the remote and rugged western Adirondacks, which lay — at that time — far beyond the sparsely-settled frontier.

In addition, the *Journal* contains much valuable information on matters of historical, social and scientific importance. There are descriptions of living and traveling conditions in the 1790s (both domestic and Trans-Atlantic) and detailed observations on scenery, settlers, houses, crops, weather and mechanical devices. Detailed notes of botanical, zoological and geological phenomena are sometimes enhanced with precisely drawn sketches.

There are interesting and often amusing comments upon American manners and customs, and some adverse criticism of such famous Americans as Thomas Jefferson, Robert Morris and Philip Schuyler. The Frenchmen were often offended or disappointed by American hospitality or by sharp business dealings or ingratitude, and they recorded their hurt feelings very frankly in the *Journal*.

Three writers contributed entries to the *Journal*. They were the two American Commissioners appointed by the Company — Pierre Pharoux and Simon Desjardins, plus Simon's younger brother, Geoffrey, who acted as the Company Clerk. Sharing diverse responsibilities for the development of the settlement, they were often separated from each other or from their headquarters. Originally they recorded their notes in separate diaries or field books, but all their records were combined and recopied into one official ledger by Geoffrey Desjardins during the winter of 1796-97.

Since all the entries therefore appear in one handwriting, it is not always possible to tell which person wrote a particular section. However, the authorship can often be deduced from its context or location. All three seemed to be accomplished writers, scientists, draftsmen and mechanics. The *Journal* reveals they were extremely adaptable, resourceful and sometimes ingenious as they battled unremittingly against the overwhelming problems of living and traveling in the northern wilderness.

An interesting development can be traced through Dr. Hough's writings on Castorland, as his opinions changed about the ability and character of these men. His original disdain turned to admiration as he came to know them through the *Journal*.

This book has been written in an effort to recount the complete history of Castorland. Information has been culled from every available source and carefully evaluated when discrepancies arose. I hope to focus attention on Dr. Hough's later historical labors, many of which are unpublished but carefully preserved in the State Library at Albany. His translation of the *Journal of Castorland* deserves greater recognition in any listing of the legacy of his many noteworthy achievements.

The original French Manuscript of the *Journal of Castorland* is at the Massachusetts Historical Society, Boston.

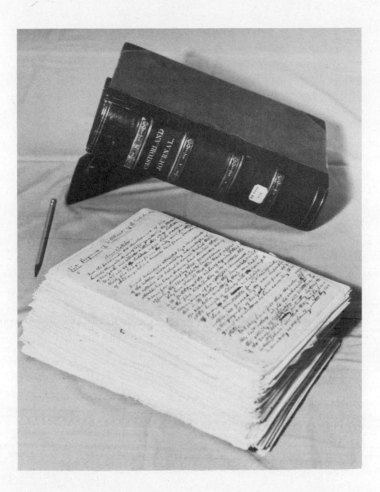

Dr. Hough's bound French transcript and his unbound English translation of the *Journal of Castorland* are at the New York State Library, Albany.

ACKNOWLEDGEMENTS

I am very grateful to the many librarians and historians who facilitated my research — the staffs of:

Union College's Schaffer Library & its Adirondack Research Center

The Manuscript & Special Collections Unit of the New York State Library, Albany

The Massachusetts Historical Society, Boston

The Gould-Hough Museum and Lewis County Historical Society, Lyons Falls, N.Y.

St. Lawrence University Library, Canton, N.Y.

Oneida Historical Society, Utica, N.Y.

Schenectady Historical Society

The following individuals have been especially helpful:

Arlene Hall, Director of the Lewis County Historical Society, furnished numerous leads to references and resource people.

Kenneth Mayhew, Chief Engineer of the Hudson River-Black River Regulating District, supplied maps, photos and general information.

Mary Teal, Lyons Falls Historian, identified for me the precise location of the first Castorland Establishment.

Lewis S. Van Arnam of Beaver Falls, N.Y. kindly showed me the remains of the Castorville mills and supplied photos of the site.

Charles P. Dunham, Jefferson County Historian, provided copies of historical materials, photographs and much regional information.

Lorena Jeresen, President of the Remsen Historical Society, shared her interest and enthusiasm and her typewritten copy of the Hough translation of the *Castorland Journal*.

Major Carl Olsen of the Public Affairs Office at Fort Drum conducted me on a personal tour of the LeRay Mansion and provided official slides of it.

Mrs. K. J. Stanton, Historian of Watertown, N.Y., was extremely informative on materials relating to F.B. Hough and his writings and research.

Mary Ann and Alex Simpson of Pittsford, N.Y. accompanied my husband and me on a two-day paddling and camping trip along the Black River.

Betty and Ken Mathes of Schenectady, N.Y. have revolutionized my world with their proficiency on word-processor and computer.

My appreciation is boundless to those who read my manuscript and contributed helpful suggestions, corrections, recommendations and encouragement. These include Alex Simpson, Murray Heller, Robert Igoe, Warder Cadbury, Lorena Jersen, Arlene Hall, Charles P. Dunham, Emily Williams and Terry Peak.

This work could not have been completed without the assistance of my husband, Ennis. He has served as critic, proof reader, chauffeur, photographer and fellow-paddler. With his help, plus all of those mentioned above, the research for this book has been an adventure and delight.

CHAPTER ONE

Formation of the
Compagnie de New York

Castorland was a small French settlement which struggled for existence in one of the wildest and most remote areas of New York State between 1793 and 1814. It encompassed lands along the Black River, between the Adirondack Mountains and Lake Ontario. This region was still an unmapped wilderness, far beyond the northern frontier, when its first settlers arrived. They were woefully ignorant about the conditions to be faced, but imbued with admirable enthusiasm and determination.

These first arrivals were two resourceful, well-educated aristocrats who were representatives of a French shareholding company. They were sent to prepare the way for an anticipated flood of later French emigrants. The difficulty of their job was sadly under-estimated, and the magnitude of the obstacles confronting them was never understood by their directors in Paris. Only gradually did they discover that they had been misinformed and misled about the precise location of their lands and boundaries, the harshness of the climate and ruggedness of the terrain, the difficulty of access and the potential for trade and development. Nevertheless, they struggled valiantly to make the best of their situation, enduring incredible hardships.

The *Journal of Castorland* is a poignant record of their hopes and disappointments, their adventures and achievements, and the daily round of labor over the first four years of Castorland's existence. It is summarized in following chapters, along with events which followed, leading eventually to the failure of the enterprise.

With the advantages of hindsight, most historians have claimed that the colony was doomed from its inception. Its founders have been dismissed as incompetent visionaries, deluded by their own wishful thinking. Such universal condemnation arises from the contrast between their original idealistic plans and the actuality of the settlement's final failure.

However, a complete study of the *Journal* yields an entirely different perspective. Contrary to the usual characterization recorded in regional histories, it is clear that Castorland's founders were not mere dupes.

19

It is now possible to understand how reasonable men were led to invest so heavily in such a difficult undertaking. Their initial plans were based upon the soundest information then available about conditions in that part of America. The principle backers of the project were highly-respected businessmen, some of whom had extensive experience with land development in America. Several contemporary European settlements in America were flourishing. The prospects for success all seemed auspicious.

This was the time, shortly after the conclusion of the American Revolution, when new lands were being developed at a tremendous rate. Former crown lands had been appropriated by state governments, and sold to produce revenue. Some were awarded as land bounties to ex-soldiers, in lieu of cash payments for their service. Settlers from the overcrowded farms of New England spearheaded the westward movement in New York State. They followed the Mohawk Valley, spreading gradually to fertile lands north and south of it.

Land speculators bought up large tracts and resold them in smaller lots to eager settlers. Many of this country's most respected citizens were among such speculators; some made sizeable fortunes from such enterprises. European capitalists also invested heavily, including many from Switzerland, the Netherlands and France. Shareholding companies were attractive to both settlers and investors, as these ventures improved their mutual lives and fortunes.

In France, the chaotic conditions during the 1790s particularly encouraged emigration. The years of upheaval which followed the French Revolution threatened the security of all the aristocrats, even those who had favored some limitation of royal authority. Almost all had become alienated by the continuing violence of the street mobs, and by the power struggles and blood baths which followed the imprisonment and subsequent execution of Louis XVI and Marie Antoinette. Most merchants, as well as members of the nobility, were accused of being royalists, and they found themselves in great danger. Thousands were arrested, imprisoned and guillotined; their lands and fortunes were confiscated.

While many helplessly awaited their fate, others sought to escape from France. Unknown dangers seemed far less ominous than the daily horrors confronting them at home. The rigors of an ocean crossing and discomforts of resettlement seemed a small price to pay for the opportunity of life in America.

Utopian schemes of settlement were popular with those who had been educated during the Age of Enlightenment. Satirical writings by Voltaire and Montesquieu had weaned them away from conventional views of government and religion, while Rousseau's romanticized visions of simple, bucolic "back to nature" existence had excited a passion for such imagined peace and security. The French of all classes were tremendously influenced by such writers, and there was general admiration for the new, democratic nation across the ocean which had torn itself free from royal tyranny. It was an inviting location for new communal enterprises.

Another major influence upon the proprietors of Castorland was first-hand information and experience of two Frenchmen who had recently lived and traveled in America. The first was St. Jean de Crèvecoeur, a widely respected author, who had written an immensely popular book entitled *Letters from an American Farmer*.[1] This work gave a very favorable view of life and travels in several states. Crèvecoeur had resided in America for two decades prior to the French Revolution. He had become a naturalized citizen, taken an American wife, and eventually bought and farmed a large estate in the Hudson Valley. Writing in 1782, he had extolled the advantages of immigration to America as a land of great opportunity for everyone:

> "There is no wonder that this country has so many charms, and presents to Europeans so many temptations to remain in it...the variety of our soils, situations, climates, governments, and produce, hath something which must please everybody....
>
> He does not find, as in Europe, a crowded society, where every place is overstocked; he does not feel that perpetual collision of parties, that difficulty of beginning, that contention which oversets so many. There is room for everyone in America...
>
> An European, when he first arrives...very suddenly alters his scale; two hundred miles formerly appeared a very great distance, it is now but a trifle; he no sooner breathes our air than he forms schemes, and embarks in designs he would never have thought of in his own country...Thus Europeans become Americans."[2]

Crèvecoeur later served as French consul in New York City until recalled by the Revolutionary government in 1790. Then relocated in France, he was reputed to be most knowledgeable about conditions in America. He was one of the earliest share buyers in the Castorland association.

The other extremely influential person was James LeRay de Chaumont, son of a prominent French merchant who had lent vast sums to assist the American Revolution. The younger LeRay lived in the United States for five years, 1785-1790, attempting to recover the money which the new republic owed to his father. He was personally acquainted with many influential Americans. Benjamin Franklin was a longtime family friend. He also became associated with Gouverneur Morris and William Constable, both of whom were heavily involved in purchase and development of American lands. LeRay, himself, invested in some lands, including Cooperstown, which was just starting to prosper spectacularly. Also during this period, he became an American citizen and married Grace Coxe of New Jersey.

William Constable was a prominent American land speculator, well known in Adirondack history as the major proprietor of an enormous tract of land in upstate New York known as the Macomb Purchase. It contained nearly four million acres. Like other promoters, Constable sought European investors, as well as American. He went to Europe in 1792, taking advantage of the unsettled conditions in France, to encourage émigré land colonization ventures. His friendship with LeRay facilitated introductions to many potential investors, and his offers attracted considerable interest.

The gullibility of Constable's purchasers is understandable, given the best information then available about the region. The basis for his land sales was Sauthier's Map of New York which had been published in London in 1779. It had been prepared for Major General William Tryon, then Governor of the Province. A flowery inscription entitled it "A Chorographical Map of the Province of New York" and went on to state that it had been compiled from actual surveys deposited in the Patent Office at New York. The map was accurate about populated areas, and certainly useful for military purposes, but it was very vague about the upstate regions pertinent to the land sales.

The Black River was not shown on Sauthier's Map, but Constable had drawn in its supposed course on the basis of information he had derived from the Surveyor-General of New York State. According to this representation, the river ran directly west into Lake Ontario from a site called "the high falls." (Today this same site is known as Lyons Falls.) In reality, the river rises in the southern Adirondacks north of Utica, and flows northerly from the falls for about fifty miles before turning, in a great loop, toward the west. (See frontispiece map.)

At that time, no one knew that the map was grossly inaccurate. Constable was known as a persuasive talker, but a man of honor; his deceit was not intentional.

When LeRay introduced Constable to his brother-in-law, Pierre Chassanis, intense interest developed in forming a settlement for émigrés in northern New York. For this purpose Chassanis organized the Compagnie de New York and contracted with Constable on August 31, 1792, for the purchase of 630,000 acres. However, he was forced to renegotiate the agreement in April of 1793 for an area of

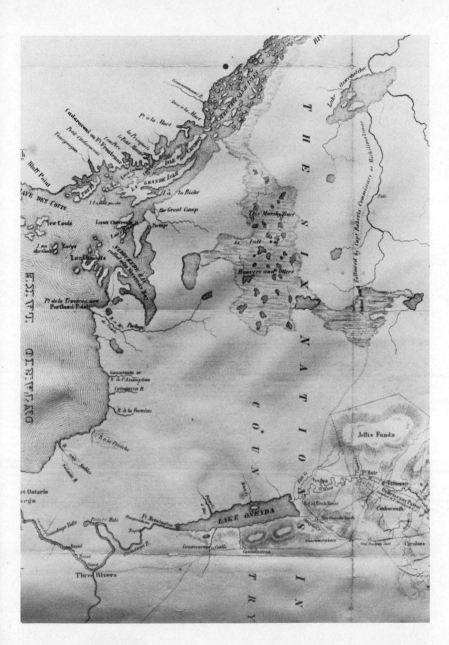

The northern section of Sauthier's 1779 Map of New York, published in London, was the basis for William Constable's land sales. Constable had drawn in the reported course of the Black River as a straight line from "the high falls" flowing east to west into Lake Ontario. The actual course varied considerably (see front map and page 75).

only 210,000 acres, after it became clear that the number of share buyers would be far below the level originally anticipated. Constable promised to donate an additional 10,500 acres to be used for roads, canals and other public improvements which would aid development.

Land speculation was a profitable business. Constable had purchased his tract for eightpence an acre (equivalent to 20 cents) and sold it to Chassanis and Company at 50 cents per acre.[3] The Company's first shareholders bought at $1.48 per acre,[4] and they expected to double their investment within a short period. It seemed obvious that land prices would rise rapidly once development got underway.

Sauthier's map contained a descriptive note pertaining to this region:

"This marshy tract is full of beavers and otters"

This notation gave rise to the name "Castorland" for the prospective settlement, since "castor" is French for "beaver."

According to the terms of the sale, the Black River was to form the southern boundary of the tract, and Lake Ontario its western boundary. The area was supposed to be roughly rectangular in shape, with the northern and eastern boundaries defined by straight lines. Constable's map showed the river entering the lake far south of its true course; this crucial error was not discovered until two years later. It caused enormous confusion and many problems which had to be resolved by litigation.

However, at the outset, the leaders of the new Company were happy in their ignorance. They optimistically issued a *Program of Settlement* and a *Prospectus* that were almost irresistible! (See Appendices I and II.) A plan was projected for an ideal settlement in which prosperity was practically guaranteed from harvests of natural materials and from trade; there was no mention of the labor and hardships inherent in such an enterprise.

Readers of today will be amused by the flowery and romantic form of expression which was typical of writings during that period. The Introduction to the *Prospectus* begins:

"The Association of which we are about to offer the Plan, will doubtless attract the notice of the Fathers of Families, as everything desireable in the way of solidity and advantage will be found united in this Enterprise. Its success can not be doubted, since it is based upon lands, the cultivation of which it at once offers to the Proprietors of these domains, alike important for their extent and fertility..."[5]

A long "Topographical Account" follows, organized into sections,

DESCRIPTION
TOPOGRAPHIQUE
DE ~~SIX~~ CENTS MILLE ACRES DE TERRES
DANS L'AMÉRIQUE SEPTENTRIONALE,

Mises en vente *par ~~la Compagnie de Plan...~~*

PROSPECTUS.

Le Bureau de la Compagnie eft à Paris, rue de la
Juffienne, n°. 20.

1792.

The Title Page of the Prospectus, printed in Paris in 1792 and bound with the original manuscript, shows an alteration made in 1793. As printed, it envisioned a purchase of 600,000 acres; a handwritten revision to 200,000 acres reflects the vast reduction of the land included in the renegotiated sale.

which gives the impression of being based upon impeccable sources. Carefully annotated footnotes cite references in such learned publications as the *National American Gazette*, *The Annals of Agriculture*, *American Geography* and *The American Spectator*. Apparently its authors were unable to comprehend the relatively immense size of New York State, the problems posed by traveling great distances through undeveloped lands, and the diversity of climatic conditions within its borders. They assumed that descriptions of any part of the State applied specifically to their domains.

Samples from the *Prospectus* best provide the flavor of this document, and the contrast between concept and reality:

> **"Location**:
> Thirty five leagues eastward from the Concession, is situated the city and port of Albany, where vessels land from Europe...Lake Ontario... offers the finest resources for commerce and fisheries..."[6]

Lacking any concept of the tremendous difficulties of transportation between Albany and Lake Ontario, they seemed to assume that arrival at the former was practically equivalent to smooth sailing on the latter. They did not yet know that Lake Ontario would be totally inaccessible to most of their lands.

> **"Productions**:
> ...the soil varies considerably, but we may determine its quality by the different kinds of trees that are found, and from the vigor of their growth, which is such, that the surface of the earth is covered with very streight *(sic)* trees, eighty to a hundred, and two hundred feet high...
> The wild Cherry tree, very valuable for joinery and cabinet work, is there found very common and of the finest quality...
> The Hickory also found there...and its ashes are very suitable for making potash...
> Upon the highlands we find Pines of various species, and especially the White Pine whose majestic appearance strikes the beholder...
> In parts less elevated...we there observe especially the Sugar Maple, so interesting to the cultivator...The extraction of the Juice requires very little expense..."[7]

Extensive descriptions were devoted to the rich harvests anticipated from maple sugar, grains, fruits, vegetables, flax, hemp and particularly ginseng. Large profits were also expected from the sale of furs, timber and potash.

> **"Clearing**:
> Everyone knows that in America, they do not uproot the trees to clear and cultivate new lands. It is customary to cut them down and then burn whatever is not reserved for building timbers and carpenter's

work... From the ashes they make potash, which sells for about enough to pay the cost of clearing...

The first years they admit the harrow among the stubble...their stumps rot away in a few years..."[8]

They did not envision the enormous effort required to cut down the trees, nor did they consider whether an ample supply of labor would be available. They were also ignorant of the dangers and damage caused by fires in clearing fields by burning.

"Climate:
...The salubrity of the climate and the fertility of the soil are admirable...They never there experience those excessive heats which in other parts of America follow the spring rains and occasion sickness...[in winter] benificent (sic) snow, which uniformly covers the ground in this season, protects the grain, fertilizes the earth, and assures to the husbandman abundant harvests..."[9]

Actually, this particular region is renowned for the most severe climate in all of New York State! It bears the brunt of storms blowing off Lake Ontario, and it is noted for the most rainfall, the deepest snowfalls, and the coldest winter temperatures (40° below zero is common). Spring comes late and winter starts early in this region; naturally, it has a very short growing season.

"Population:
It is not surprising that a country so rich in all the gifts of Nature, and so well calculated to satisfy every human want, should attract industry and population, so that each year is marked by a rapid progress. The visible increase of the State of New York, and especially of Montgomery County...will ere long animate our lands..."[10]

They assumed that proximity to the Mohawk Valley and to Lake Ontario indicated easy communication. In fact, they were so far from populated areas that mere survival was a constant struggle. Even after a road was constructed, at great cost and effort, it took at least four days for a horse and wagon to trek the 40 circuitous miles from Castorland to the nearest sources of supply at Old Fort Schuyler. In wet seasons the road was often impassable, due to overflowing streams and swamps.

"Goverment and Religion:
...Justice is everywhere administered equally. The laws are founded upon Liberty and Toleration, and the respect which the Americans pay to all Religions is the first pledge of Manners, from whence comes that spirit of gentleness and benevolence which characterizes them."[11]

Their view of American manners soured very quickly after they obtained some first-hand experience here!

27

They assumed that the Black River would be navigable throughout its length, providing easy access from interior lands to Lake Ontario and to the St. Lawrence River, the latter providing an alternate route to an Atlantic port. In fact, insurmountable waterfalls at several locations prevented navigation from the lake, a cruel blow to their expectation of easy transport.

Having thus convinced themselves that opportunities were unlimited, they devised a "Program of Colonization" which was an elaborate plan for transporting the French manorial system to Castorland with certain idealized provisions linking private and public ownership of land. As envisioned in the *First Program of Settlement*:

"...the value of this vast estate might be enhanced by the activity of cultivation and settlement, if the proprietors were to become mutually interested in their own labors, and that they might become, in some way, as one family, united by common interests and common wants..."[13]

In order to maintain this "central unity of interest,"[14] one-half of the property was intended to remain in common ownership until 1814, while the other half was being developed. Initially, therefore, each share was to consist of 50 acres, with an additional 50 acres to be allocated after 21 years had elapsed (presumably, by then, its value would be greatly enhanced). In addition, each share included two lots in each of the two planned cities, with a similar provision of immediate and delayed allocation.

The two cities were intended to serve as centers of culture and trade, and each was planned in great detail. One was to be a port, called "Basle," located on or near Lake Ontario. The second, designated "Castorville," was to be located in the interior. 2,000 acres were allocated to each city, and, without any concern for topography, locations were established for central markets, schools, churches, and lots designated for artisans' workshops and for residences.

There were elaborate schemes for equalizing the value of all shares. Lot values were determined by proximity to the cities' centers. Contrary to reason, it was assumed that all of the land would be capable of cultivation, and equally attractive. No share would contain land which had no usage or value!

Copy of a Share of Castorland Stock (courtesy of Charles P. Dunham, Jefferson County Historian).

A Constitution was adopted which stipulated elaborate operating procedures to foster a combination of private enterprise and communal advancement. The Company was to be governed by a Director (Pierre Chassanis) and four Commissioners in Paris (initially these were Guyot, Guinot, Maillot and la Chaume, all of whom were merchants,) while two other Commissioners (Pierre Pharoux and Simon Desjardins) were to reside in America and oversee the Company affairs there.

While 100,000 acres therefore were to be held communally for 21 years before being divided among the stockholders, another 100,000 were to be apportioned as rapidly as possible after completion of a survey and a map. It was assumed that such a map would be prepared quickly, but in order to further encourage rapid development from the start, an exception was made for those who took up early residence in America. They were to be allowed to choose their land prior to completion of the survey, provided that each choice did not contain more than ten lots and not more than 2,000 feet of frontage upon navigable waterways. Additional acreage was to be sold to generate income for land development.

2,000 shares were sold at the start of the enterprise; there were over 40 shareholders. Some planned to emigrate as soon as possible, but others bought mainly for speculation, intending to remain in France. The largest number of shares were purchased by Jean-Baptiste Mesnard (370 shares), Jean-Nicholas Livry (300), Pierre Chassanis (204), Etienne Guinot (132), James LeRay de Chaumont (100) and Antoine-Francois Charpentier (100). Of these five, only Chassanis and LeRay played significant roles in the later history of the settlement. The American Commissioners, Desjardins and Pharoux, held 60 and 25 shares, respectively. St. Jean de Crèvecoeur was listed third among the signers of the Constitution, although he held only ten shares.

During violent street riots which followed the assassination of Marat, as Robespierre was taking over control of the government, the Constitution of the Compagnie de New York was formally adopted. Its founding members met at Chassanis' quarters in Paris for this purpose, on June 28, 1793. 41 shareholders, or their legal representatives, solemnly signed the Constitution; the list of signatories includes the number of shares each one owned.

Thus Castorland was launched — amid fears for the Old World and high hopes for the New.

CHAPTER TWO

1793 — Voyage to America
and First Explorations

Entries in the *Journal of Castorland* began on July 1, 1793 with an account of business details preparing for the trip to America by the two newly appointed American Commissioners.

Surprisingly little information is available about these men who were to occupy such important positions in the formation of the Castorland colony. Pierre Pharoux was the younger of the two, and had already achieved a reputation as a brilliant architect and engineer and some experience as a land surveyor. His salary was fixed at $600 annually.

Simon Desjardins received no pay, apparently of his own choice. He was a wealthy man of broad experience and abilities who had been prominent at the royal court. He had served as Chamberlain to Louis XVI, and his wife had been a maid-of-honor to the Queen.[1]

The responsibilities of the two American Commissioners had been defined by the Company's constitution. Their major tasks were to verify the property's boundaries; direct a survey and division of the land into lots of 50 acres each; erect houses, stores and mills; build necessary roads and obtain stock and provisions to assist forthcoming settlers. In addition they were to arrange land leases and sales, record all business transactions, keep a journal and report on all matters to the Director and four other Commissioners in Paris.

After their appointment, Pharoux and Desjardins lost no time in setting forth for America. They left France within a few days, accompanied by Desjardins' wife and two children, two servants and his younger brother, Geoffrey.

They embarked at Le Havre on July 8th on the American sailing ship *Liberty*. The vessel was badly overcrowded, with forty passengers crammed into accommodations they considered barely adequate for twelve. The cross-Atlantic trip took two months, with time passing very tediously, according to the *Journal*. There were bouts of seasickness, complaints about the quantity and quality of food and drink, and many petty annoyances from fellow passengers, some of whom they described in amusing, if disparaging, terms:

"During this period, characters developed themselves, and when once displayed, no further pains were taken to keep up a mask of appearances...We had a merchant, with a *comédienne* from Havre, the latter having thought it proper to leave behind her, a husband, some children and some creditors; a miniature portrait painter with his dear 'friend,' formerly a chambermaid at Havre; and an English *Chevalier d'industrie*, with his pretended wife and niece, both lately *citoyennes* of the Hotel d' Angleterre, and not over modest frequenters of the Palais Royal. But the most boisterous party, was that of Baucel, the litigator, with his wife and bawling family of four children, the youngest at the breast...

The *Comé*dienne, professing to be jealous of an élégante of the Cape, who was on board, thought proper to court a piece of high tragedy, and poisoned herself by swallowing a vial of mercury...but was saved by the timely administration of a dose of oil...

The wisest of the company were six young persons, who amidst these disordered scenes, behaved themselves with a propriety that would have done credit to those older..."[2]

Scientific observations were interspersed among other notations in the *Journal*; entries displayed a naturalist's interest in tropical fish and phosphorescent seas.

Highlights of the voyage included three dangerous encounters with British ships. Because France and Britain were at war, their naval vessels often stopped neutral ships and impressed enemy citizens. Therefore, all aboard the *Liberty* were alarmed when a British "corsair," disguised under the French flag, stopped their ship off Bordeaux. After checking their papers, however, the captain permitted them to continue the voyage. They were menaced by a second British ship in the West Indies, but were able to dodge away east of the islands and avoid further detection by steering clear of all main shipping lanes.

As they approached the American coast, navigational errors nearly caused a disaster. The captain had calculated that they were still 80 miles off shore, when, in fact, they were fast approaching land at night, under full sail, with the captain and most of the crew asleep. Pharoux happened to climb the shrouds at a propitious time, and it was he who detected the breakers upon the New Jersey shore and alerted fellow passengers on deck. They managed to change course in the nick of time, saved only by extremely quick action and a high tide.

The next morning, as they entered New York harbor, they had to dodge another British ship, aided by a rain shower which obscured visibility. Finally arriving on September 7th, they were delighted with their first views of New York:

A view of Battery Park in New York from the Hudson River, about 1793, from an original engraving by Archibald Robinson.

Another early view of New York Harbor by J. Milbert.

"On the approach of evening, the country presented a striking and picturesque landscape, and upon passing the Narrows, the City of New York, illuminated by its reflections, was displayed to our view, but the tide being low, we were forced to drop anchor in the bay. The barking of dogs, and the noises that came from the shore, struck our ears most agreeably, after having been becalmed for two months in the solitudes of the ocean.

September 8: In the morning we enjoyed a magnificent view of the roadsted of New York, and of the city located at the point of the island formed by the North and the East Rivers. We breakfasted with delight upon fresh bread and butter, and with coffee which they had taken to the vessel . . ."[3]

When the ship finally landed, the Desjardins were dismayed to find that no suitable lodgings were available for them in New York because the city was overflowing with Philadelphians who had fled an epidemic at home, and with 4,000 French refugees who had escaped a slave uprising on the island of St. Domingo. The family was therefore forced to live upon the ship for another three days while the men hunted for accommodations and transacted some business.

Letters of introduction were delivered to various personages from Crèvecoeur and from Gouverneur Morris, the latter's addressed to George Clinton, the Governor of New York. Morris was then serving as U.S. minister to France.

When Dr. Hough was engaged in translating this part of the *Journal*, he obtained a copy of Morris' letter from the *Clinton Papers*, and inserted its full text (intended for a lengthy footnote) because of its unusual historical interest. It discloses a complexity of motives in writing, ranging from mere civility to public interest to self-interest, since Morris was also involved in various land transactions with Constable in the same region as Castorland. As he was also peripherally involved in Castorland's administration several years later, the letter is of particular interest:

"Letter from Gouverneur Morris to Governor Clinton

24 June, 1793

Dear Sir:

A gentleman of my acquaintance having asked for letters of introduction for the bearer, it has appeared proper that I should take the liberty of presenting him to you. Mr. Desjardins, a gentleman of fortune in this country, has purchased, as I am informed, some lands in the State of New York lying on the Black River and Lake Ontario. He is on his way to take possession and to form settlements. I understand that he will be followed by several of his countrymen and I own to you that this appears to me a desirable circumstance not only for our state in particular but for the United States in general, because it will not only tend to the speedy settlement of our northern region, but placing in the neighborhood of the ancient Canadians, people of the same language, manners and religion, renders them a barrier so much the more useful...in case of a rupture. It is not therefore merely as a compliment of civility that I send this gentleman (who is I am told a sort of chief in the business) to you: but that your penetration and good sense may turn his efforts to the best account for the public. At the same time, I should suppose that it might be useful to open at the public expense the needful roads into that country, although at this distance from the scene, I on that point, can only...conjecture. From my view of things here, I can venture to say however, that any decided step in favor of the French settlers taken by the State, would go far to turn the current of wealth and population about to flow from this Country into the heart of New York. If therefore anything of that sort should happen, I would deem it a favor if you would communicate it to me in such manner that I might disseminate properly the idea.

I am with sincere esteem, and a just remembrance of old times My Dear Sir,

Your Obedient Servant,

Gouverneur Morris

(Clinton Papers, No. 6167)"[4]

Temporary lodgings were finally found in a private home in New York for the Desjardins family, but they spent a week searching unsuccessfully for a house to rent as a permanent residence there. This failure resulted in Desjardins' decision to establish his home in Albany, instead:

"...not withstanding the ennui that a residence in a small city promised us."[5]

Customs officials caused difficulties over the enormous amount of baggage which the family had brought. In addition to many personal belongings, there was a whole houseload of furniture,[6] chests containing a library of 2,000 books and many baskets of wine. Customs attempted to confiscate all of the books and the wine, but the affair was finally settled through the helpful intercession of William Seton, their banker. Desjardins wrote philosophically:

35

"The customs house clerks contented themselves with retaining some bottles for trial, under the universal law of all customs houses in both hemispheres."[7]

Among the many business calls they made in New York, the most important was to James Constable, brother and business agent of William Constable. There they received the dismaying news that work had not yet started on marking the Castorland boundaries, although they had been promised the job would be finished before their arrival. James Constable assured them that the arrangements for the survey were made, and the work would be done the following spring.

They had hoped they could begin their settlement immediately, but now realized this would be impossible. Nevertheless, there was much else to do. Soon after, they set out for Albany, sailing up the Hudson River and recording interesting and amusing observations about scenery, settlements, travel conditions and American manners:

"**September 20**: Left New York for Albany on the sloop *General Schuyler*...

The navigation of the North River is very picturesque, and from New York to the Tappan Zee, the shores are steep rocks. Along New York island there are many houses and country seats agreeably located. The Tappan Zee is a great enlargement of the river, and beyond this we enter the Haverstraw Bay, another considerable enlargement, and then we come in sight of the Highlands.

The strait between these enormous mountains opens a very crooked channel, where in sounding we can scarcely find bottom. We anchored at Verplank's Point as the tide left us, and waited for it in the morning to take us into the defile.

September 21: During the night we had occasion to observe the American Way of making love. The Bennington Merchant courted the New York lady all night, and went out five or six times to get her little glasses of Madeira Wine. Her married sister was present at all this, and laughed heartily at everything, but it greatly offended our French ladies, and prevented them from sleeping. In the morning, these tender lovers, reclined alternately upon each other's breasts, and combed each other's hair, than which nothing could be more amusing to them, but it was extremely shocking to French delicacy. But every country hath its customs, and we advised our ladies to not appear surprised at anything...

The captain charged us twenty shillings, or two dollars and a half, for our meals for four days, and ten shillings for the passage, and we were treated with perfect civility. They sometimes make the passage in 24 hours, and sometimes in eight days, according to the wind."[8]

The "fine appearance" of the City of Albany was a pleasant surprise to them, but they were disappointed in not being able to find a suitable house for rent. However, satisfactory temporary lodgings were arranged for the family, and the men set about their business as rapidly as possible.

Discussions with businessmen and officials, both in New York and now in Albany, helped acquaint them with local conditions and anticipated problems. It was not until this time that they began to perceive the difficulties of frontier living and travel conditions, particularly during the winter. However they resolved to make an exploratory trip to Castorland that fall, hoping to make at least a preliminary map of their new estate. Geoffrey Desjardins was appointed Company Clerk; it was decided that he would remain in Albany during their absence and look after the family, while also taking care of correspondence and business affairs.

In gathering information for their journey, Simon Desjardins and Pharoux called upon a number of prominent people. Although they had brought letters of introduction, they were often disappointed by their reception:

"In France with letters of recommendation to the principal persons of a town, at each place, a stranger would be received with hospitable dinners. But in this country, they take your letter, ask you to sit down, bring a glass of Madeira Wine, and the whole affair is ended. Most of them do not invite you to another visit, much less do they offer you dinners, lodgings, etc., but if you wish to treat them at a tavern, the personages to whom you are addressed, will see you very willingly . . ."[9]

They had other difficulties in adjusting to the American scene. Tradesmen frequently overcharged them, taking advantage of their unfamiliarity with local customs and prices. Such mistreatment enraged them, violating their sense of justice.

On one occasion a liveryman rented them a carriage for two days for a trip to Schenectady, 15 miles away. He quoted a price of one dollar per day, but upon their return insisted that they pay an additional dollar "for the horse"! After futile protest, they paid it grudgingly, recording their resentment in the *Journal*.

Schenectady was the departure point for all westward bound boat trips along the Mohawk River. Several times they traveled the road between the two cities, and this prompted further complaint about American customs:

". . .to escape the expense of hospitality, every good American puts a tavern sign on his door, if located on the public road; and in their inns we sometimes can find neither bread, nor meat, nor a bed."[10]

View of Albany waterfront and Hudson River sloops by J. Milbert.

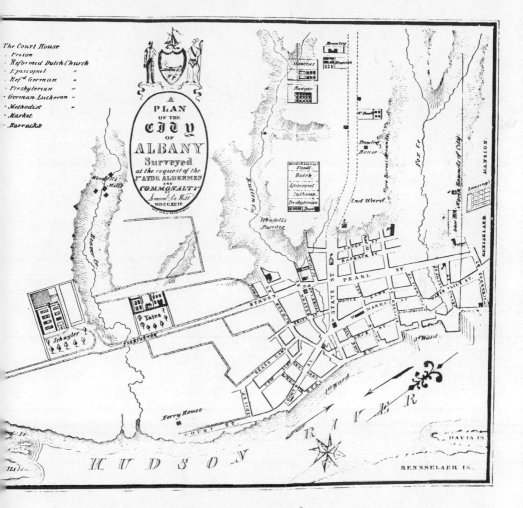

1794 Map of Albany.

They were often unhappy with the beds they did find, as it was customary to change bedsheets only once a week, regardless of their condition or former occupancy.

In the midst of preparations for their trip, they were joined by Marc Isambard Brunel, a fellow passenger from their ocean voyage. A former French naval officer, he was adept at mechanics, engineering, surveying and architecture, in addition to sailing and navigation. Such an extraordinarily capable young man was a valuable addition to their party.

His motives for joining them were not totally philanthropic; he had just fled New York to avoid meeting some former shipmates presently visiting there. He feared prosecution as a naval deserter, since he had incurred their enmity in previous political brawls when he had defended the royalist position. Therefore, it was expedient for him to join the Castorland group temporarily, conserving his own slender resources while enjoying a challenging adventure.[11] (Later in life, Brunel achieved an international reputation, and won an English knighthood for his engineering achievements. However, in 1793 he was merely another young French émigré, barely escaping from France at great risk.)

Before leaving Albany, Pharoux and Desjardins sought more information about the Castorland area from Simeon DeWitt, the Surveyor-General of New York State. He attempted to be helpful but could provide no further maps or details. He did advise them, however, to travel via a water route, through rivers and lakes, to Castorland rather than attempting an approach by land. This was because the nearest roads ended at least 30 miles south of their tract, and he knew little about the terrain beyond, except that it was wilderness.

General Philip Schuyler, whom they also visited, seconded this advice about the water route, and recommended that they employ Major DeZeng as guide and translator during their trip. DeZeng had traversed most of the route during the previous year, and claimed familiarity with the region. He lived in Little Falls, and worked for the Inland Navigation Company (of which Schuyler was President) which was then engaged in constructing a lock for boats around the waterfalls. Schuyler was willing to grant him a leave in order to serve as guide. Although somewhat dubious of his value, the Castorland party agreed to hire him, noting:

"It was better to be cheated by one person than by everybody."[12]

This first journey to Castorland took about three weeks — a major adventure and achievement, considering the distance (300 miles through mostly uninhabited country), and the inaccuracy of their maps.

They started from Schenectady on October 3rd, traveling by boat with hired men rowing and poling the vessel up the Mohawk River for the first leg of the journey — nearly 100 miles from Schenectady to Fort Stanwix (now the city of Rome).

Customarily they would rise before dawn, commence traveling at daylight, and stop for breakfast at eight or nine o'clock. They were eager to proceed as rapidly as possible and use every hour productively, so they would not stop before dark. Unfortunately, they had little sympathy for their hired help, who were not as strongly motivated and were unwilling to keep such a rapid pace. Arguments, quitting, and rehiring new men caused frequent difficulties.

It was on this journey that Desjardins' and Pharoux's strong character and determination were revealed through lengthy entries in the *Journal*. They were well-educated men, gifted with inquiring minds, keen observational powers and great sensitivity to natural beauty. They noted settlements, living conditions, crops, mills, ovens, farming implements, birds, animals, trees and other plants. Observations from the first day of travel along the Mohawk are typical of such records:

"...The banks of the river are adorned with fine farms, upon low and fertile ground called 'bottom lands.' At a short distance beyond, the surface rises into rocky hills, covered with woods. Generally these flats have but little breadth. They have preserved the large trees along the banks, to defend against the ice, the timber and the rocks which the Mohawk brings down in its freshets. The lands are very well cultivated...

We observed everywhere along the banks, pebbles of quartz and other ferruginous rocks, with some of marble and others of gypsum. Not far from this we observed slate rocks...

At four o'clock, we landed to rest our boatmen, who had within the distance of a mile, surmounted six rapids. At this place, we had an opportunity to observe the excellence of these bottom lands. The farm buildings where we landed were well built, and beautifully located, and nearby was a little tannery, proving the industry of its owner. A plow, much resembling that of Normandy, was drawn by three horses, and guided by one man. The soil beautifully sown, was of the richest mould, and very deep. Upon the bank which was adorned with fine trees in excellent preservation we found some superb Capillaire, (a common indigenous fern), already tinted by the autumn frosts. The inhabitants call it 'Maiden's Hair,' and drink an infusion of it in place of tea.

We observed upon many of the goldenrods an insect gall of very considerable size as compared with the plant. These galls were as large as pigeons' eggs, and were of a violet color, contrasting beautifully with the delicate green of the plant, and the golden yellow of its blossoms. So far from injuring its growth, we saw several flowers coming directly out of the galls.

At a very fine farm, two miles beyond, we saw them boiling cider in large kettles. After reducing it one-half in volume, over the fire, they mix with it barley, sassafrass, spruce boughs...and some other ingredient of which we were not informed. This cider, which we drank in a silver goblet, holding at least a pint, was very pleasant. As strangers, they made us pay sixpence a quart, while our boatman, as Americans, were charged only threepence...

Most of the inhabitants above Schenectady thus far, are of Holland origin, and they take great pains to inform you that they are Dutch and not English...''[13]

The French were amazed at how deftly their boatmen poled the batteau over rapids, but it was necessary to hire wagons for two major portages. The first was around Little Falls, where a lock was under construction, and the second was from the Mohawk River at Fort Stanwix (now Rome) to Wood Creek.

Before reaching Fort Stanwix (which had previously been called New Fort Schuyler — causing endless confusion until the name was changed), they passed through the community of Old Fort Schuyler (now Utica). Their first night of camping occurred between the two villages, and they relished the experience:

"...we resolved when night came on, to sleep in the midst of the forest. We accordingly landed, and for the first time, pitched our tent, built a fire, made our beds, and arranged our packets so as to make convenient seats. Having made our cooking arrangements for the evening and morning, we partook of a frugal supper, and slept from nine til six, as sweetly as on the best beds in Europe.''[14]

It was nearly another hundred miles from Fort Stanwix to Oswego on the shores of Lake Ontario. The route traversed Wood Creek to Oneida Lake, then the Oneida and Oswego Rivers. There were a variety of obstacles along the way, including shallows, rocks, rapids and waterfalls. At the beginning of Wood Creek, they were delayed by low water until a miller upstream chose to discharge some from his mill pond, a state of affairs which was most unsatisfactory for travelers. Wood Creek was so shallow, narrow and obstructed with overhanging branches that they sometimes had to hack their way through with axes, while wading to lighten the boat.

On one such occasion, Pharoux and Desjardins explored along the banks while the others were occupied in assisting the boat's passage. Pharoux attempted to wade across one creek which appeared to be shallow, but:

Wood Creek, near Fort Stanwix, was a narrow, tortuous passage
through which boatmen had to hack their way with axes.

"...at once sank waist deep into the mud. If he had not luckily seized a branch...he would have remained stuck in the mire, and would have sunk deeper into the pool, before assistance could have been rendered... [he was] radically cured of his curiosity for traveling in the woods without roads or paths."[15]

They had never seen such a wilderness, nor conceived of such grandeur, and their description was both precise and poetic:

"On every hand it was a fearful solitude. You are stopped, sometimes by impassable swamps, and at other times by heaps of trees that have fallen from age, or have been overturned by storms, and among which an infinite number of insects, and many squirrels find a retreat. On every hand we see the skeletons of trees overgrown with mosses, and in every stage of decay. The Capillaire and other plants and shrubs spring out of these decaying trunks, presenting at once, the images of life and of death."[16]

Contractors had been hired to clear away some of the obstacles which impeded the navigation of Wood Creek. The Castorland group met one work party along their way and were amazed at the primitiveness of their methods:

"...we met the men and oxen of the contractors, busy in removing from the creek some fallen trees...If this contractor, would use a windlass, or only a cable and pulleys fastened to the trees along the bank, he would do thrice the amount of work in half the time: but no mechanical appliances were used, and everything was done by the sheer force of men and animals. They appeared not even to know the use of a ladder, much less of a crane, or of the simplest labor-saving power."[17]

It was a relief to reach Oneida Lake after their slow and tortuous passage through Wood Creek. However, the lake seemed as rough as an ocean after the placidity of river and streams. During the traversal of its 20 mile length, they saw an island on which a French family named Desvatines lived in isolation. The family was away at the time, so they resolved upon a visit during their return trip.

After a difficult descent of the Oswego River, the Castorland party finally reached Fort Oswego at the entrance to Lake Ontario, and here an unexpected problem developed. Oswego was one of several northern forts still held by the British, long after the ending of the Revolutionary War. An American garrison had been sent in 1783 to take over its command, but the British had refused to evacuate on the pretext that debts were still owed to British subjects. Not eager to renew hostilities, the American command had acquiesced, and this situation remained unresolved for 13 years, during which period the forts were under command of British authorities in Canada.

Wood Creek widened as it flowed downstream to its connection with Oneida Lake.

Because Britain and France were at war at that time, the fort's commander was suspicious of Frenchmen who might be spies, and he forbade their passage. DeZeng attempted to negotiate, and finally secured permission for them to proceed if Brunel remained behind as hostage. However, the commander would not permit Brunel within the fort, but insisted that he camp alone across the river. They pretended to agree to this condition, but circumvented it by hiding Brunel under a tarpaulin in the bottom of the boat until they were safely out on Lake Ontario.

There they hoisted a sail to speed their way on that vast inland sea. The boatmen were accustomed only to rivers and small lakes, and they were terrified of the high waves, particularly when they encountered a severe storm. It took all of Brunel's sailing experience to keep the small boat from being swamped, and to navigate eastward when they were out of sight of land.

Several days were consumed in searching for the mouth of the Black River along the eastern shore of the lake. On this portion of the journey Major DeZeng was more liability than asset, because he pretended familiarity with the area, although he knew it no better than they did. They finally found Black River Bay on October 20th, far north of its expected location, and were thrilled to set foot at last upon their own lands:

"Finally, we supped and slept for the first time on our own domains."[18]

However, with winter fast approaching, they could spend less than a week in exploration. Therefore they divided forces, with Desjardins examining the bay area on foot, planning to choose a site for their projected port city, while Pharoux confidently set out with two days' provisions, to travel the river eastward, expecting to reach Baron Steuben's settlement after about 30 miles. They had heard that Steuben was their nearest European neighbor, and wanted to make his aquaintance. Pharoux's trip was blocked by his discovery of the "Great Falls" at what is now Watertown. This was a major disappointment, since they had assumed the river would be navigable throughout their lands, providing easy access to the interior. The falls were an insurmountable obstacle to boats, and the forests and swamps along the shores obstructed land travel.

On October 26th they started their return trip and managed to complete it in two weeks, despite storms and various other difficulties. While Brunel prudently bypassed Fort Oswego on foot, Desjardins and Pharoux had to bribe the fort's commander with gin, gunpowder and lead to prevent being held prisoner. Then retracing their way up

46

the Oswego River, they had to wade in freezing, waist-deep waters to haul the boat over rocks and rapids.

Particularly noteworthy in this account of their journey and in many subsequent adventures is a remarkably matter-of-fact tone when reporting extraordinary hardships, efforts or achievements. Although these Frenchmen were fresh from civilized lives amid the comforts of court, estates and cities, they somehow quickly developed the stamina and skills to cope with wilderness camping and travel in near wintry weather. They seemed to possess an almost religious sense of mission, in which personal comfort and security were of little importance. In these early days they were undaunted by adversity, although they reflected wryly that patience and courage were "useful qualities" in American endeavors. They scarcely mentioned such emotions as hopes and fears during the account of this trip, confining themselves to long, detailed descriptions of events, people and places.

Returning through Lake Oneida, the party visited with the Desvatines family whom they described as a "French Robinson Crusoe."[19] These fellow exiles had fled to America seven years earlier with all of their possessions. A series of unfortunate speculations in land and trade had left them destitute after several years. Finally, they had sold their furniture, retaining only a fine library. Two years previously they had established themselves on an uninhabited island in the middle of Oneida Lake. Their white neighbors would not assist them without payment, but neighboring Indians had helped them survive their first winter there. Despite the care of three young children, Madame Desvatines had labored alongside her husband in building a log cabin, clearing six acres of land and planting vegetables and orchards. After achieving an amazingly fine homestead despite lack of ready cash, they were dispossessed! The State sold a large tract of land to the Roosevelts which included their island, and once again they were forced to start life anew. Mr. Scriba, one of the proprietors of the Roosevelt Patent, offered them a lot in a new community he was establishing on the lakeshore, to be known as New Rotterdam.

At the time the Castorland group visited with them, the Desvatines' log cabin was still unfinished on their new lot, and wintry blasts penetrated the walls so that the place was barely habitable. Despite such hardships, the "wife and children were jovial as cupids."[20] Desjardins and Pharoux felt pity and admiration for them, but Brunel must have experienced even deeper emotions.

A later biographer of Brunel, Richard Beamish, recounts this meeting in such personal, romantic terms that it would seem his information was derived from hearing first-hand recollections:

"During this exploration, a little incident occurred which made a lively impression upon the mind of Brunel, and to which he never afterwards alluded but with emotion...

Children's voices were distinctly audible: 'Viens Papa — Viens Mama, voilà un bateau.' Who shall describe the effects of these simple sounds upon the hearts of exiled travelers as they broke the silence of an American solitude? What visions of home recollections must have been presented to their affections, and with what eager interest they must have sought the dwelling of their expatriated countrymen, may be conceived but cannot be described.

There in the backwoods, was a family who had fled, as they had, from the horrors of the revolution, supporting themselves by the work of their own hands, and indebted to the forbearance and kindly natural instincts of the lawless Indians, for that life and that peace which had been denied to them at home."[21]

When Hough included the above description as a footnote in his translation of the *Castorland Journal*, he noted that the unnamed family must have been the Desvatines at Oneida Lake, although Beamish stated the incident had occurred on the Black River.[22]

Desjardins and Pharoux felt that the Desvatines had been victims of American avarice and greed, and this sympathy, along with some of their own experiences, led to increasing disallusionment with American manners, honesty and common trust. They recounted two examples of poor trust and ingratitude which occurred on their homeward journey:

"...one of Mr. Scriba's carpenters asked passage for payment, as far as Fort Schuyler. We told him we did not want his money, but that since he was sick, and wanted to go home, we would cheerfully take him along. He seemed astonished at our refusing his money...

We soon had occasion to witness another trait of this character in Briton, one of our boatmen. On our return across the lake, he had taken a hard cold, and this had gained upon him on the river. With his half dollar a day all summer, he had bought nothing, and his pantaloons of coarse stuff were badly torn, so that he was in fact nearly naked. M. Brunel had a pair still very good, which he gave him. He was astounded at the word '*give*' and asked him to repeat it several times. Nor would he accept the garment, until in the presence of the two other boatmen, M. Brunel had declared that he *gave* them to him, and that he would never ask anything for them...He accepted the gift, without thanks...nevertheless he afterwards threatened to quit us on the way...."[23]

Because of their interest in seeing more of the country, and hoping to meet Indians who might give them more information about the Castorland area, the party split up before entering Wood

Creek. While Brunel accompanied the boat and baggage, Pharoux and Desjardins walked south from Oneida Lake to visit an Indian friend of Desvatines, Schenando, who accommodated them cordially in his own cabin. There they were astonished to meet an old French trapper whom they did not recognize as non-Indian until he spoke to them. He had been kidnapped and adopted by Indians 40 years earlier, and had adapted to their way of life and dress.

At nearby Oneida Castle, some State officials, including Simeon DeWitt, were in the area, attempting to negotiate a land sale treaty with the Oneida Indians. He gave them some food and news of the Desjardins family, who had moved from lodgings to a house in Albany.

The two Commissioners then traveled eastward to Fort Schuyler to unite with Brunel and the rest of their party. Staying at Post's Inn there, they met Gerrit Boon and several others who proved to be prospective neighbors. Boon was a Dutch land developer employed by the Holland Land Company and was in the process of establishing a community at Olden Barneveld, five miles south of Steuben's, and fifteen miles north of Fort Schuyler. He was able to inform them about roads in the area.

Then resuming their journey homewards, down the Mohawk River, they came again to Little Falls. DeZeng, as administrator of the construction project on the new locks, was proud to show them around. As engineers, Pharoux and Brunel were both familiar with the construction of French canals and locks, and they were appalled at the American project:

> "It would scarcely be believed in Europe, that in building a navigable canal, they had laid up dry walls, of broken stone, five or six feet high, without any widening at the base, and with only six feet of sandy soil on the outside...After blasting the rock here and there, without any plan or system, so that the excavation looks like a huge trough, they have built the locks of carpenters' work, and the spaces between the cheeks of the locks and the rock, are filled after General Schuyler's economical style, with broken masses of loose rock, without mortar, for cement is an article unknown in these parts..."[24]

They discussed the project's shortcomings with DeZeng, who told them:

> "...he was only charged with carrying out the views of General Schuyler, the President of the Company, who did not like to be contradicted in his opinions, and drew a thousand pounds a year as the head of the enterprise. This did not keep us from remarking, that these thousand pounds might have been better spent in paying an European engineer,

and that the country should know better than to give such a sum uselessly to one of the richest citizens of the State, by whom the confidence of the company should be borne as an honorary office...''[25]

These honest, but tactless, remarks must have been repeated to the General, for the Frenchmen later perceived a coolness to them from that personage, and attributed it to this conversation.

After another day proceeding down the river, they visited with Colonel Fisher of Fort Plain, who received them with warm hospitality. In their description of this visit, they reveal an ability to laugh at themselves as well as others:

> "The table was better served than American suppers generally are, as they usually consist of only bread, butter, etc. We did honor to it with our appetite, and one might have admired the way we disposed of the turkey, fowl and fresh pork. The Colonel begged our permission to eat with his hat on, as he had been scalped by the Indians in the late war...After supper he conducted us to an extremely neat chamber, furnished with two good beds, in which we rested with all the more pleasure, as for more than a month, we had slept in our blankets on the ground."[26]

On the next morning, Colonel Fisher showed his guests around his farm, and they took great interest in his barn and in innovative arrangements for winnowing and storing the wheat. Long technical descriptions with mechanical details are included in the *Journal*.

The party finally reached Albany again on November 9th, and found their affairs there in good order. The Desjardins family was comfortably located in a rented house. One might presume that the men were entitled to a rest and sojourn with the family after such a long demanding trip. However, they were indefatigable in pursuing the interests of the Company.

After only three days in Albany, Desjardins and Pharoux set out on a business trip to Philadelphia and New York, with Brunel accompanying them. En route, on a Hudson River sloop, they encountered William Inman who owned the tract of land adjacent to their own at the High Falls on the Black River. He showed them a map of the area which was much more accurate and detailed than their own, giving them their first inkling of the true course of the Black River. Also, he claimed ownership of the waterfall, which they had assumed would be on their own property.[27] Because of the importance of water power for mill operations, this too was disturbing news, leading them to develop considerable apprehension over their boundaries. They did not immediately accept Inman's claim, but courteously asked to copy his map and confirm the information the

50

following year. The problem could not be resolved until they were able to make their own survey.

After conducting some business in New York, they traveled to Philadelphia by a combination of boat and stage coach, the latter a new vehicle to them which they found uncomfortable, dangerous and lacking in civilized services:

"Started at two in the morning. It was very dark, but fortunately the horses knew the road, and we passed many small bridges without railings, although scarcely wider than the track of our coach, and this without attention of the driver, who used little besides his whip. These stages...are as hard to ride in as a cart, and are without springs. They are closed with leather curtains, fastened to the rods that support the roof, so that they keep out the cold, the rain, the dust and the wind. The roof is so low, that when it jolts, if you are a little tall, your head is thrown violently against the boards of which it is formed. There is only a footrope, which exposes ladies and persons unaccustomed to mounting a carriage, to risk of accident. The price is four cents a mile...They will not answer for the baggage, and each one puts his sack or little trunk under his feet, and is obliged to take it out and replace it at each change of coach, and at each lodging place, as the conductor, who according to the custom of the country receives nothing for drink, attends strictly to his own business, which is that of taking through his stage..."[28]

In Philadelphia they presented letters of introduction to national officials at the Capital. Senator Robert Morris, a well known financier and land speculator received them coldly — possibly because he perceived Castorland as a rival to a French colony he was sponsoring at Asylum in Pennsylvania. Thomas Jefferson was also less cordial than they expected:

"...Mr. Robert Morris...received us without ceremony, seeing that he could gain nothing from us. Mr. Jefferson, Minister of Foreign Affairs, did not even offer us seats, but we took the liberty of helping ourselves. He asked us if there were many French intending to come to America. We replied, that according to present appearances, many of the best families would come before long, to seek in this country the tranquility of true liberty. At this he made a grimace that amused us greatly, and all the more so because we knew his hatred for foreigners, which he did not even disguise in his *Notes on Virginia*. Europeans are distrusted here... In short, the Americans of all ranks and conditions look upon us as children do, when busy in eating something good, and others come with whom they see they must divide the honeycomb. That 'the sun shines for all', is not the motto of this country. To Monopolize all, Concentrate all, — everything for self, nothing for others — such is the governing principle of *this nation*. We were so rebuffed by these American receptions, that we resolved, (although perhaps we should not have

51

done...) not to deliver the President a letter of recommendation which the American ambassador had given us..."[29]

Such an anti-French view of Jefferson may be perplexing, as our history is full of references to his pro-French proclivities. It can be explained by the fact that American officials were more sympathetic to the French Revolutionary Government than to the refugees from it. They were having great difficulty at that time in maintaining their neutrality during the war between Britain and France. Representatives of the new French republic were overly sensitive to imagined slights, and they were offended by the sympathetic reception which monarchist émigrés often received from Americans. They had protested the welcoming of such émigrés by American officials. The American dilemma is clearly stated in a letter by George Washington to Alexander Hamilton, written in reference to a visit by Tallyrand:

> "...I do not hesitate to declare that I find it difficult to hit upon a line of conduct towards...emigrants that is satisfactory to my own mind... by avoiding what might seem incivility on one hand, or unpleasant political consequences on the other.
>
> I can perceive very clearly that the consequences of receiving these characters into the public rooms will be driving the French Minister from them..."[30]

After such disappointing receptions, Pharoux and Desjardins could find nothing pleasant about Philadelphia. Accustomed to the gracious streets and buildings of French cities, Pharoux was very critical of the American capital city:

> "A sojourn in Philadelphia appeared to us as sad, as the city is uniform. The famous market, of which travelers have so much to say, has nothing remarkable about it except its length. The city is built in lines, the streets are all at right angles, and everything is so uniform, that it is very embarassing to a stranger. The view of the Delaware is obstructed by dingy and obscure houses whose foundations are laid in the mud of the harbor, so as to shut out of view both the river and the shipping. There is not a public square. The building where Congress meets is a pile of brick, as is also the library, over the door of which they have placed the fine statue of Franklin, like a saint in a niche, so that the beauty of the work can not be seen..."[31]

The harshness of their judgments softened a bit upon later reflection and after visiting with French friends who informed them about recent degrading behavior by some of the French refugees from St. Domingo:

> "...Not withstanding our dislike of the Philadelphians, we agreed that

our dear fellow countrymen had given some occasion for the distrust with which we had been received. In fact...the unfortunate victims who fled hither, had among their number many abandoned wretches...Their conduct has not been such as to edify the Quakers of this country. They had passed much time in gambling and other disorders, so that the Americans who should have distinguished the honest ones among them, took the scum of our nation as the representation of the nation itself."[32]

Back again in New York City, they occupied themselves with business affairs for another ten days. They called upon James Constable again, and upon Nicolas Olive, a French merchant who had just moved to New York and was also a shareholder in the Castorland enterprise. They also visited Baron Steuben, who owned a large tract of land some 20 miles south of Castorland; he received them very hospitably and persuaded them to build their projected road via his settlement, offering to share the expense for their mutual benefit. A warm friendship quickly developed, partially because of their common heritage of European manners and hospitality.

After these affairs were concluded, Pharoux spent the winter in New York, handling some Company business there but mainly engaging in architectural work. He designed a city tavern, public baths and private residences for the Livingston and Harrison families.

Brunel returned to Albany with Desjardins, but did not take any further part in the development of Castorland. Although he remained a good friend, he became fully occupied with his own career, then working on the canal which ultimately connected the Hudson River with Lake Champlain.

When Desjardins and Brunel traveled back to Albany in December, 1793, their experience illustrated the frustrations inherent in sailing upon the commercial Hudson River sloops, particularly in winter. Brunel was unexpectedly delayed, and he missed the boat upon which they had planned to sail together. He then embarked on a later sloop which soon passed the first and arrived in Albany without any difficulty. Meanwhile, Desjardins' boat encountered one problem after another. First it ran aground on some rocks, and had to await a rising tide before getting free. Then it was hampered by ice formations in the river and uncooperative winds, as well as an incompetent captain. After many delays, the captain finally decided to terminate the trip at Hudson, 30 miles south of Albany. The passengers were compelled to complete their journey by land, and Desjardins did not arrive until several days after Brunel.

During their first winter in America, both Desjardins and

Pharoux taught themselves English and achieved sufficient proficiency that they had no further need for interpreters.

So the year 1793 drew to a close, setting a pattern for the following years. The warmer months were used for exploration and settlement, while city business was transacted during the inclement winters.

It took several men to pole a batteau upstream, against the current and over minor rapids.

CHAPTER THREE

1794 — Founding of the Settlement

1794 was the year of truth for the Castorland colonizers. Reality slowly replaced fantasy as they came to grips with the many unanticipated problems, but during this first year their unbounded enthusiasm never failed. They seemed to have no doubts that fair dealing and hard work would overcome all obstacles. Simon Desjardins adopted a military term for the *Journal,* referring to each year's work at Castorland as a separate "campaign." He worked eagerly on preparations for the 1794 campaign all through the preceding winter and spring.

Pharoux and Desjardins petitioned the state legislature for permission, as foreigners, to hold real estate in their own names and also on behalf of Pierre Chassanis, Director of their Company. The right was granted to them but denied to Chassanis, since he was not a resident.

Other major business transactions were time consuming and worrisome. Inadequate financing was a major problem at the outset of the project and throughout the ensuing years. It has been presumed that income would be generated through continuing land sales in France and America, but such optimism proved to be unrealistic. Desjardins was able to raise one significant sum during the spring of 1794 by selling 20,000 acres to Nicolas Olive. Olive was the French merchant who had recently moved to New York and had originally purchased 10 Castorland shares (1,000 acres). His additional purchase now made him one of the largest shareholders. Olive also assisted in other matters involving banking and correspondence, and he opened a store in Albany to simplify their procurement of necessary supplies for the settlement. He promised to establish additional stores later on in Fort Stanwix and in Castorland, itself.

The funds provided by Olive's purchase were used to hire surveyors. First they engaged Benjamin Wright to cut a road through the woods from Steuben's Patent to the High Falls on the Black River. Philip Frey was employed as their Chief Surveyor for the first year and given the major task of confirming Castorland's boundaries and laying out individual lots of 50 acres each within the tract. His assistants were Webster and Cantine who directed parties of unskilled workmen.

Constable's surveyors also started work that spring, although according to the terms of their contract his survey should have been completed prior to the French arrival, with boundaries already marked and mapped. Actually, the two teams worked simultaneously throughout the summer, comparing notes frequently. William Cockburn was head of Constable's team, with Charles C. Brodhead as Chief Assistant.

In April the Desjardins family changed their Albany residence, moving to a larger and more comfortable house. It also served as Company headquarters, and wife, children and servants remained there while the men were away during the major part of the year.

Preliminary arrangements continued for the 1794 campaign. A wagon was purchased and an enormous variety of supplies. They hired a young Frenchman who had emigrated to America with Baron Steuben. He was Jean Baptiste Boussot (referred to always afterwards as "Baptiste") — a skilled woodsman and drover who became their foreman and one of their most faithful and trusted employees.

In the middle of May the Desjardins brothers finally set out for the Black River, with Pharoux planning to join them in June after completing some work with Brunel on the Champlain Canal. From this time on, Geoffrey Desjardins shared key responsibilities, and they worked together on advance arrangements during the trip, hiring laborers and procuring more supplies. Impatient as they were to reach Castorland, and despite the burden of their chores en route, they still found time for scientific observations along the Mohawk:

> "May 18, 1794...I observed along our route, that the rapids were all formed at mouths of creeks, by the stones and gravel, which these streams when swollen and overflowed by the melting of the snows, sweep into the river, where they pile up and form bars. These can not be carried away by the main current of the river, since, as the water subsides, the force of the current is lessened, and soon ceases to move these materials further. The formation of islands is due to the same cause. They begin by rapids, which bring down new deposits of rocks, gravel and sand each year, which gradually heap up to the level of low water, and finally of high water, when plants and acquatic shrubs find root and grow. These form a lodgement for mud and sand, which every freshet brings down, and for these reasons we always find islands at the foot of the rapids of rivers, and below the mouths of creeks. The rapids and islands are always proportioned to the force and volume of the confluent waters.
>
> It is thus with the rapids and islands of the Schoharie, and the East

and West Canada Creeks, the three principal tributaries of the Mohawk, which have also the most considerable islands, and the most difficult rapids. This physical law demonstrated by experience, proves the absurdity of the Commissioners of the Canal Companies, who gravely proposed to dig a passage for bateaux in these rapids...They do not foresee that the cause which formed the rapid continues; that the next spring freshet would fill in their channel, that the rapid would appear again..."[1]

As they proceeded up the river, it was sometimes expeditious for the brothers to separate in order to handle various arrangements. The *Journal* carries separate entries on those occasions.

This year, after reaching Fort Schuyler, they planned to take a different route than on the previous year's journey. They intended to go by land, rather than water, hauling the supplies needed for establishing their settlement.

They had hoped to rent several wagons at Fort Schuyler, but none were available at reasonable prices. Therefore, after buying many provisions, they had to arrange for storage. Only the most essential goods were taken on the first trip.

Finally they set out, headed north toward Castorland, a distance of some 40 miles. Near the half-way point, Baron Steuben's 10,000 acre tract lay in the Adirondack foothills. It was a welcome stopover point. Very crude roads led as far as Steuben's; these were hard to follow, since they were little more than unmarked paths, often inter-sected by other unmarked paths. They were so narrow and uneven that the wagons had great difficulty traversing them and breakdowns and accidents were frequent.

On the first day's travel, a succession of mishaps so delayed the teamsters that finally Desjardins and Baptiste went on alone on foot, leaving the wagoneers behind to make repairs. Desjardins was ill with dysentery and exhausted, so they were looking forward to their arrival at Steuben's, anticipating a warm welcome. It was late evening when they arrived, and at first the servants did not want to admit them, since Steuben was away. Finally they were allowed entrance, but not treated with the deference which Desjardins considered appropriate:

"...The servants, who seeing us on foot, and covered to the chin with mud, did not make haste to receive us. At length the gardener, recollected having seen me in better plight, at the Baron's house in New York... They then invited us in, but said that no one could be allowed to enter the Baron's chamber. They made up a bed in the garret, and proposed that I should sleep with Baptiste, as if we were household domestics. When I asked the gardener whether he slept with the Baron, they saw their error and made apologies. This would have been very diverting to me had I been in good health..."[2]

Baron Steuben

Sketch of Steuben's log cabin.

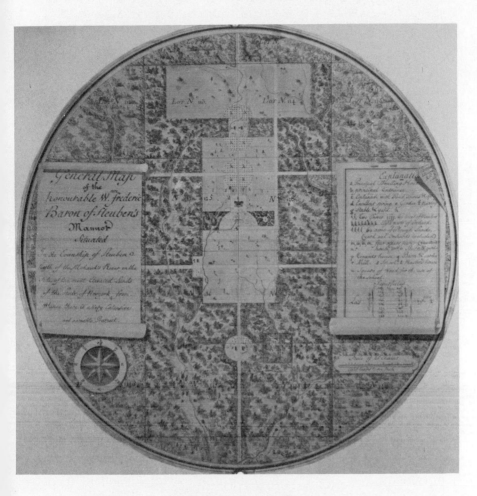

Pharoux's Landscaping Plan for the Steuben Estate.

The original drawing is 20 inches in diameter and is signed by Pharoux in upper right corner of cartouche. (Courtesy of Douglas M. Preston, Director of the Oneida Historical Society).

When the Baron returned a few days later he welcomed them warmly and offered them all the assistance at his disposal.

Work had already started on building a road north from Steuben's but it progressed very slowly. Workmen had to hack their way through 20 miles of wilderness, lay causeways over swamps and detour along streams to places where they could be forded.

Frustrated by the delays, the Frenchmen nevertheless used their time productively. Studying the lands around them, they recorded many botanical and geological observations. Pharoux laid out some landscaping improvements for Steuben, including a pond to assist irrigation. Desjardins designed a machine to aid boats in bypassing rapids.

However, during this interval, Desjardins' main occupation was handling the transportation of their supplies. He finally bought more wagons and oxen and directed construction of a warehouse at Steuben's to serve as a way-station for their goods. The difficulties he encountered were typical of those which plagued them throughout their years at Castorland. Workmen were hard to find, expensive, often troublesome and apt to quit without notice. The roads were alternately filled with dust or mud, both severely impeding travel. Streams were difficult to ford and sometimes were impassable during and after heavy rains. The wagons overturned or broke down frequently and oxen sickened or wandered off, causing frustrating delays. Food and rum had to be rationed strictly in order to last between supply trips; constant supervision was required to prevent workmen from stealing provisions.

Finally Pharoux went ahead· with their team of surveyors to explore the southern part of Castorland, while the Desjardins brothers accompanied their supply wagons, dogging the slow footsteps of the road builders.

June presented a problem new to their experience — blackflies! Those familiar with northern forests are aware of this seasonal plague, but the French were totally unprepared and suffered cruelly along with their work crews, bogged down in the swamps and wilderness where refreshing breezes could not afford relief. Desjardins described their predicament with his usual preciseness:

"Today for the first time, I experienced the torment of gnats, which the Canadians appropriately name 'brulots' (incendiaries!)...This little insect, by thrusting its little proboscis shaped like a dart into the skin, occasioned the most acute itching, followed by a swelling and sometimes by inflammation...This insect no sooner finds you within reach, than it falls upon you with its lances. It is more troublesome than the musketo...'[3]

Because of their discomfort and his impatience to reach Castorland, Desjardins was exasperated with the slowness of the road-cutting, and he complained about the workmen:

"Our men worked with an indifference and a laziness that I have never seen equalled, and of which an European could scarcely form an idea."[4]

Although he admired liberty and equality in principle, it was clear that he was missing the subservience of the lower classes to which he had been accustomed in Europe!

Insects continued to torment them during this interminable stage of road construction, but at least Desjardins recovered some sense of humor despite the discomforts:

"The musketos and brulots defended their natal country most valiantly, and the neighboring marshes furnished recruits in such numbers, that we could scarcely sleep at night."[5]

Meanwhile, Pharoux and his party of surveyors reached the High Falls (now Lyons Falls) on the Black River. There they built a raft and crossed over to their own land where they constructed some temporary bark shelters and started work on a canoe 27 feet long. This involved cutting down a pine tree which had a diameter of four feet and hollowing it out with hand tools. Pharoux carved a small model for the workmen to follow.

The High Falls constituted a drop of 63 feet, and were particularly impressive and beautiful in the spring:

"Above the High Falls, the junction of the Moose and Black Rivers forms a quiet basin, in which the waters are held by a long and very even belt of rock, over which they flow across the whole breadth, in a sheet having a slope of two feet, to the opening of the rocks of the cataract, where they plunge in an impetuous torrent, widening as they descend. The spray of the fall rises continually in a cloud, on which are painted the prismatic colors when the sun shines, and one can see a great rainbow when the fall is viewed from above..."[6]

Their hopes were dashed that the falls would be upon their property, as their own survey measurements confirmed Inman's claim to ownership. This was disappointing as the power would have been very useful for mill operations. There wasn't another suitable site for lumber or grist mills for many miles.

Finally the entire party was reunited at High Falls when the road was completed. It terminated on the western side of the river and a crude raft served as a ferry to their site on the eastern bank. At this time their work crew included 22 men who were divided among the

Sketch of the High Falls (now Lyons Falls) from Haddock's History of Jefferson County (1895 edition).

62

Observations.

Stations. Directions. Distances. _convert le pied et à une chaîne de distance._

1. N. 24° 40' W. 20 chaînes — 0. un petit ruisseau.

	à 4 50	Le pied de la montagne très rapide. La rivière
	à 10 0	à une chaîne et demie de distance.
	à 11 .... *	sur la pente du côteau; environ 60° d'inclinaison
	à 12 .... *	
Détail des 20 chaînes.	à 15 .... "	Le sommet faisant plateau de jeunes chênes
	à 16 80	hemlocks et pins.
	à 20 .... 9.	Tourné à l'angle droit à la rivière. Elle est à cinq chaînes 90 links. pente 60°

333. 2. N. 67° 0' W. 15 chaînes 706. Sur le plateau de la montagne, principalement chênes et pins. bois anciennement brûlés. à 13. On est dans la direction d'une partie du tournant de la rivière.

3. S. 55° 0' W. 8 ...... 13. sur le même plateau. La rivière est à cinq chaînes, quarante links.

4. S. 47° 0' W. 7 ...... 78. même plateau; même bois. La distance à la rivière est de 4 chaînes.

5. S. 28° 0' E. 3 ...... 82. Plateau et bois id. Toujours eau tranquille depuis le camp. La rivière est à 3 chaînes de distance.

6. S. 10° 30' E. 8 ...... 67. Plateau et bois id. à une chaîne demi-pied d'une monticule plus élevée que la montagne. à 2 ...... 30. Le sommet de la monticule. à 7 ...... 0 La rivière est à deux chaînes. 50 links. à 8 ...... 67 La rivière est à 1 chaîne. Côte très escarpée de 70°

7. S. 9° 30' E. 7 ...... * sur le penchant rapide de la hauteur, pins et quelques hemlocks.

Pharoux' survey notes of the course of the Black River from
Hough's French transcript of *Journal*

various essential tasks: surveying, transporting supplies, clearing land, erecting fences and cutting logs for construction of a cabin.

The *Journal* contains a sketch of their initial building plans. (See page 4.) Two cabins were to be constructed, each 32 by 20 feet long, connected by a covered gallery 42 feet long. They were to be placed near the bank, overlooking the river and within sight of the High Falls.

Their next major undertaking was construction of "an American oven in the woods" which enabled them to bake 40 loaves of bread at a time. Their detailed description of this construction was also accompanied by a sketch.

They also included a long description of the balsam tree, which predominated in the surrounding forests. It was an unfamiliar species to the French; they ascribed to it precious qualities for treatment of wounds and for lung and venereal diseases.

The survey, however, was their major interest and predominant task. Their eastern boundary was supposed to be a straight line running north, but they found that the river's meanderings intermixed their lands with Inman's. Their boundaries were hopelessly confused because of the unexpected course of the river. Instead of bordering upon Lake Ontario, their only access to it was at the mouth of the Black River, and major waterfalls at two points obstructed navigation from the lake. This barred easy access to trade with Canadian settlements at Kingston and along the St. Lawrence River. Not only was Castorland much more isolated than they had anticipated; it also contained less acreage than they had purchased. Preliminary protests were immediately dispatched to Constable, even while explorations continued.

In the meantime, Pharoux started mapping the area. On July 4th he discovered a river entering the Black from the east, and he named it Independence River in honor of the American holiday. It still bears that name today. A high scenic bluff overlooks the junction of these two rivers, and the view from there was so attractive that he chose it as a site for his own future home.

An Indian canoe was found concealed along the riverbank, and Pharoux had no compunctions about appropriating it. An extra boat was a great asset in carrying men, messages and supplies.

As the Castorland party slowly became accustomed to the wilderness, they started to live off the land, supplementing their bought provisions by hunting, fishing and planting. They ate fish, turtles, hares, eagles and deer.

Development plans were slowed by injuries, illnesses, disagreements and resignations among the workmen. Everything took longer

Pour dix-huit employés à l'arpentage. D'après le règlement des rations
il fallait un baril de rum, deux barils de porc et trois barils de farine
pour nourrir ces dix-huit personnes pendant un mois.

Plan d'un four américain dans les bois

Sur un plancher de grosses bois l'on fait une aire avec un rang de petites
et un lit de sable uniforme bien battüe. Sous forme ensuite un cercle de
trois pieds de diamètre, intérieur avec un rang ou deux de grosses pierres, et
puis on met quelques rangs de pierres plattes, le tout maçonné avec de
l'argile, en observant de laisser une porte. Pour cintrer la calote, on
emplit l'intérieur ou l'on fait un petit dôme avec sable et copeaux de

than they had anticipated! However, at this time they were still full of optimism about their eventual success, and they learned rapidly to make the most of their meager resources. Their labors were divided among construction of the first cabin, clearing land and preparing a garden.

Occasional visitors relieved their isolation. The Topping family, who settled seven miles south, were their first neighbors; later a family named Butterfield located only one-half mile away. Occasionally friendly groups of Indians passed by, on their way to or from Canada; some of them spoke a little French and cordial relationships were established. Three hungry Canadians from Kingston were found lost in the woods, rescued and assisted on their way. They were also visited by two Township Roads Inspectors who registered their new road in compliance with current legal procedures.

Work never stopped during the daylight hours, and often continued into the night by firelight. However, despite the fatigue and anxiety connected with their affairs, interest in natural phenomena never failed. Interspersed among the surveying notes and work records in the *Journal* are observations and descriptions of unfamiliar plants, insects, fish, birds and animals. Sometimes these descriptions were accompanied by sketches, such as the following of bloodroot, leek, and diver (probably merganser):

> "*The Bloodroot* is a good vermifuge for children and is infused by putting some little pieces in rum. The root is very bitter, and when broken there oozes out a fluid resembling blood, from which it derives its name.
>
> *The Leek, or Ramp,* is an elongated, bulbous white wild onion, and on its stem it bears a white flower, the parts of which are shown in the margin. This stalk is brown below, and green toward the blossom and its roots are like whitened threads. The flower has a light, agreeable odor of the onion, and much stronger than that of the garden plant, and more like the garlic. It is good to eat, and would improve by cultivation.
>
> *The Diver* is an aquatic fowl, about a foot from the end of the bill to the tail, feathers grey on the back and whitish on the breast, a streight *(sic)* serrated beak somewhat rounded toward the end, feet webbed like the duck, and of a greyish color, three articulations in the toes, and the fourth without a membrane. Two feet in the extreme span; wings small and tail short."[9]

Pharoux carefully mapped the course of the river and his field books included sketches of crooks and turns, points of interest, possible mill sites, navigation hazards, notes on soil, timber, topography, islands, marshes, shoals, reeds, rocks, etc. Some of his surveyors were assigned to laying out lots on the eastern side, marking boundary lines along the intervals.

observations

Blood root, (racine sanglante). C'est un bon vermifuge pour les enfants. On en infuse quelques gouttes seulement dans un peu de rum. cette racine est très amère. Lorsqu'on la rompt, il en sort des gouttelettes de liqueur semblable à du sang; ce qui lui a fait donner son nom.

Leek or Ramp (oignon ou ail sauvage.) Cet oignon est blanc, allongé et bulbeux. une tige s'en élève et porte une fleur blanche dont le détail est ci-côté. Cette tige est brune dans le bas et verte vers la fleur. Les racines sont comme des filets blanchâtres. La fleur a une légère odeur d'oignon assez agréable. Beaucoup plus forte que l'oignon des jardins et approchant de l'ail; celui-ci est bon à manger et serait plus doux s'il était cultivé.

Diver (Plongeon). C'est un oiseau aquatique d'environ un pied du bout de la tête à la queue. plumes grises sur le corps et blanchâtres sous le ventre. Son bec dentelé et droit un peu arrondi vers le bout. Pattes avec membranes comme le canard, de couleur grise. Trois articulations palmées et la quatrième sans membrane. Deux pieds d'envergure. Petites ailes et queue courte.

This page from Hough's transcript of the *Journal* is a very close rendition of the original drawings of bloodroot, leek, and diver.

On July 21st, Pharoux reached an area he dubbed "Long Falls" (now Carthage), 41 river miles from the High Falls. There he found navigation impeded by a series of small waterfalls and rapids which extended for 1½ miles. It afforded good mill sites and he chose it as a place to establish a second base of operations and headquarters for the northern part of the survey. Geoffrey Desjardins was put in charge of operations there, while Pharoux went back and forth as needed. Huts were constructed to shelter men and supplies, and a portage path was marked and cut around the rapids.

Mapping the Long Falls was a taxing job for Pharoux. He established the latitude precisely by shooting the sun at noon with his astronomical instruments. A very prominent rock was called "Meridian Rock," and he used a triangulation system to figure other measurements. Along with his detailed technical notes and drawings are more mundane descriptions of discomfort: it was dangerous, exhausting and painful work, hopping on and off rocks, often falling into the water, wading about on slippery, unseen underfootings and suffering from blistered, sunburned legs.

Near the end of August, Pharoux and his surveyors reached Black River Bay — so far from their sources of supply that, when hampered by bad weather or other delays, they sometimes ran out of provisions. He complained of the gluttony of his men in describing one such occasion:

> "No more provisions remaining, we tried to fish and caught some large catfish which we had broiled over the coals. Our men took care to help themselves first, but fortunately Americans do not eat either the heads or livers of fish, so that from the refuse of our men, I made a scanty meal."[10]

Meanwhile, as Pharoux traveled back and forth, work progressed slowly at High Falls and Long Falls.

Two prospective settlers arrived from France and were warmly welcomed. One of them was Louis Crèvecoeur, the youngest son of the famous author; he was only 17 years old, but already possessed the same enthusiasm and optimistic outlook which characterized his father. His companion was a young man named Huerne. Both were interested in choosing land, and they were taken downriver in the canoe as far as Long Falls, so that they could look over available lots. The *Journal* laconically records that the entire distance was covered in a single day, with the current aiding the oarsmen. They started early and arrived after nightfall, at 10 P.M. The return trip going upstream took 2½ days.

Young Crèvecoeur selected his plot and wanted to settle there immediately, but Desjardins dissuaded him from this attempt with great difficulty since the youth lacked the experience, assistance and supplies which were essential for building a cabin so late in the year. Without shelter and supplies it would have been impossible to survive the winter, he pointed out. Discouraged by such advice, the young man was unable to wait until the following year. He went off to New Jersey, bought 220 acres of land, and lived there for two years before returning to France.[11] Huerne was more reasonable, and he promised to bide his time and return at the beginning of the following season.

As Pharoux continued final details of map making, his preliminary work was sufficiently accurate to disclose the extent of Constable's misrepresentations. Desjardins set forth on a trip to New York in August to confer with James Constable on the matter. Heading south from Steuben's, he was pleased to find a new road, via Gerrit Boon's Dutch settlement at Olden Barneveld, which was a vast improvement over their earlier route to Fort Schuyler.

In New York, Constable could give him little satisfaction. He did acknowledge Desjardins' grievances, but claimed that he lacked authority to make any changes in the contract himself; all that he could do was write to his brother in Europe.

Frustrated and angry at such lack of recognition and redress for Constable's mistakes, Desjardins started back toward Castorland. He stopped over in Albany for several days longer than he had planned because his wife was severely ill. (This was one of the rare times he mentioned his family in the *Journal*, aside from his concern in establishing a home for them.) Using this delay in Albany advantageously, however, he took time to discuss the boundary problem with Simeon DeWitt, the State's Surveyor-General, who "confessed" that latitude lines drawn upon official maps of that part of the state were only theoretical. DeWitt promised to order an official state survey of the area.

Desjardins also met with some other prominent French émigrés who had come to Albany. They were the Marquis and Marquise La Tour du Pin,[12] former acquaintances who became good friends during their American sojourn. They bought a farm several miles north of the city where many notable émigrés, including Talleyrand, visited them.

Meanwhile, back at High Falls, progress was hampered by shortages of both men and tools. It took much longer than anticipated to complete their first log cabin. Work upon it was subject to constant interruption for needs with a higher priority: clearing more land, cutting wood, working on crops, caring for stock animals and hauling endless mountains of supplies from Fort Schuyler. The supplies then had to be divided and transferred to various surveying groups at distant locations, as well as to the work party at the Long Falls. This continuing transport effort sapped their small productive manpower.

When Charles Brodhead completed his surveying work for the Constable team, late in the summer, he accepted employment with the Castorland group and proved to be a stalwart friend as well as an exceptionally capable and hard-working employee.

A letter written in September illustrates typical difficulties and their personal style of communication. Pharoux, then stationed at High Falls, wrote to Geoffrey Desjardins at the Long Falls:

"My Friend,
    I send you the little canoe and five men, with Mr. Brodhead, which is all that I can collect, besides the three men that remain here to finish our work. It will be absolutely necessary for Mr. Brodhead to have five men with him. He should even have a sixth, to take charge of the provisions. I shall remain at the Falls, to work on the report, and it would be needless for me to be where you are to look after the sending and distribution of provisions, which you are very well able to do. I am more needed here for the preparation of plans, and the Field Books. I shall await with impatience and uneasiness the return of M. Desjardins. The great canoe is out of service. The men I have sent with Mr. Brodhead, are Harrison, Francois Perrot, Caish and Bowman, but I must confess to you confidentially as to Harrison and Francois, that they should not be sent down to the lake: the first, because he is only hired for a month, and he will ask for his discharge if he is asked to go farther than the camp, and the other, because the debility consequent upon his sickness will not permit him. Moreover, my friend, one man more to aid in carrying provisions, and another to stay with you, appeared to be indispensable..."[13]

When workmen became ill or disabled in those days, it was not customary to give them time off until their recovery. Instead tasks were assigned to them within the limits of their capacity, and continued work was expected.

An epidemic of dysentery, called "bloody flux," interrupted this pattern. It severely disabled almost all the workmen and surveyors, and two were so badly afflicted that they died. Panic set in among the survivors. Frey and all of his surveyors quit, some because they were sick and the others because they feared the contagion. This infuriated Pharoux, who termed their desertion a "mutiny." Since Frey did not fulfill his contract, they parted angrily.

Originally Pharoux discounted the seriousness of the illness, noting it was "aggravated by fear and discouragement,"[14] but he changed his mind later when he too succumbed. Severe dysentery was a frequent problem in those days, and treatments varied widely. The usual American remedy was rum, but Pharoux and Desjardins had previously observed that this was more harmful than beneficial. They preferred limiting the diet to rice and rice-water which is a favored modern treatment; such a practice was then scorned by most Americans, including some doctors.

When Simon Desjardins returned on the 18th of September, he was much alarmed by the widespread illness and continuing desertions, but unable to prevent either. Eventually, only he, Pharoux and Baptiste were left at High Falls, the last disabled by a leg wound. Then these three were also stricken by the disease. Desperately seeking assistance, they sent Baptiste on their only horse to get help from Steuben's, and Pharoux and Desjardins followed on foot, after burying those valuables which they were unable to carry. Their neighbors were so afraid of the contagion that they refused to help. The Baron sent his servant with another horse to assist them in reaching his house, where rest and care resulted in their eventual recovery.

However, by the time they regained their health and strength it was already October, and winter was too close to permit a new start upon their work. They had to postpone remaining plans until the following year, and devote their final efforts to merely safeguarding their possessions. They hid the canoes in the forest, buried their grindstone, boarded their animals and sold their surplus supplies. Upon departing, they left a sign in both English and French which invited Indians who wintered in the area to use their cabin, but take care to avoid accidental fires.

Returning home through Fort Schuyler, they were so disgusted with the filthiness of the tavern there that they preferred to sleep in their tent. Their trip down the Mohawk was impeded by an early winter storm. On October 23rd and 24th, a severe blizzard deposited more than two feet of snow in the Mohawk Valley. Through the storm they continued rowing down the river in their open boat, suffering greatly from cold and exposure.

After they reached Albany and settled themselves at home, a dispute ensued with Frey over payment of his wages and reimbursement for his surveying expenses. Despite his failure to complete their job, he submitted a bill which they considered "inflated." They requested an itemized statement, and asked DeWitt to arbitrate the disagreement. The latter's reply was ambiguous; he clearly preferred to take neither side. Meanwhile Frey served a legal paper upon them, attesting "under oath" to the correctness of his bill. Fearful of a slander suit, Desjardins and Pharoux prudently, but reluctantly, agreed

71

to pay his requested amount. However, they returned his affadavit with indignation, stating that:

> "Frenchmen never resorted to such papers, and that the simple word of an honest man was worth more than all the oaths that could be drawn up . . ."[15]

After this incident, they wanted no further dealings with Frey, and chose Brodhead to be their chief surveyor for the following year.

Thus, the 1794 campaign ended on a disappointing note. After the expenditure of enormous effort, the settlement had barely gotten a start, the survey was still incomplete and their boundaries remained in doubt.

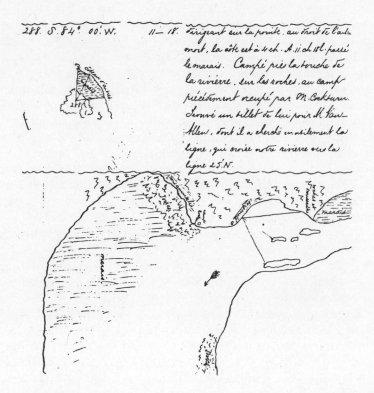

Pharoux's sketches and descriptions of the course of the Black River included notes on rapids, reeds, shoals, and landscape details such as woods, swamps, and natural meadows. These were useful later in locating hayfields, campsites, navigational hazards and possible mill sites.

CHAPTER FOUR

1795 — Consolidation and Disaster

By 1795 the founders of Castorland had fully realized the difficulties of their position and were making determined efforts to overcome them. Their three major concerns at the beginning of the year were settlement of the boundary dispute, more financial support and better road access to Castorland.

Resolving the boundaries depended upon communication with William Constable, who was still in Europe, and correspondence was maddeningly slow. While awaiting his response, they again devoted the winter months to financial and legal affairs with additional journeys to New York and Philadelphia.

They were hopeful that State officials could be persuaded to construct and maintain a public road from the Mohawk Valley through Castorland to Kingston, Ontario. In behalf of this "Canada Road" project, they made a formal petition to the legislature, and also attempted to secure the interest and support of some of its prominent members through visits and letters. A major blow to such efforts was the saddening news of Baron Steuben's death during the winter. In addition to their sense of personal loss of such a good friend and neighbor, they missed his considerable influence on such public matters as the road[1] and other legislation so vital to the development of the region.

In February William Constable finally wrote to them from France, after he had received the surveyors' reports. Responding to their complaints, he agreed to the need for some boundary adjustments, but his suggested solution infuriated Pharoux and Desjardins. Constable proposed that their land deficit should be resolved by the addition of land on the east, from other tracts which Constable had sold to proprietors named Watson and Greenleaf. These lands were mountainous and unsuitable for settlement, as well as being even more inaccessible than those near the river.

They wrote another lengthy letter to Constable,[2] listing and clarifying their five main grievances which can be summarized as follows:

73

First, Constable's survey should have been completed by 1793 according to the terms of the sale in Paris. They had expected to find their tract mapped and boundaries marked upon their arrival. Much confusion and inconvenience had been caused by the delay.

Second, many deficiencies resulted from the faulty map on which the sale was based. They had purchased 220,500 acres, with their boundaries described as:

west- Lake Ontario's shoreline (10 or 11 leagues — about 30 miles)

south- the Black River

north- a line at N87W latitude (to connect with the northwest corner
of the Totten and Crossfields's boundary)

east- a straight line running due north for nine miles from "Inman's
corner."

Instead, they found that the true course of the Black River cut them off from Lake Ontario, except at Black River Bay. It reduced their acreage by "about one-third" to a mere 180,000. The river's curves interspersed their land with Inman's, and intersected the northern boundary twice, interrupting the continuity of their tract. Their land was thus broken into six parcels, necessitating trespassing to get from one to the other by land.

They insisted that Constable should remedy these deficiences by giving them uninterrupted title to all lands on the eastern bank of the river, and adding fertile valley lands west of the river.

Third, Survey errors needed correction because Constable's surveyors had run lines with a compass, ignoring magnetic deviation from true north. It was customary and accepted practice that boundaries conform with lines run "in the exact direction of the meridian."

Fourth, they reminded Constable that the State of New York had reserved 600 acres for government use on Black River Bay in its original sale of the Macomb Purchase. Surveyor Cockburn had located this reserve upon the Castorland Tract, but their own study of the Macomb Purchase records and conference with Simeon DeWitt led to the conclusion that the reserve belonged north of them on Macomb's Lot Number Four, and should not be deducted from their own bay frontage.

Fifth, they complained of delays in obtaining the papers essential to their land titles because of a missing signature by Constable's wife.

The letter concluded with an appeal to Constable's sense of honor and equity, asserting:

"Without doubt Sir, you have sold this in good faith, and we have bought it in the same...We trust that the equity of our cause will not fail to arrest your attention, and that our quality as strangers, will give us a further claim to obtain exact justice from an upright man."[3]

CONTRAST OF CASTORLAND'S ANTICIPATED AND
ACTUAL SIZE, SHAPE AND LOCATION:

N 87 W Latitude

Lake
Ontario

Anticipated course of Black River

High Falls

According to Constable's map, the Castorland plot should have been
approximately rectangular shaped. Borders were expected to be the
Black River on the south, Lake Ontario on the west, a straight line
extending to the corner of the Totten and Crosfield Purchase on the
north, and a straight line on the east, running nine miles north from
Inman's northwestern corner. The total acreage was to be 220,500.

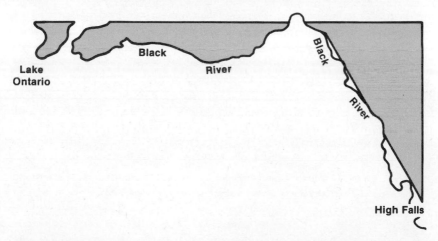

Black

River

Lake
Ontario

Black

River

High Falls

Instead, Castorland's surveyors found that the true course of the
Black River cut them off from Lake Ontario except at Black River
Bay and their land totalled only 180,000 acres. Furthermore, Inman's
lands were interspersed with theirs along the eastern bank, so that
riverfront access divided their lands into six separate plots.

Constable's reply was ambiguous. He was disposed to concede points which affected him alone, but insisted he must consider the rights of other purchasers in adjusting the boundaries.

Desjardins and Pharoux concluded that Constable's proposed solutions were unjust and unacceptable. They finally filed a legal suit against him and the matter remained unresolved for the next several years, becoming increasingly complicated as the surrounding lands became settled and residents claimed title to lands under dispute. (See Chapter Six for details of the final settlement.)

In the meantime, while the legal arguments continued, major efforts were devoted to developing the settlements at High Falls and Long Falls. The spring of 1795 was occupied with advance preparations for renewed occupancy.

They hired a French Canadian couple, Louis and Marguerite Ferlent, to live and work at Castorland throughout the year at an annual salary of $80 plus keep. Other workmen were hired for the season, including a millwright, carpenters, wagoneers and two Indians. Father Perrot, an acquaintance from their trip through Oneida in 1793, joined them and worked throughout the summer as a common laborer. A year's supply of provisions were purchased and a stock of animals including goats, sheep, cows, horses, two watch dogs and another team of oxen.

Desjardins was forced to spend nearly a month at Fort Schuyler while arranging for provisions and trying to hire additional workmen, but he sent the rest of the group ahead to High Falls to begin operations there. It was June 18th when the party reached High Falls, and they were pleased to find most of their belongings in good order, since Indian hunters had used their cabin during the winter. However their two canoes, which they had tried to hide by burying, had been found and misused. One was lodged upon a rock with its end crushed; the other was cracked and leaking but still usable.

A young man named Louis Tassart was among the party this year. He had been employed by Nicolas Olive to select his tract of 20,000 acres and begin a settlement upon them. During June and July, Tassart worked cooperatively with the Castorland group, joining forces on such common chores as hiring workmen, purchasing supplies, driving wagons and baking. It was a matter deemed worthy of note in the *Journal* when he produced the first meat pie ever baked at High Falls! Its contents included duck and turtle.

Plunging into their second year of work with renewed ambition, the Frenchmen often worked 18 hours a day and drove their help to do likewise. However, their achievements were always limited by

William Constable
(Engraving from a painting by Gilbert Stuart).

conditions beyond their control. The oxen, cows and horses were a constant source of problems. Left to forage in the woods, they frequently disappeared and caused many delays. The black flies were so vicious that workmen quit because of them and a dog died after multiple bites.

The shortage of laborers and frequent disagreements with them hampered their work. The men insisted on having Sundays off, a "religious scruple" which seemed totally unreasonable to Pharoux. Rum rations were also a subject of contention. A "mutiny" developed because the surveyors who had worked for them during the previous year had received a larger allotment of rum than was presently offered. Pharoux insisted that had been proper because they had been living outdoors, and pointed out that their neighbors gave no rum at all for equivalent work. He would not compromise upon this matter, asserting:

> "He would never allow them to dictate to him the law, upon a question which ought to depend upon his good will alone."[4]

There is a distinct change in the tone of the *Journal* during this second year of settlement. Where the first had contained mostly terse, factual, unemotional accounts, they now recorded more hopes, fears, complaints and worries. It became less of a business document and more of a personal diary. Authorship of some entries is clear from the content; in other cases it is not always possible to tell whether the writer was Pharoux, Simon or Geoffrey Desjardins. The location of the writer was often the only clue to a series of entries. Among all three, however, it is possible to perceive a sense of disallusionment; a common theme was complaints about various sharp dealings by Yankees.

Again the summer's work was varied; slow progress was discernible. Dividing their forces as before, Simon Desjardins directed the affairs at the High Falls Establishment, while Geoffrey took charge of the headquarters at Long Falls. Pharoux ranged widely, often working with Charles Brodhead and his party on the survey. They were endeavoring to complete the mapping and tract divisions in Lower Castorland, on the northern part of their lands.

At High Falls the log cabin was partitioned, creating an office and supply room which could be locked and separated from the living quarters. They started construction of a stable and a second log cabin for the Ferlent family. Repairs were made to boats and rafts, and furniture was built. They planted, fished, hunted, reaped hay from natural meadows, baked, made soap, enclosed a spring, erected fences, chopped wood and cleared more land. Each activity was time and energy consuming. There were many complaints about the workmen. One referred to their "insubordination and idleness, the general faults of this country..."[5] and continued at great length, concluding:

> "In short, one ought to have the charge of men, to realize all the difficulties that are encountered, and to know what patience he is obliged to exercise. Some persons who don't know any better may say, that there is nothing to be done, to accomplish a work but to undertake it; but then will find, that men will not engage unless at an exhorbitant price, especially by the day, and that then they will do no more than they are obliged to. It is impossible to give an idea of their faithlessness, for they will never execute their tasks with fidelity; — if you pay them in advance, they will leave their work unfinished, and if you refuse to pay them thus, they will likewise abandon you. Through these means, the work that ought to be finished in one month, will remain unfinished in six...The wisest course, although it appears to be the most costly, is to hire by the day..."[6]

Despite their daily frustrations, however, they did not lose their interest in natural phenomena. The *Journal* includes interesting descriptions of insects and snakes:

> "The dragon-fly preserves under her elegant form...ferocity...We saw one holding an ant between her paws, and tearing it to pieces. In the evening observed an insect resembling the gnat in form, but clothed with the most brilliant colors. Examined a large fly, striped white and black, which makes a buzzing about the vagrant-fly, takes it up and devours it...Saw a dragon-fly with the body of a scarlet red. Caught a beetle smaller than a May-Bug, with the body and legs of a bronze color, sprinkled with gold."[7]
>
> "Killed two snakes striped yellow and black, with the belly white. These reptiles are not venemous. Noticed a beetle that was green, black and bronze colored. It carried on its belly a swarm of little ones, as large as rape seed, of a yellow color, resembling little spiders with long legs."[8]

Obtaining provisions from Fort Schuyler and supplying their northern parties continued to be an endlessly demanding task. It took the wagons at least four days to traverse the makeshift road to or from the town, occupying men and oxen who were badly needed elsewhere. (When the oxen were not on the road, they were used for hauling logs and other heavy work.) The trip to town was always very difficult and uncomfortable because of the poor road conditions and also because "The musketos helped themselves freely at our expense."[9] Workmen quit so frequently that attempts were always made, on such trips to town, to hire additional laborers. One most welcome addition to their workforce was a cat; it was a great help protecting supplies against the mice and squirrels.

Because of supply problems, Desjardins refused to sell supplies to visitors, who often arrived ill-equipped, expecting to purchase provisions. Desjardins explained that they could not "keep tavern" as was the customary practice, but he did provide a free breakfast when necessary. Few strangers were able to appreciate his supply problems — on one occasion he had 26 people sleeping in the cabin at High Falls when bad weather detained passing hunters as well as his group of surveyors.

The selection of a mill site occupied a great deal of time. Pharoux considered every possible location, making careful measurements and calculations of power potential and details of construction. The nearest suitable location was on Otter Creek, but it was finally rejected because it lay on land still under dispute.

They finally chose a site at Long Falls for mill construction. This decision was reached reluctantly, because the 41 mile distance from the main establishment at High Falls was a major drawback. However, it was overbalanced by the natural factors at that location, which simplified the necessary construction and offered the best opportunity for rapid completion.

The work party at Long Falls, supervised by Geoffrey Desjardins, included two carpenters, two Indians, a blacksmith, two or three laborers and one of their wives who served as cook. In addition to starting construction of two mills, they built a forge and charcoal pit and another log cabin. The Indian carpenters proved to be better workmen than the Whites, until one night when they got drunk. They quit the following morning in embarassment over their behavior and started home. However, on their way they met Brodhead, who persuaded Hitto, the elder of the two, to join his survey party. This was particularly fortuitous, for Hitto later saved his life.

The tedious pace of the daily round of work is best appreciated by reading typical excerpts:

"**Saturday, August 8,1795: At the Establishment** — I had the two Canadians clear out the yard and burn the chips, cut and split the wood fit to burn, sort it out and pile it ready for use. In the afternoon they cut brush in the pasture, and got ready some bread to take to M. Pharoux's camp...Baptiste was employed on the floor and in splitting pine planks.[10]

Monday, August 10th: At the Establishment — The two Canadians worked on the clearing. Baptiste...worked on the floor. Marguerite has made soap with good result, and which will effect much saving. In the afternoon Perrot, being wounded on the leg with an axe, was employed in drawing nails of various sorts from the barrels.

Stations	Directions	Distances	Observations
			exactement au droit du rapide. roches escarpées sur le bord opposé. une petite isle basse un peu avant du meme côté.
18.	S. 63° 00' W.	4 chains 73 links	*A partir du commencement des d. roches jusqu'à la pointe ou est le rapide au dessus d'une chûte.*
19.	S. 70° 30' W.	2 ... 22	*au long du rapide en tournant.*
20.	N. 85° 40' W.	9 ... 57	*au long du rapide. Pierre bleue par assise à 9 chaines, la chûte.*
21.	N. 69° 30' W.	2 ... 57	*à la chûte. Elle tourne rapidement formant un angle d'ogive et est resserrée entre des assises de pierre horisontales.*
22.	N. 55° 45' W.	2 ... 36	*au tournant de la chûte en quittant la riviere. côte de sable au dessus des bancs de pierres; pente de 30°.*

Campé dans cet endroit à cause de la grande pluye. Essayé à prendre le niveau de cette chûte; mais il m'a été impossible de le faire. J'évalue la hauteur totale, depuis la partie au dessus des rapides jusqu'au dessous à quinze pieds. La chûte peut avoir 8 à 9 pieds ... dessus la rivière.

A page from the original *Journal* showing sketches and notes by Pharoux pertaining to one of the waterfall sites considered for mill construction.

At the Mill — Sent back Cross and Robinson in the canoe to get provisions at the High Falls, and with them was sent a letter informing M. Desjardins of our operations. Had some trees cut down, and cleared a place for the log house at the mill. Placed and leveled the foundation logs of the house. The great number of large trees, the roughness of the ground which is encumbered with rock, the want of cattle, and the scanty supply of our help, occasioned many delays. Nature has indicated the place for a supply canal. We only want some powder, and a couple of men who are accustomed to work in mines. The surface indicates that the rock will be easy to raise."[11]

South of Castorland, lands were being settled gradually. Desjardins was pleased to hear of the expected arrival of 40 new settlers on Inman's tract nearby. Happy at the prospect of having more neighbors, however, he had learned to be skeptical of plans:

"We are most anxious to have them execute all their projects, as the prosperity of their establishment will contribute to that of our own; but we have remarked that in general, the imagination is as active, as the execution is slow in this country."[12]

Some potential land buyers visited Castorland, but none chose to settle there. Also disappointing was belated news that Huerne and young Crèvecoeur, who had so eagerly chosen lots the previous summer, had both reneged on their commitments and settled on lands elsewhere. One impecunious Frenchman and son, named DeJean, arrived fresh from France. Although they could not afford to buy land, they hoped to settle and keep a store at High Falls. Receiving encouragement from Desjardins, the elder left to bring on his wife and four other children, while his son stayed on as a workman for a while; his father never returned.

The first disharmony at the leadership level occurred over a disagreement about the location of Olive's tract of land. Pharoux and Desjardins strongly recommended that it be located somewhere between the High Falls and the Long Falls; they particularly favored sites on Otter Creek or the Independence River. These were close to sources of supply and the lots were already marked and mapped. However, Louis Tassart, Olive's representative, insisted upon a location at Black River Bay, even though he had not yet visited that area, and the mapping and survey work there were not completed. Letters were exchanged with Olive, who sided with Tassart, and acrimony seems to have developed. Desjardins and Pharoux took offense because their advice was rejected.

Late in August a shortage of funds and provisions required Desjardins to leave Castorland for a short trip. He managed his

Contemporary photo of the Black River shows it is still wild and beautiful today.

business in Albany in only one day, but required more than the usual time coming and going, trying to locate provisions which were in short supply.

As their boundary dispute still remained unsettled, they were eager for any pertinent news. One item of interest was that surveyors employed on Macomb's Tract Number Four, to their north, had quit work because of illness, supply difficulties and "extraordinary variations of the needle"[13] due to widespread deposits of iron ore. Similar magnetic problems had been experienced by Cockburn's surveyors. This news seemed to lend weight to their own case.

By September, Pharoux and Brodhead had nearly finished the survey work. All that remained was mapping the area around Black River Bay at the mouth of the river, subdividing and marking the lots there. Notes and sketches from the field books were copied into the *Journal*. As in the previous year, the work was slowed by the great distances from the sources of supply. They were about 30 miles from the Long Falls and 75 from High Falls. When deliveries were delayed they sometimes went hungry; at other times they had to interrupt the work in order to come in and get supplies.

Rain was unusually heavy that summer, often causing delays in the outside work, as well as impeding transportation and provisioning. Chores that could be done indoors were saved for the rainy days in order to keep the men fully occupied.

However, affairs were progressing reasonably until a catastrophic accident occurred. Pharoux and two other men were drowned on September 21st. They had been accompanying a party of surveyors on a trip from Long Falls to Black River Bay. Tassart was a member of the group, going along in order to choose lands for Olive on Black River Bay. Pharoux's intention had been to leave the others and proceed around the cape (now known as Cape Vincent) to Kingston on the northern shore of Lake Ontario. He wanted to investigate Canadian sources of labor and supply for the coming year. It had rained heavily nearly every day that week, and the river level had risen ten feet in the past two days. The *Journal* account of the accident was written by Geoffrey Desjardins at the Long Falls camp:

> "**September 19, 1795:**...Messrs. Pharoux, Brodhead and company set out, happy and in good health...
>
> **September 20:** The river having risen considerably, I sent the carpenter to secure our canoes in case of need...It rained incessantly...
>
> **September 21:** The rain continuing...I occupied the men under cover... At three o'clock I observed some persons on the other side of the river, whom I recognized as belonging to M. Pharoux's party, and felt alarmed

84

These pages from the original *Journal* contain survey and field notes of the Black River Bay area.

lest some accident had happened. Half an hour later, my fears were realized, on the arrival of Messrs. Brodhead and Tassart, with one of their men, who informed me that yesterday morning, as they were endeavoring to cross the river on a raft, they had been drawn into the falls by the violence of the current, and that M. Pharoux and two men had perished... The place selected for crossing was narrow, and consequently rapid, and the great flood had still further increased the velocity of the current, which prevented them from touching the bottom with their poles, or of offering any resistance...

The zeal of M. Pharoux had led him to disregard the representations of M. Tassart, and even the fears of the Indian, who had refused to cross with them. The dread of losing time in making another raft, and the belief that there was no danger, occasioned this inestimable loss that has befallen us. I had urged M. Pharoux to give up this journey, as the season was so far advanced...but his anxiety to procure at Kingston information as to provisions, men, etc. which we might depend upon next year, and above all, his desire to verify for himself, the operations on Penet Square[14] and in Lower Castorland, drew him onto the end of his career...Money, instruments, provisions, all were lost, and his men lost all their effects.

This unfortunate event happened yesterday morning at half-past nine o'clock, and of the seven persons who were on the raft, four only were saved. Our friend looked upon the danger with firmness. They went down the first two rapids without breaking, and he did not cease encouraging his men till the moment when they were precipitated over the third fall, which is more than 15 feet high. Their raft went to pieces, and they disappeared in the cauldron of the falls..."[15]

The falls at which the accident occurred were those they called the Great Falls (now Watertown). It is clear from the above account that the cause of the disaster was the unusual flood conditions resulting from such excessive rain. It had so deepened the waters and increased the current that their poles failed to touch bottom, and they lost control of the raft. They had used this method of crossing the river for two years, and probably at the same place so that the raft could be reused. Pharoux was over-confident, failing to recognize the new dangers posed by the unprecedented floods. It is interesting that the equally experienced Brodhead accompanied him, while the inexperienced Tassart evinced better judgment.

Hough's *History of Jefferson County* gives another account of the accident which differs from the *Journal's* report. It quotes an obituary notice, published after Brodhead's death in 1853, in a Utica newspaper:

"On one occasion when they had approached the river, having journeyed through the woods without noting their route by the compass, they arrived at a part of the bank which they recognized, and knew to be a safe place of passing. Making a raft of logs, they started from the bank, and began to pole across. When in the midst of the current their poles failed to reach the bottom, and simultaneous with this discovery, the noise of the waters below them revealed the horrid fact that they had mistaken their ferrying place, and were at the head and rapidly approaching the Great Falls of the river, the passage of which threatened all but certain death. Instantly Mr. B. ordered every man who could swim to make for the shore, and he prepared to swim for his own life. But the piteous appeals of Mr. Pharoux, a young Frenchman, of the party, who could not swim, arrested him, and he determined to remain with him to assist him, if possible in the awful passage of the falls. Hastily directing his men to grasp firmly to the logs of the raft, giving similar directions to Mr. Pharoux, he then laid himself down by the side of his friend. The raft passed the dreadful falls and was dashed to pieces. Mr. Pharoux with several of the whites and Indians was drowned, and Mr. Brodhead himself thrown into an eddy near the shore, whence he was drawn senseless by an Indian of the party."[16]

The two accounts of the accident disagree over the number of men lost and the actual cause of the accident. Many writers have accepted and repeated the latter version, that "they mistook their crossing place."[17] However, it seems more reasonable to believe the *Journal's* account rather than one written more than 50 years later and based on second or third-hand reporting. Since it is impossible to resolve the differences, it must be sufficient to take note of them and go on with the story.

An unsuccessful search was made for Pharoux's body. However it was not found until the following year, when it washed up upon an island in Black River Bay and was found by another surveying party. His remains were buried on the lands where he had hoped to build a home for himself, at the junction of the Black and Independnence Rivers.

The entire Castorland party was grief-stricken at Pharoux's death. Geoffrey Desjardins could not accept the truth, and kept hoping that, against all reason, some miracle had enabled Pharoux to survive:

"Not withstanding what Mr. Brodhead had told me, I climbed many times upon the rocks, fancying to myself, that my friend had been able to save himself by gaining the shore, and that he had come up to opposite our place; but all in vain!"[18]

Simon Desjardins was so upset that he could hardly eat for days, and he recorded his depression and sadness along with his first foreboding that the settlement might fail:

"Mr. Brodhead arrived in the evening, and I was scarcely able to revive his drooping spirits. Yet while endeavoring to console him, and revive his courage, I could not help inwardly recapitulating in my mind, all the obstacles, delays and misfortunes that we had encountered in everything we had undertaken, and I could not but feel a foreboding that our Company was destined never to succeed..."[19]

The late summer floods also caused many other problems. ptiste was nearly drowned trying to cross a creek along their road ich was normally easy to ford. The road became such a quagmire t wagons and horses could hardly move, and supply trips were pended for nearly a month. Provisions ran low, and finally the n (unused for so long) became unusually wild and hard to handle.

Slowly the Desjardins brothers recovered from the shock of aroux's loss. They rallied their forces and continued working. The t accomplishment was choice of a site for the future city of torville, four miles up the Beaver River from its intersection with Black. There were good mill sites on rapids above the head of igation, and fine fresh water. (Today this area is known as Beaver ls.) After selecting the site for Castorville, they planned a road to nect it with High Falls (a distance of 20 miles) and Long Falls (an litional 15 miles).

Louis Ferlent, their year-round caretaker, became ill and was sent a hospital in New York City "for treatment of the stone." He rned early in October "cured of gravel," but still not well.

They remained at Castorland until the end of November this ond year of the Establishment, but as snow and cold became severe, work force dwindled away. Without Pharoux, the survey could then be completed. Operations at Long Falls were closed on tober 2nd, in order to concentrate the small work force that was left High Falls. In leaving the area, Geoffrey Desjardins noted:

"I have had the Indian hut, built near the coal pit saved, to give our Indian brethren an example of respect for property."[20]

At High Falls they were able to finish building the stable and the ond log cabin, which contained three rooms, for the Ferlent family. ey also constructed a sled for moving supplies over snow. Finally y departed on November 30th, leaving the Ferlents and a workman med Robinson planning to stay over the winter.

En route southward, they visited with their neighbors, the pping family, and were entertained with a drink of spruce beer, ich they described as "highly praised by Cook, and the Americans, t to our taste it is very poor."[21] Despite their dislike, they included recipe in the *Journal*:

"Spruce Beer:

For a barrel of 32 gallons, boil in a large kettle, twelve pounds of spruce boughs, and turn this decoction into the barrel, and after it is settled, add a gallon of molasses, then fill with cold water, and stir the whole together with a rod."[22]

Snow accumulated as they journeyed southward. Although there had been none at Castorland as they left, two feet crowned the mountain at Steuben's.

While passing on through Boon's settlement they had an amusing encounter in a tavern. An indignant householder made a claim upon them for damages to his garden, caused by their goats eating some trees while passing. Desjardins paid without protest, grateful that only a small sum was asked. He noted:

"The twelve shillings did not go out of the tavern, where they drank to the health of the French goats."[23]

As they passed through Fort Schuyler, Desjardins arranged for supplies to be delivered to Castorland during the winter by sleighs. He expected that the transport over the snowdrifts would be easier and cheaper than by wagons over the terrible roads.

Finally reaching Albany again, he spent most of the winter working in the Company office in his home. It seemed habitual for him to work as long hours at his home as he did in Castorland; his wife and children are seldom mentioned. Holidays were not causes for interruption in his work schedule. No mention was made of Christmas observances; his entry for December 25th lists a full account of the usual business activities. He did not celebrate the New Year either, commencing a business trip to New York City on December 27th, and arriving on the 30th.

The total achievements for the second year were discouraging. All he could report, despite enormous efforts, were the two tiny clusters of cabins and sheds at High Falls and Long Falls. He had contracted for an access road to be cut to Fort Stanwix, which was rapidly out-stripping Fort Schuyler as a source of supply, but the road was not yet usable for wagons since it still lacked bridges and causeways. Pharoux's death had delayed the completion of the maps and land subdivisions around Black River Bay. The boundary dispute with Constable still remained unsettled.

Contrary to their expectations, no new settlers had joined the colony; even Tassart's endeavors on behalf of Olive had failed to produce another settlement. It seems to have resulted, however, in development of some coolness between Olive and Desjardins, leading

89

to a loss of confidence in the latter and foreshadowing further problems in the future.

   Pharoux's loss may have been a critical factor in the ultimate failure of the colony. If he had lived, it is possible that his energetic and ingenious contributions might have made a crucial difference. At this stage, however, no one could foretell the future, and the Desjardins brothers continued to exert every effort to overcome their problems.

Current view of the Black River.

CHAPTER FIVE

1796 and 1797 — Desjardins' Downfall

By 1796 Desjardins felt that his settlement was sufficiently well established beyond the subsistence level that more rapid progress could be anticipated. He was in New York ready to transact business and financial matters by the first day in January, but letters from France awaiting him there contained a disagreeable surprise. Instead of providing the expected funds for another year of support, the Company demanded reimbursement, with interest, for their earlier investments.

This demand produced a financial crisis. After various consultations, Desjardins decided that his only hope of raising funds was to conduct a public sale of 14,000 acres of land. Shares were offered at the price of $1 per acre, but this bargain price failed to attract any buyers. Finally the banker, William Seton, alleviated Desjardins' desperation by purchasing 2,216 acres at $2 per acre. This revenue enabled him to meet his most essential obligations, but severely limited plans for new undertakings in Castorland.

In past years Mr. Olive had been helpful in business matters, but now his store in Albany was failing, and he reneged on promises to establish new stores in Fort Stanwix and in Castorland. Desjardins wrote despairingly:

> "It is however impossible for the Castorland Project to succeed, unless Commerce lends its hand to Agriculture."[1]

William Constable had finally returned to New York, and at last Desjardins was able to confront him personally about the boundary disputes. The results were disappointing; Constable appeared to be "selfish" and "hard."[2] Not only was he unwilling to adjust the boundaries favorably; he even opposed their petition for the Canada Road, since an alternate route would be more advantageous for other lands he wished to develop.

Desjardins did not give up easily. He sought legal help from Alexander Hamilton, and continued lobbying for a road through Castorland, mustering whatever support he could through introductions to influential people.

At the end of January, the work party, which had planned to spend the winter in Castorland, was forced to abandon their residence because of a shortage of supplies. The Black River had not frozen over sufficiently to bear sleighs with the provisions which had been ordered for them. Therefore they had to struggle through the snowdrifts into Fort Schuyler for the remaining winter months, unable to return until the spring.

Traveling by stage coach, Desjardins visited the town in February, was surprised to find his party there, but he arranged further purchases and deliveries and gave orders for necessary wagon repairs.

These advance preparations enabled an earlier start than usual for the 1796 campaign. Before the beginning of May, the Desjardins brothers started toward Castorland once again, and as previously their record of the journey up the Mohawk reveals their indefatigable pace and the wide diversity of their interests and knowledge. They included technical notes on various kinds of mills which they studied and on the "dykes" and flumes at the falls in Canajoharie.

Unexpected expenses ate into their limited money supply. Some of their animal stock had starved to death or been lost during the winter, and replacements were needed. Costs of supplies and transport had greatly increased. Hired laborers cost nearly twice what they had been paid the previous year, and were in short supply because everyone available was employed on building a canal from Fort Stanwix to Wood Creek. Nevertheless, the routine of life at High Falls slowly resumed.

Visitors became more frequent as neighboring lands were developed to the south and those along the opposite bank were being surveyed. Sometimes they accommodated such visitors by renting them a canoe or providing meals or lodging; such services were often paid for by a few hours of work rather than cash.

Newer settlements surpassed Castorland because of superior resources. Particularly thriving was the one founded by Gerrit Boon of the Holland Land Company at Olden Barneveld (later called Trenton and now Barneveld). Boon had also established a new "upper" settlement (now Boonville) which was only eleven miles from High Falls. This latter developed a store, grist mill, saw mill and ashery which were of great advantage to the French as nearer sources of supply than Fort Schuyler or Fort Stanwix. Most of the settlers were New Englanders, but a sizeable group of Welsh bought land at Steuben's.

Despite the increased traffic and some improvements in the road since its earliest days, the 40 mile trip between High Falls and Fort

Gerrit Boon
(Portrait at the Boonville Historical Society).

93

Schuyler was still difficult and hazardous. When overtaken by darkness, it was necessary to stop and camp in the woods, even if only a mile or two from habitation. Otherwise they risked getting lost or wandering into fallen trees, mudholes or swamps. Desjardins described one occasion on which he made the familiar journey. After spending the night at White's (formerly Steuben's):

> "...There being no bread at White's we went on three-fourth's of a mile further, to Platt's, for breakfast. Started from thence at nine o'clock, and arrived at five in the evening at Topping's, six miles and a half from Castorland, after having been twice mired with my horse: the last time, in coming out of Sugar River, where I had to throw my cloak over my horse's head, to prevent him from struggling, and I was placed in great peril..."[3]

The major project for this year was a start upon the two grand cities envisioned in the Castorland *Prospectus*. Surveying parties worked in both areas — Black River Bay and along the Beaver River — exploring, mapping and laying out lots.

Brodhead was directed to select the site for the port city, either upon Black River Bay or at the basin below Great Falls, if the bar in the river could be made passable for sloops. This port is hereafter referred to as "Niaoure," the Indian name for Black River Bay, instead of being called "Basle," its previous designation. Brodhead chose a site several miles up the river near the present location of the village of Dexter. They hoped that the port would facilitate access, trade and shipping via Lake Ontario and the St. Lawrence River, even if they could not pass Fort Oswego.

Greater priority was given to very detailed plans for the inland city, Castorville. It was to include 250 acres near the falls of the Beaver River. Desjardins was delighted with the site, and described it in lyric detail:

> "...I could not but admire how Nature had in this place varied her forms which are always sublime and beautiful. There is here no impetuous torrent, plunging in mass down a precipice of 63 feet, as at the High Falls, nor a turbulent chaos, the image of destruction, and the overthrow of creation, as at the Long Falls, where the river takes a mile and a half to descend a like distance...There is here a cascade, which the art of Le Notre could never equal. This fall of at least five feet, is divided by different islets of rock, covered with trees, and adorned with a verdure, which makes them appear like other cascades of varied form. The great foaming torrent, plunges majestically down in the middle, and the others as it were accompany it. While the tranquil waters of the upper basin, reflect as in a mirror, the little islands of rock and verdure that sprinkle the surface, they form a striking contrast with those of the lower

basin, rocky and foaming. The cascade on the city side, appears as if it was expressly arranged, for improvement, and need only a canal to bring the waters into the city, and not only serve the lumber mills, but also for locks to pass up bateaux...."[4]

After his visit to the Castorville site, Desjardins was impatient to return to High Falls, and was disgusted with the slow rowing of his workmen against the current. He complained about the laziness of American oarsmen who merely "caress the placid surface of the stream."[5]

Back at the Establishment (the High Falls settlement), difficulties with workmen continued. They quit on many pretexts, including the voraciousness of the black flies. Louis Ferlent, who had completed his year's contract, was infirm and dissatisfied, but unable to find another job. Reluctantly he signed on to stay another year, and his health continued to decline. As Desjardins unhappily observed the greater prosperity of newer settlements where the settlers themselves were land owners, he concluded:

"Establishments ...where the laborers are hired are foolish and ruinous enterprises."[6]

Nevertheless, they persevered.

Their gardens were much more extensive this summer: they planted beans, peas, corn, potatoes, oats, pumpkins and barley, lending variety to their diet and saving the hauling of food supplies. A smokehouse and second stable were built, and more fields were fenced. They installed a Franklin stove in one cabin to supplement the fireplace.

A major theft caused a dramatic interruption in their progress, on the evening of June 28th, 1796. While they were eating supper, a robber entered their office through a window and stole two watches and a small locked trunk which contained all their money (about $600), important papers and valuable instruments. The theft was not discovered until bedtime, and they were unable to take any constructive action until daylight, spending the night in fruitless suppositions. The next morning, they found and followed the thief's tracks. Across the river they located a spot where he had opened and abandoned the cumbersome trunk. They found the handle of a broken file, the tool he had used for this purpose, and this later proved to be significant evidence in identification of the robber. Some papers and brass surveying instruments were also recovered at this spot, but maps and other valuable records had been burned and the money was missing. Baptiste and Desjardins hurried south to report the theft and try to find the robber, and lists were circulated of the items stolen, with detailed descriptions to help identify them. Eventually the thief was located — a former employee named Crocker — and arrested and indicted by a grand jury at German Flatts (now Herkimer).

While in a tavern, discussing the prosecution of the affair with the judge, Desjardins was shocked at the unceremonious treatment they received. The two had ordered their dinner and were about to sit down when their chief witness Mr. Merrill arrived, along with the constable and the prisoner. These travelers were also hungry:

> "The thief, as well served as the rest, and without any distinction, was placed without ceremony at the same table with the judge and myself... so that the curious people, who are not rare in this country and whom the rumor of our affair had drawn together at the tavern, asked which of us was the thief?"[7]

Crocker was jailed for a subsequent trial term, but Desjardins was able to recover only part of his money, since some had already been spent. This intensified their financial problems.

He returned to Castorland via Fort Stanwix (now Rome) which had begun to replace Fort Schuyler (now Utica) as the main regional commercial center. In the town he purchased a lot for a future store, and then traversed, for the first time, a new road which he had previously ordered cut as a direct link with Fort Stanwix. It was not yet completely finished, but since its length was only 28 miles, it significantly shortened the distance their supply wagons would have to travel.

They started preparations for construction of a bridge across the Black River to replace their makeshift ferry. It was to be located at the road terminus, below the falls. Transportation and communications were finally becoming easier, and new neighbors were settling closer and closer.

In July Desjardins contracted for another new road to be cut through the woods from High Falls to Castorville; the distance was shorter by land than water. Other work continued slowly at the Establishment, hampered by a succession of other difficulties — floods, sickness (dysentery was endemic), and fires which got out of control, threatening forest and buildings.

At the end of July, Desjardins set out on another trip to New York to try to raise money. He planned to return via Canada, visiting Niagara, Detroit, Kingston and Montreal so that he could explore the possibility of more advantageous trade and labor from Canadian sources.

However, a new blow fell upon him in New York — news that a new administrator, Rudolphe Tillier, had been sent out by the Company from Paris to take over management of Castorland. Tillier was a Swiss businessman and former judge, a member of the Sovereign Council of Berne. He also had some previous American business experience, since there is evidence of his being a merchant in Philadelphia in 1783.[8] Some of the Castorland funding had come from Swiss creditors; they must have wanted closer fiscal involvement in the project.

Europeans were so ignorant of the great difficulties in establishing a wilderness settlement that they could not understand Desjardins' slow progress and constant requests for additional funds. They suspected him of mismanagement and hoped another man could produce more satisfactory results.

It is probable that Nicolas Olive was also involved in this decision, since he participated in the Company's business and financial affairs in America and was a large stockholder. Some distrust must have developed between him and Desjardins after the disagreement about the location of Olive's lands, and various reports by his trusted employee, Louis Tassart. Desjardins had refrained from adverse reports to Olive about Tassart, but clearly the other had not been so charitable after they had clashed. Desjardins began to suspect some collusion against him, and recorded his suspicions in the *Journal:*

"Perhaps these gentlemen are trying to get the advantage of me."[9]

He waited in New York for Tillier's arrival, offended and apprehensive. Their original meeting must have been an uncomfortable one; after it Desjardins wrote:

"If he is a sensible man, he will not report until he has examined."[10]

A dramatic denouement ensued — one to which previous historians have paid no attention, although it seems apparent that the clash of personalities between Tillier and Desjardins must have been one of the major causes of the failure of Castorland!

A picture emerges from entries in the *Journal* of Desjardins transformed into a classically tragic figure — unappreciated, ill-used, full of smouldering anger. Each was a proud man, jealous of his prerogatives. Their mutual dislike increased as they journeyed toward Castorland, with Tillier rejecting every friendly overture and maintaining a shield of reserve and suspicion. He refused an invitation to lodge at Desjardins' home in Albany. The latter retreated into a haughty, self-justifying defensiveness, and his apprehension increased when Tassart joined their party in Schenectady, by prearrangement between Tillier and Olive, who described Tassart as "an indispensable man."

Upon their arrival in Castorland in early September, Tillier began to examine the lands and records and gradually take over direction of workmen and affairs. Desjardins continued to keep the *Journal*, recording the daily round of activities, sprinkled with comments indicating discord and disagreements, his hurt feelings and forebodings.

There was one pleasant exception to his increasingly dismal entries. On September 28th he wrote with some surprise:

"Mr. John Smith of Whitestown sent me a cheese, which is the first present I have received in America."[11]

During that fall there were finally some additions to their company. Tillier had brought along a French storekeeper, Victor Colinet, to whom he gave responsibility for year-round provisioning. Four French people arrived directly from Paris to take up residence in Castorland: a couple named Riedain; a young bachelor, Henri Boutin; and another young man only identified as being the son of a friend.

Although originally enthusiastic, they quickly became disallusioned, and Desjardins acidly commented upon this development:

"...Our newly arrived from France, have found the *real*, very different from the *ideal*, that they had formed. They had looked upon Castorland as a Normandy, or a suburb of Paris, where they had nothing to do but to come and live — they did not suppose when they came here, that in order to eat bread, they must get flour, etc."[12]

Nevertheless, the new settlers did remain and adapt themselves to the circumstances. They were the first private residents of Castorland, taking up shares for development, rather than primarily employed by the Company. Madame Riedain shared in some of the cooking and domestic chores while her husband and the other men were concerned in choosing their plots. Boutin selected 500 acres of land near the Long Falls (which later developed into the town of Carthage) and Riedain, who was acting for Chassanis, selected 1,250 acres at the mouth of the Beaver River. Initially they planned to spend their first winter living together in the Company cabin at the Long Falls, until they could build their own cabins the following spring. However, as they slowly became aware of the problems and hazards involved in that scheme, they changed their minds and decided to winter in Fort Schuyler.

Desjardins wrote very critically about their hasty choice of plots before they had a chance to see all of the lands available. They had not even visited the Black River Bay area before making their choice. He stated in very strong terms that it was against the Company's best interests to designate ownership of plots before their mapping was fully completed. As an example of the type of problem caused by premature land designations, he cited a current cause of contention about the lands which he had sold to Nicolas Olive overlapping those chosen for James LeRay in Paris by Tillier. Desjardins asserted that Tillier had a conflict of interest in acting as personal representative for James LeRay as well as being the Company Administrator.

At this point in the *Journal*, the conflict is heightened by a mystery! Two notes, in a different handwriting from the rest of the *Journal*, were inserted on loose sheets of paper. They defended the actions taken by Tillier and LeRay, and expressed indignation concerning the slurs on the integrity of both these gentlemen. They insisted that Tillier's purpose was to take charge of the interests of the stockholders as well as those of the company:

> "Oh! for this time he should have been more careful! It had been agreed that Mr. Tillier should be charged with the interests of the shareholders, as well as those of the Company...Mr. Tillier was perfectly right. Mr. LeRay was right, since he had sufficient confidence in the integrity and justice of Mr. Tillier..."[13]

One of the notes makes a counter-attack upon Desjardins, questioning why he had already selected 3,000 acres for himself if premature land designations were against the interests of the company:

> "...The selections of M.M. Olive and LeRay did not overlap, and if the choices that M. Desjardins calls premature, gave embarassment in the completion of the map, why did M. Desjardins make the selection of 3,000 acres for himself and his relatives, before it was finished?"[14]

The authorship of both these notes is uncertain. Hough believed (and this writer concurs) that they were written by Tillier; they are both typical of his flamboyant style of expression, and a motive for defending himself is obvious. However, in a footnote elsewhere, Hough did acknowledge the possibility that James LeRay might have written them;[15] each had the opportunity after the *Journal* was sent by Desjardins, via Tillier, to the Directors.

By this time, LeRay had become one of the Paris Commissioners, and must have been involved in the decision to replace Desjardins by Tillier.

This disagreement was only one of many which occurred that

fall. Meanwhile, the work continued at the Establishment, despite the developing rancour. In October preparations began for the winter season.

Louis Ferlent died; nevertheless his widow and three children planned to remain at High Falls over the winter, in addition to Colinet (the store keeper) and three workmen. Supplies were stockpiled well in advance this year, to free them from dependence upon winter deliveries. Lumber supplies were ordered so that they could work on building furniture when bad weather necessitated indoor work.

More disagreements are mentioned in the *Journal*. Tillier countermanded Desjardins' orders to the workmen, and he revoked the Castorville road contract. He rejected the mill site at Long Falls, on which so much effort had already been expended the previous year. Desjardins' hurt feelings show through the recording of a trivial incident:

> "M. Tillier remarked that we had too many dogs. (We had only two of our own, and two which the Indians had left with us to keep while they were on a journey.) I gave mine to M. Brodhead."[16]

Relations between the two men continued to deteriorate. During the following week, Desjardins wrote:

> "...this new administrator has appeared shocked, whenever I mingle in any affairs, and his plan appears to be to take exactly the opposite course, in everything that I do. After some disagreeable moments, I have resolved to follow my own course, and absolutely take no part in anything. But as I don't want to stay in the chimney corner, any better than he does, I have set myself at work on the roads in the vicinity...an exercise that engages my time, and distracts my thoughts."[17]

Geoffrey Desjardins and a lately arrived cousin of the family were witnesses to his humiliation, but unable, of course, to intervene. As Company Clerk, Geoffrey took his orders from Tillier, and was occupied with correspondence and record keeping.

Some snow fell on November 1st, and Tillier, who clearly did not relish hardships, resolved to leave the next day, despite Desjardins' insistence that departure was not necessary before December 1st. In final preparations for the winter, Tillier wrote out detailed instructions for the workmen who were to stay on, although most of them could not read. He read the particulars to them, and made them sign with a cross. Desjardins noted smugly:

> "...he has not the least doubt but that everyone would do exactly as he had enjoined upon them."[18]

It is obvious that Desjardins hadn't the least doubt that matters would not go as smoothly as Tillier anticipated.

So Tillier departed, with the brothers accompanying him, and Simon Desjardins sadly recording:

"I left Castorland with a presentiment that I should never return, and that I had encountered all the pains and perils on my part, only that a newcomer should enjoy, or rather squander, the little I had done with our slender means. It was a little hard for me to quit, at the moment when the survey was finished, and the condition of the Company would furnish the means sufficient to realize the plans I had formed, and to contribute to the prosperity of the country, of which I hoped to be one day called the founder."[19]

The two Desjardins spent the next five months in Albany, preparing duplicate records of all accounts, working with Brodhead on the final map and survey report, updating the *Journal* and completing the last field books. The final map included 4,828 numbered, marked lots of 50 acres each. Geoffrey recopied the complete *Journal*, incorporating notes and field records which had been recorded separately from different locations. Tillier, who was spending the winter in New York City, demanded that all records be sent to him there.

Desjardins discontinued detailed, daily *Journal* entries, limiting most of the final months' entries to lists of correspondence received and forwarded and other business records. However, he entered one personal note of satisfaction on December 8th, when Tillier acknowledged, on the basis of the newly completed survey maps, that the lands he had chosen for LeRay did overlap those previously sold to Olive by Desjardins. This petty triumph was clearly balm to Desjardins' wounded ego.

In February, Riedain and his wife, who must have been short of funds, insisted upon returning to High Falls. Colinet vainly protested against keeping them at the Company's expense.

In April Tillier received further bolstering of his legal supremacy over Desjardins as Company Agent. He decided that he would remain in New York and appointed Louis Tassart to be his representative in administering affairs at Castorland. The elevation of this young man must have been galling to Desjardins; he had a low opinion of Tassart's integrity and capability, despite frank acknowledgement of some good qualities. In their two years of acquaintance, they had originally formed a cordial relationship but this had deteriorated after the disagreement over location of Olive's lands, and the tragedy of Pharoux's death, which Tassart had attributed solely to Pharoux's poor judgment.

Desjardins was now placed in a most uncomfortable position. Tillier gave him the choice of staying in Albany and handling business affairs there, or returning to Castorland to work under Tassart's direction. Obviously this ultimatum offered choices that were equally untenable. Neither alternative offered him opportunity to exercise his considerable experience and independence.

Most historians who have written about Castorland ignore this dilemma (if, indeed, they even knew about it) and merely say that Desjardins "quit." This is contrary to the intentions he clearly stated on the final page of the *Journal*:

> "**April 8, 1797**...M. Tillier has received news from the Company. He gives me the choice of going with M. Tassart, or of remaining here. Believing that the welfare of the Company should decide upon what is best, and not finding it convenient to leave the establishment to the disposal of M. Tassart alone, I judge it preferable to go with him."[20]

There is no detailed record of subsequent events; they constitute another mystery which appears unsolvable. Tillier was responsible for keeping a journal after this time, but it has not survived. Some other records do exist about legal transactions and business details, and there are a few recorded personal reminiscences from several sources. All of these are described in the next chapter. However, there is no indication of whether Desjardins actually spent any more time at Castorland. He must have resigned eventually, but the overwhelming evidence in the *Journal* of his steadfast character and his strong interest in the settlement seem to lead inevitably to a conclusion that he was forced out, rather than electing freely to disassociate himself from the settlement.

Since Desjardins occupies no further part in the story of Castorland, after having been a principal for so long, it seems appropriate here to digress from the settlement's history and tell what little more is known of his own.

Desjardins drew no salary as an American Commissioner. No reason for this was stated in the Constitution, which did provide a stipend for Pharoux who held equal office. It seems reasonable to infer that this situation was a result of Desjardins' own choice, and that he preferred to serve the common interest without charge. He was personally wealthy, as indicated by the extensive possessions he brought from France to America — furniture, library, wines, two servants, etc. — all perquisites of a rich man. He clearly stated his attitude toward the responsibilities which should properly accompany wealth, in his uncomplimentary remarks about General Philip Schuyler who drew a salary from the canal company (stated in

Boats on the Mohawk River.

Chapter Two). He strongly felt that public figures should not derive personal profits from positions of public trust.

Two sources of information give us glimpses of Desjardins in later life. One indicates an attempt to found a private settlement on his own share of Castorland lots. He had chosen 3,000 acres for himself on Point Peninsula — the spit of land which juts out into Lake Ontario. A footnote by Hough indicates that it was actually 3,002 acres in the area known locally as "Portuguese Neck."[21] This was a fine location, fronting on both the bay and the lake. If the projected port city had ever been built, its value would have been further enhanced. Desjardins was entitled to receive 3,000 more acres at the Company's final distribution of land, so he anticipated a holding of 6,000 acres by 1814. It is possible he may have purchased the additional 3,000 earlier than that date.

A two-page footnote by Hough in his translation of the *Journal*, gives information about Desjardins' plans for his private holdings:

> "...he subsequently formed a project for a magnificent community here, of which we have seen a printed copy: without date, but evidently issued early in the present century. After setting forth the fact that the State of New York is one of the most flourishing in the Union, with the largest revenues in proportion to its expenses, that its people are least taxed, etc., he proceeds to set forth his plan for a 'Rural Establishment,' which bears strong resemblance to some very recent schemes...
>
> The scheme included 6,000 acres, and was to be conducted by Simon Desjardins-Pont-Vanne, in the Portuguese Peninsula of Lower Castorland. The property of the Company was to remain undivided and the land was to be applied as follows:

Dwelling and 50 acres for each of the Secretaries	200 acres
For Powder Mill and its dependencies	10 acres
For Lime kilns	20 acres
For Brick and Potteries	10 acres
For Potash and Pearlash	20 acres
For Two Fisheries.	20 acres
For Tannery and Leather dressing	10 acres
For Iron Foundry	10 acres
For Copper Foundry	10 acres
For Glass works	20 acres
For Botannical Garden	60 acres
For Natural Meadows	600 acres
For Village divided into small tracts, 9 allotments.	900 acres
For Orchard and Manufacture of Cider	100 acres
For Woodlands	4000 acres
	6000 acres"[22]

104

LOCATION OF DESJARDIN'S LANDS ON POINT PENINSULA

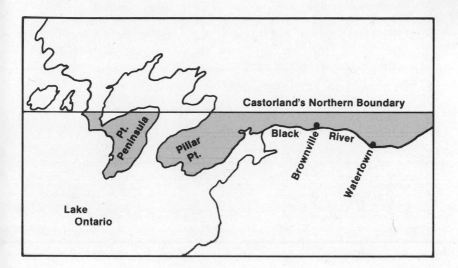

Actually the correct total for the acreage listed is 5,990, but there is no way of knowing whether the error was Desjardins', or whether Hough may have omitted copying one 10 acre item. After completing the above list, Hough added a final comment with his personal opinion of the plan:

> "This scheme proved to be of no more substance than Moonshine. We are not informed of the details or history of the speculation."[23]

Desjardins' optimism in projecting another speculation may have been warranted. Since the British had finally vacated Fort Oswego in 1796, the waterway access to his lands was now easy from both American and British shores. Canal construction had eliminated portages on the Mohawk, so that boats could travel more easily all the way from Schenectady to Lake Ontario.

There is no information as to why Desjardins' scheme was never carried out; we can only assume some repetition of the frustrations and disappointments which blighted his earlier hopes.

A local history of Jefferson County states that the first settlers on Point Peninsula arrived in 1808 by ox team, and that the first road was not built until 1818.[24] We do not know whether such settlers were associated with Desjardins' plan, but it seems unlikely, in view of the last information relating to him.

A final view of him is derived from a letter written in 1859 by James LeRay's son, Vincent. It was directed to Dr. Hough and included his recollections and information about Castorland, of which he had become a neighbor in 1808. He refers to Desjardins in disdainful terms, probably reflecting his father's point of view:

> "...I will mention...one...who was not a settler, but an owner, to give a sample of the spirit which moved that class of men in Castorland. He owned half the peninsula opposite Sackett's Harbor. The most flourishing town in that part of the State, was, according to Mr. Desjardins' calculation, to rise at the isthmus which was to be cut, and the best harbor on Lake Ontario to be made. He had formed such ideas of the rise of the land in consequence, that he never would sell an inch. The emigrants, persuaded that there could be no owner where there was no settler, poured upon the tract, which was good land, and took up every part of it. Mr. Desjardins getting old, gave up, it seems, the idea of seeing the northern city rise, since squatters had taken up possession of it, as of a common farm land. He sold the tract, and died a few years ago in Versailles, the survivor of all the persons whom we have mentioned, as settlers in Castorland."[25]

It is not known when Desjardins returned to France, but he must have been a disappointed, if not embittered, man.

CHAPTER SIX

Subsequent History of Castorland

Seventeen years elapsed between the end of the *Journal* in 1797 and the official end of Castorland in 1814. Although no official record of those years exists, by piecing together information from a variety of sources, it is possible to outline the main events and glimpse many fascinating details.

The administration under Rudolphe Tillier lasted until 1800 and was clearly a stormy period. His personality seems to have been unstable and abrasive, antagonizing both would-be settlers and the directors in Paris. Hough relates:

> "Tillier is remembered as a man somewhat advanced in years, fond of display, vain, visionary, and as the sequel indicated, unworthy of confidence, if not a downright villain."[1]

He proved to be a poor choice for the job, lacking any zest for the adventures and discomforts of frontier living. He attempted to govern Castorland from his residence in New York City through orders to his representative, Louis Tassart.[2] It is not known how long Tassart occupied this position.

Tillier's most important achievement was the conclusion of the revised agreements with William Constable[3] which were based upon the records and arguments previously presented by Pharoux and Desjardins. Constable finally recognized the validity of most of their claims, and signed a new legal document in 1797 which redefined Castorland's boundaries. He conceded some, but not all, of the points which Desjardins had tried so hard to establish.

A new map was drawn, based upon William Cockburn's survey, replacing the inaccurate Sauthier map. The Black River became Castorland's western boundary, eliminating the checkerboard pattern of ownership with Inman along the river bank. This resulted in the French tract being divided into three pieces, rather than six; the major area (called Upper Castorland) lay south of the Great Bend on the Black River and contained all of the land on the eastern bank. A narrow strip lay west of the Great Bend along the northern shore of the river, stretching to Black River Bay, and a third part, Point Peninsula, jutted into Lake Ontario.

107

FINAL SETTLEMENT OF CASTORLANDS BOUNDARIES

**CASTORLAND PRIOR TO
THE BOUNDARY SETTLEMENT**

The final settlement of the Castorland boundaries in 1800 eliminated Inman's minor holdings on the eastern bank of the Black River, so that their lands were divided by the river's curves into three parcels, rather than six.

Additional lands were added from the mountainous Adirondacks on the east to make up the land deficit.

**CASTORLAND AFTER
THE BOUNDARY SETTLEMENT**

A second agreement was signed in March, 1800, adding 30,000 acres to the southern part of the tract on its eastern side, giving it a triangular shape. These new lands were not the fertile farmlands which Desjardins had demanded, but were hilly, heavily forested terrain, extending into the western Adirondacks. These changes are illustrated in Brodhead's Map of the Macomb Purchase, issued by the Surveyor-General of New York.

While Tillier transacted business in New York, life continued at the settlement in Castorland. Supplies were now more easily obtained, and more buildings must have been erected at High Falls, as well as a settlement begun at Castorville on the Beaver River.

These developments can be inferred from records left by other settlers, who were then spreading onto lands to the west and north of Castorland. One of these was Noadiah Hubbard, who passed through High Falls in November, 1797, and wrote a letter in which he mentioned "the log city constructed by the French."[4] He later settled in Champion near the Long Falls, on the western side of the Black River.

The first settlers enroute to the area which became Lowville arrived at High Falls in late March, 1798.[5] This was a party of several families from Westfield, Massachusetts, who spent two weeks there with the French while building a boat with tools borrowed from their hosts. It was a large, flat-bottomed vessel, 25 feet long and 7 feet wide — larger than any craft the French had built. It was launched on April 10th, only two days after the river was free of ice. Overloaded with people, animals and supplies, the boat nearly capsized! With some difficulty, the settlers regained control and had to store some of their supplies on shore for subsequent trips.

By this time, Castorville was starting to replace High Falls as the chief Company settlement. These settlers at Lowville became their nearest neighbors, and obtained their first lumber from a French sawmill which had begun operations there.[6]

Several French families attempted to settle in Castorland during Tillier's administration. They were appalled by the difficulties they encountered, unprepared for the severity of the winters, the shortness of the growing season and the remoteness from civilized society. They lacked the skills necessary for frontier existence and were unwilling to perform manual labor. They were helpless without servants. The glowing promises of the Castorland *Prospectus* were finally revealed as out of touch with reality.

Most of the families who attempted to settle during this period left after a short time, sending angry complaints back to the directors in Paris. They felt that Tillier should have made more effort to facilitate their settling. In turn, he complained that large numbers of unprepared settlers were too large a drain upon communal resources, overtaxing their capacity for supply and transportation.

One notable exception among the settlers was Louis Francois de Saint-Michel, who came in 1798[7] with his convent-educated daughter, to manage the Sistersfield Estate on the Black River. It was jointly owned by the three daughters of M. Lambot, a Paris notary, and was located a few miles south of Long Falls. Saint-Michel had been a nobleman, serving as Royal Forester under Louis XVI, and was one of the very few upperclass French who managed to adjust well to his change in fortune and environment. He and his daughter were much admired and respected by both French and American neighbors, unlike many of their haughty fellow countrymen. They lived simply in a crude cabin and were noted for their friendly, warm and gentle manners and the natural dignity with which they performed humble tasks. The girl married a neighboring Frenchman, was widowed, eventually remarried, and finally settled on the Deer River nearby. Her father resided with her during his declining years and died in 1830.[8]

American settlers were more self-sufficient than most of the French, but they did not populate Castorland either, although similar lands all around were being developed. Those interested in buying plots were able to procure the neighboring lands much more easily, because of delays and difficulties in obtaining clear titles on Castorland land purchases. Aside from the obvious time-consuming problems in obtaining legal papers from across the Atlantic, an additional difficulty had arisen. In 1798 a federal law was passed which restricted land ownership by aliens, so Chassanis had to transfer nominal ownership of Company lands to his brother-in-law, James LeRay, who held American citizenship. By now LeRay had become a major stockholder, as well as a Paris Commissioner, and was therefore much more involved in Company affairs. The legalities of the title transfers, however, were not completed until 1801, thereby impeding local sales.

Much of the blame for Castorland's slow progress, however, was attributed to Tillier. As adverse reports about his manner and activities reached Paris, Company officials became alarmed and tried to take a more active hand in directing the development of the settlement. Such efforts proved counterproductive, as they gave detailed instructions about matters on which they lacked any first hand knowledge. The ultimate absurdity was their ordering of the precise route of a road to be built from High Falls to Castorville, then to Long Falls, and finally to the St. Lawrence River where the village of Clayton stands today. The terrain was difficult, but the map-makers in Paris were adamant. Their folly was later described:

> "...even roads were laid out on the maps, without any knowledge of the localities — but it is true, in beautiful straight lines. I would hardly dare state such a fact, if a sample of this folly was not known in this country, where the traces of a road once opened, but of course never traveled... was to cross an almost impassable precipice; but orders were imperative, and the road was made on both sides..."[9]

Aside from the problem of crossing from one cliff top to another, there were additional difficulties in crossing numerous streams, because the road lacked any bridges. A man on horseback might manage to ford or swim some of them, but crossing was impossible for wagons. One later historian flippantly observed that such a road could have been traveled only by an "äeroplane."[10]

One attempt Tillier made to encourage development did turn out well. During 1798 he became acquainted with Jacob Brown, a 23 year old Pennsylvania Quaker who was then teaching school in New York. Tillier interested him in the job of founding another settlement in Lower Castorland, near Black River Bay, as well as acting as Land Agent for the Company in that area. Brown was excited by the opportunities offered, seeing prospects for himself and his family to recoup former wealth lost through "an unfortunate speculation."[11] Tillier traveled to Philadelphia to convince Brown's father of the soundness of the enterprise, and the elder Brown bought a considerable tract of land at $2 per acre.

Jacob Brown closed his school during the winter, and set out for Castorland early in 1799. He preceded his family by several months, passing through High Falls for the first time in March, en route northwards. Apparently he inspired confidence in all who met him (showing early those qualities of leadership which later elevated him to the position of Major General during the War of 1812, and finally Commanding General of the U.S. Army).

Brown chose lands near the head of navigation on the Black River, about seven miles from the Bay. The tract included excellent mill sites near where Philomel Creek entered the Black River. The homestead later developed into the village of Brownville, named after its founder. Few people today realize that Brownville and vicinity were initially part of Castorland.

Although Brown started construction of a log cabin as soon as possible, it was still unfinished when his family arrived in May. They

111

came via the water route through Lake Ontario, a much easier mode of travel for a large party with heavy goods.

The Brown family was a large group — some 20 people including his parents, 16 brothers and sisters and other relatives — all of whom managed to crowd into his 20 foot square cabin which still lacked roof, windows and doors. A piece of sailcloth from their boat was stretched across the timbers for a temporary roof, while openings for the door and windows were closed with makeshift arrangements of quilts and blankets.

A story is told that Jacob's mother surveyed her new windowless home with great dismay, and then declared:

"Well, Jacob, thee has got us all here, but thee has not a board to make us a coffin, nor a spade to dig us a grave."[12]

The tale continues that she did not smile for the next six months! Finally, Jacob made a trip to New York City for supplies, and upon his return he solemnly presented her with a spade. When she asked:

"What will thee do with a spade amongst these roots and stumps?"[13]

he alluded to her first remark, upon her arrival, airily stating:

"Oh, some of us may die!"[14]

This sally was said to have provoked her first smile.

The Browns were among the first of a large number of hardy American pioneers who settled between the Black River and the St. Lawrence in 1799 and 1800. However, only a few were within the narrow strip of land of the Castorland territory. Brownville developed faster than any other settlement in that area[15] due to the large family labor force and their varied capabilities. They constructed roads, mills, bridges, opened a store, manufactured potash, cleared fields and raised crops. As the family prospered, Jacob built a new home and married a woman from Williamstown, Massachusetts. Brownville did not appear to have much connection with the French settlements in Castorland. Its best lines of communication lay via Lake Ontario.

Meanwhile, back in Paris, more concern mounted among the directors as they received complaints from dissatisfied shareholders. They attempted to obtain firsthand information about Tillier's administration through reports by trusted envoys in America. One was Patrick Blake, son-in-law of Monsieur Lambot. Another was Father Pierre Joulin, a close associate of James LeRay. Tillier was outraged by the investigations of these gentlemen and he refused to let them examine his books.

Jacob Brown
1812 oil painting, artist unknown.
(Courtesy of Charles P. Dunham, Jefferson County Historian).

Sketch of mills at Brownville, about 1820, by J. Milbert.

The directors had already lost confidence in Tillier by the spring of 1798, at which time Gouverneur Morris was planning his return to America. Morris was a close friend of LeRay and a business associate of William Constable. He owned a large neighboring tract of land, northeast of Castorland. The directors attempted to persuade Morris to take over administration of Castorland, but initially he was reluctant to get involved. He finally agreed to assist in a limited way, and bought some Castorland shares also.[16]

Morris did not take an active role in Castorland affairs, but he encouraged the hiring of Jacob Brown and in September of 1799 he appointed Richard Coxe (Mrs. LeRay's brother) to replace Tillier in directing all operations in Upper Castorland. Coxe arrived in Castorland in June of 1800 and then forcibly took possession of the store, mills and property at High Falls, Long Falls and Castorville.

Tillier was stripped of all his legal powers and he fought this dismissal furiously. In January, 1800, he advertised in Albany newspapers, cautioning the public to trust no Castorland agents except himself. He disclaimed their authority for sales, acts or deeds. In October he had a printer at Rome, New York, publish French and English editions of a long, rambling document justifying his administration, defending his honor and accusing Chassanis of fraud.[17]

Writing of himself in the third person, he immodestly praised his own struggles against vast obstacles, his fair dealings with all parties, and his own zealous attention to Company affairs. He claimed that his reports and his journal proved the regularity of his administration. (This mention of his journal is the only indication of its existence, but no historians have been able to find it.)

Five of the complaints made by Tillier against the Paris directors are undoubtedly justified and indicate some reasons for the failure of the colony. First, funds were insufficient and always late. Second, effective administrative decisions could best be made by persons on the spot; government from afar was necessarily ill-informed, resulting in poor management. Third, land shares should have been allocated only after the purchaser had a chance to see the land in question. Land designations made in Paris produced too much dissatisfaction. Fourth, the Company's policy of reserving alternate shares from sale (so that their value would appreciate) impeded sales and was difficult to maintain. Fifth, the necessity of confirming all American transactions in Paris also impeded local land sales because of the delay in obtaining clear titles.

Other complaints by Tillier appear a bit paranoid; in fact it was later asserted that he was "deranged" at this time.[18] Tillier accused

115

Chassanis and others of plotting against him, sending spies to frame false allegations, and of attempting land fraud by transferring land titles to LeRay:

> "...Mr. Blake arrived...R. Tillier received him with kindness, and in such an hospitable manner that any other person would have thought he merited some acknowledgment. Mr. Blake on the contrary, became his calumniator...
>
> In the meantime one Pierre Joulin, also arrived at New York, appearing to be secretly charged with the interests of the company... R. Tillier saw that Mr. Joulin did not treat him with the same good faith and candor that he used towards the said Joulin...He was bound by close and secret ties with Mr. Blake...
>
> The indignation of an honest man in such a case must be great, and Tillier can not refrain from expressing his feelings...Finally the plot of which these gentlemen were the agents is unveiled...the character of P. Chassanis and LeRay de Chaumont, whose interests appear to be joined and confounded together...are injurious to the interests of the company..."[19] (The full text of Tiller's charges are in Appendix IV.)

Chassanis published a reply, defending himself in detail against these charges, concluding:

> "...If Mr. Tillier wished to prove that his administration, as he says, has been pure, and that it was free from reproach, he has failed to show the result...We will render him justice, if, by the establishments formed and his model accounts, he can show a good employment of his time and of the funds which he has received. His obstinate refusal upon these points, forces upon us the suspicion that he can not report an honest administration..."[20]

The quarrel smouldered for several years, involving legal suits which were eventually won by the Company. There seems to have been sufficient truth in both charges and countercharges to indicate maladministration by all parties involved.

Meanwhile life did continue at Castorland itself, although certainly hampered by the quality of leadership. There are two descriptions of Castorland in 1800 which reflect different vantage points.

One description derives from a letter written in 1859 by Vincent LeRay, son of James LeRay. Since he did not personally appear upon the scene until 1808, his information must have come from family or Company records in Paris, possibly a report by Coxe after he evicted Tillier:

> "In 1800, after contracting a debt of more than 300,000 livres, all their expenses had produced only one saw-mill, 18 log houses, and 82 acres of

TRANSLATION

OF A

MEMORIAL

OF

RODOLPHE 'TILLIER's

JUSTIFICATION

OF THE

ADMINISTRATION

OF

CASTORLAND,

County of ONEIDA, State of NEW-YORK.

ROME:
PRINTED BY THOMAS WALKER.

OCTOBER – 1800.

Cover page of Tillier Memorial.

clearing. So few settlers had been obtained, that there were only 11 log houses, and 130 acres cleared, in addition to those of the Company. Several roads had indeed, been made, and at a great expense; but besides being ill made, or injudiciously laid out, the want of population soon rendered them useless...."[21]

A more favorable description was written by an obviously enthusiastic person who appears to have been serving as an agent for a Castorland shareholder. It is a letter dated September 4, 1800 and is too long to quote here in its entirety. However, it seems to indicate a flourishing settlement:

> "...Our chief place, situated on the banks of the pretty Beaver River, and from thence so appropriately named *Castorville*, begins to grow. It is still only, as you may justly think, but a cluster of primitive dwellings, but still it contains several families of mechanics, of which new colonies have so frequent need. Several stores, situated in favorable places, begin to have business. The Canadians...come hither to buy the goods which they need, as well as sugar and rum, which, from the duties being less at our ports than at Quebec, are cheaper with us than with them..."[22]

The unnamed writer also buoyantly described the geography of the region, trees, crops, and the abundance of birds, fish and animals. He recounted that the colonists are a mixture of many nationalities — Scotch, Irish and Americans as well as French — and he mentioned some of them by name. He referred to the loss of Pharoux as a setback to the development of the colony. His description clearly referred to all of Castorland, not merely to Castorville. Then he gave an account of his own efforts, on behalf of his employer. It is not clear to which waterfall he was referring, in his first sentence as "the great falls." This term had been employed by Desjardins and Pharoux to designate those at what is now Watertown, but the falls above Castorville also fell in three stages:

> "I have placed your habitation not far from the great falls, but far enough distant not to be incommoded by the noise, or rather uproar, which they make in falling three stages. The picturesque view of the chain of rocks over which the waters plunge their tumultuous commotion, the natural meadows in the vicinity, the noble forests which bound the horizon; the establishments on the opposite bank; the passage of travellers who arrive at the ferry I have formed, all contribute to render the location very interesting, and it will become more so when cultivation, industry, and time, shall have embellished this district, still so rustic and wild...The house is solid and commodious, the garden and farm yards well enclosed.
>
> I have placed a French family over the store and am well pleased with them. I think, however, they will return to France, where the new

118

government has at length banished injustice, violence and crime, and replaced them by the reign of reason, clemency and law...

I want nothing but hands. You who live in a country where there are so many useless hands and whose labors are so little productive there, why don't you send us some hundreds of those men?...What conquest would they not achieve in ten years! And what a difference in their lot!..."[23] (See the full text of this letter in Appendix VI.)

The letter's author is not named, but he is described as an agent for one of Crèvecoeur's friends, certainly also a Parisian shareholder. It was included in a book published by Crèvecoeur in Paris in 1801.[24] Its placement in an Appendix, rather than the main body, suggests that it may have arrived just in time for inclusion in the publication.

Hough reprinted the letter in his 1854 *History of Jefferson County*, playing down its importance by stating: "...from its romantic style it scarcely merits notice in history."[25] However, at that time (before discovery of the *Journal*), Hough knew very little about Castorland and did not know that Crèvecoeur was a shareholder. He seemed to believe the letter was fictional.

However, the extensive detail indicates that it is genuine, and very valuable as the only authentic description of affairs in Castorland after the ending of the *Journal*.

Another indication of ongoing life in Castorland is a record of a wedding in 1801. The bride was Mrs. Marguerite Charton, 27 years old, described as:

"...an educated French widow, who had left her native country in company with her brother, a Catholic priest, to seek in America that life of freedom of opinion which had been denied so many of her countrymen at home...She was a devoted monarchist..."[26]

She married 28 year old Guiliame Coupert (later Americanized to William Cooper), the first settler on the north side of the Black River in Jefferson County. A formal marriage settlement was recorded with the French consulate in New York pertaining to the division of property in case of death or separation. One of the official witnesses at the wedding was Henri Boutin, previously mentioned as the first settler at Long Falls.

Long Falls eventually developed into the village of Carthage, but that was not until many years later. Henri Boutin, who had settled there in 1798, had made a substantial clearing for his home and crops in his first years of residence. However, he was drowned shortly afterwards[27] and the land was not reoccupied until eventually acquired by the LeRay family in 1815.

After Boutin's death, the only settler residing at Long Falls for several years was Jean Baptiste Boussot, who had formerly been Desjardins' foreman. He possessed only a small plot, earning his living by operating a ferry and an inn. He must have married about this time, as both his wife and inn were described in strongly critical terms by Washington Irving, who spent a night there in 1803:

"...A dirtier house was never seen. We dubbed it 'The Temple of Dirt'...The landlady herself was in perfect character with the house, —a little squat Frenchwoman, with red face, a black wool hat stuck upon her head, her hair, greasy and uncombed, hanging about her ears, and the rest of her dress and person in similar style. We were heartily glad to make our escape."[28]

Before leaving the house, Irving wrote a poem on the wall over the fireplace:

"Here sovereign Dirt erects her sable throne,
The House, the host, the hostess all her own."[29]

Some time later another prominent visitor passed by, Judge Cooper, founder of Cooperstown and father of James Fenimore Cooper. He appended a more philosophical couplet to the foregoing, based upon his greater tolerance of frontier conditions:

"Learn hence, young man, and teach it to your sons,
The wisest way's to take it as it comes."[30]

A digression from the history of Castorland is appropriate here, to complete the story of Baptiste's life. He continued to operate his ferry until a bridge was built in 1813. He fathered six children,[31] the oldest being a son named George who was the first child born (in 1805) in that area.[32] Baptiste lived to a ripe old age respected by some, but not by all, who knew him.

Baptiste was described in most disdainful terms by Vincent LeRay:

"...With more order or system, he could easily, in such a position, have realized an independent fortune...The population covering the meager field of his slothful farming...others came to rival and dethrone him ...and he left a world that was getting along without him!"[33]

One possible reason for LeRay's irritation with him may have stemmed from the fact that Baptiste operated the only distillery in the Long Falls area. All later settlers purchased land through LeRay's land agents, and all their titles bore clauses forbidding the erection of distilleries.[34]

A much more favorable view of Baptiste was recorded by the historian, John Haddock, who grew up in the town of Carthage

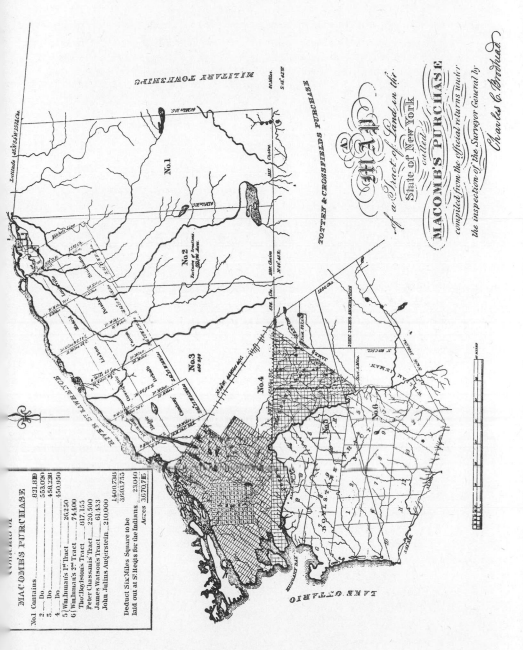

Official Map of Macomb Purchase.

(formerly Long Falls) and recorded boyhood recollections of Baptiste and his wife:

> "No one was refused a passage across the river or a shelter under his roof because they had no money to give in payment. Both himself and wife were well known for their generosity and activity... The writer well remembers this remarkable old pioneer... He was of medium stature, and for a man of his age quite active, but then quite deaf, very polite in manner, somewhat eccentric, yet bearing the impress of a life of hardy adventure... He lived to the advanced age of 93, dying... in 1847."[35]

Returning now to the chronology of Castorland, it appears that the settlements at High Falls and at Castorville started to decline rather rapidly after the turn of the century. Aside from the lawsuits between Tillier and the Company, there were other factors.

In Paris as well as in America, there was dissension at the leadership levels. Since James LeRay was now the nominal owner of Company lands, as well as being a major shareholder, he bore many legal and financial encumbrances and obligations. He was very frustrated that his advice did not prevail over the other Paris Commissioners, and finally resolved to develop his own holdings independently. He employed Jacob Brown to represent him, as well as Castorland, as land agent, and Brown worked for LeRay until 1807.[36]

By this time, LeRay owned considerable tracts, and he kept adding to them. In addition to his Castorland shares, he and Gouverneur Morris were also involved in the Antwerp Company — another syndicate which, on paper at least, was contemporary with Castorland. It too was a shareholding company formed in 1793 by European businessmen on lands purchased from William Constable. Chassanis had originally been involved in this venture also, but had turned his assets over to LeRay along with other nearby lands. These holdings lay directly north of Castorland. As far as is known, this company never undertook any settlements, its financial resources also being inadequate. Morris and LeRay represented the Company in America, each taking title to 220,000 acres in 1800, complying with the law against alien ownership. Eventually this company also failed, and LeRay bought much of its enormous tract, reselling smaller plots to local settlers as opportunities arose.

James LeRay and Gouverneur Morris had long been close friends as well as business associates, and they performed many services for each other. When Morris had returned to the United States in 1798, he had taken responsibility for escorting Mrs. LeRay and her two youngest children, who were coming to visit her family in New Jersey. This obligation was not a light one: the two month voyage was rough, dangerous and full of hardships. Provisions were inadequate, the captain and crew incompetent, the weather was stormy and the ship leaky. Morris often had to correct the captain's navigation, and sometimes care for the children personally when Mrs. LeRay and the nursemaid were indisposed.[37]

Frequent correspondence linked Morris and LeRay, and mutual favors ensued. Morris, in America, requested LeRay to find him some suitable servants in France and send them over:

> "...a *chasseur* who understood fishing...he would be useful to me, and a cook is a physical necessity. No good domestics can be had here, not even women. None of those imported can, I think, be depended on unless they be somewhat advanced in years."[38]

After Morris had established himself at Morrisania, his estate just north of New York City, he served in Congress as U.S. Senator from New York. However, in addition to his public duties, he was involved in a variety of land speculation schemes. He owned property in Pennsylvania and in western New York, as well as small parcels of land north of Albany near Ballston and Glens Falls, and a very large tract bordering the St. Lawrence River. He also held shares in Castorland and in the Antwerp Company to its north, with responsibilities for some directorship for both.

In the summer of 1800, he set forth on a long trip north, stating his purpose:

> "...to visit some property of my own, and some which was confided to my care by others, in the northern parts of the State..."[39]

He preferred traveling by boat, rather than horse or extensive walking, because he was handicapped by a wooden leg. He enjoyed camping along the way when not in the vicinity of cities or good inns, and normally carried along his valet who doubled as fisherman and cook, in addition to a boat crew. Their provisions included full, comfortable camping regalia.

Starting in the middle of July, he traveled up the Hudson, and then via Lakes George and Champlain to Montreal. After a short visit there, he embarked upon the St. Lawrence River from which he had direct access to his largest tract. He enjoyed spending several days along his own waterfront, fishing, camping and making small excursions on shore. The hunting was good also; they shot some partridges and ducks.

Then they proceeded further up the St. Lawrence into Lake Ontario, encountering rough water and gale winds. Morris prided himself upon his navigation and sailing skills and was confident of his ability to handle the boat, but recorded in his diary:

"The boatmen do not like to go out...waves would not disgrace the Atlantic."[40]

Nevertheless, they rounded the various capes and islands which lay at the entrance to Lake Ontario, and finally entered the outer part of Black River Bay. He referred to it by two names: the Indian "Niarme" (which appears in a variety of spellings in different sources) and the English name "Hungry Bay" (so called because an English expeditionary force had sickened and died there in 1777 after they had run out of provisions). Morris noted the fine harbor and included, in his diary, a description of the bay and surrounding lands. They camped there that night, in the middle of August, pleased to:

"...stretch ourselves on the bosum (sic) of Old Mother Earth and resign ourselves to that repose which is the exclusive property of Health, Temperance and Exercise."[41]

Morris then proceeded across Lake Ontario, along the eastern and southern shores, until he reached Niagara, where he spent a week.

On his return trip, in September, he spent three more days in the Black River region, this time meeting and conferring with Jacob Brown. Morris sailed up the river to the first clearing, where Brown met him, and together they toured the lands bordering the bay, most of which belonged to LeRay. In his diary, he termed them "excellent."

Boats could not ascend the river past Brownville, and Morris did not attempt at that time to visit the area beyond the falls. He then retraced his route back to the St. Lawrence and resumed his homeward trip. Undoubtedly, he wrote an account of this trip to LeRay.

In 1802 James LeRay was finally able to rejoin his family in America. He took up residence in New Jersey near his wife's family. Late in the following summer he made his first visit to his northern lands, and this time Gouverneur Morris acted as his guide.

On this trip they followed the same water route which Desjardins and Pharoux had first taken in 1793 via the Mohawk River, Oneida Lake and Oswego River to Lake Ontario.

Describing the trip in his diary, Morris wrote of the personal attention required to outfit a batteau suitably for such a trip. When they arrived at Schenectady, he was dissatisfied with the size and fittings of a boat he had ordered in advance. He insisted upon a larger one, and spent an entire day personally supervising the installation of fittings and lockers to hold their equipment.

Gouverneur Morris

They left Schenectady on September 1st, 1803, and had to portage at Little Falls because the locks were being rebuilt. Pharoux's former criticisms seem justified in the light of Morris' comment:

> "Locks are *now* going on well and will be *properly executed* — the masonry will not cost as much as the old wooden locks."[42]

When they reached Lake Ontario, their boatmen responded similarly to the wind and waves as the 1793 voyagers had; Morris recorded that he had to use a combination of "authority and indifference" to handle their fears and complaints. It was the 16th of September when they reached the Black River region and entered the bay recently named "Chaumont" in honor of LeRay's familial home. This time they spent ten days in the area, mostly in the vicinity of Brownville, where Morris much admired the "prosperous settlement" of the "industrious and intelligent" Browns.[43]

Richard Coxe as well as Jacob Brown met with them there, so Castorland affairs must have been discussed extensively, but are not mentioned in Morris' diary. LeRay toured his lands by horseback, in company with his brother-in-law, Coxe, and was pleased with them.

The weather turned cold and stormy in late September, and they experienced an unpleasant adventure at the beginning of their homeward-bound trip. They had planned their return via the St. Lawrence River and Montreal.

On the day they started, the winds were contrary and there were many delays. It was late before they reached Lake Ontario, and enroute their pilot became ill and darkness overtook them. Navigating only by memory and some very faint moonlight, Morris sailed through the dangerous waters around Cape Vincent and the large islands at the mouth of the St. Lawrence. They had to cover 18 miles after sunset before finally reaching a sheltered stopping place. Part of the time it was raining, and they were all drenched. They camped that night alongside a small house which was too full to accommodate them indoors. The only assistance its inhabitants could provide was some dry straw to keep them off the wet ground:

> "It is near midnight before all arrangements made, we settled to bed under our tent where the matresses laid on...straw, and a large fire before us. We are comfortably lodged and are lulled to slumber by the pattering rain. How delicious after Fatigue, Danger and Anxiety to enjoy Repose in Shelter from the Storm with the consolatory reflection that we are not obliged on the morrow either to surmount its fury or lie windbound in a solitary Cove!"[44]

LOCK AND CANAL, 1797
Located at upper dam; oldest existing
lock and dam in America. Seen from Railroad and Turnpike.

This view of the lock at Little Falls is from Greene's *The Old Mohawk Turnpike Book*. Its caption implies that the lock looked this way in 1797, but diary notes by Gouverneur Morris in 1803 indicate that Pharoux's early criticisms were justified, because the original wooden construction had to be replaced by masonry.

The above words were recorded just before Morris settled down to sleep, but his anticipated night of rest was rudely interrupted:

"...a little before day the wind shifted to the northwest with a heavy squall which blows the fire into our Tent, menacing us with a sudden conflagration. Before we can take measures to provide against that danger, the tent is blown down and a heavy shower drenches us completely."[45]

LeRay became ill from exposure and so did the boatmen; Morris treated them all with his own supply of medication. However, LeRay's fever was very high and he was unable to continue the journey. After a few days, Brown and his surveyors conveyed him back to the shelter of Brownville to recuperate, while Morris continued the boat trip without him. Despite a long convalescance, LeRay's impression of his lands was so favorable that he resolved to settle there himself when possible.

Meanwhile, other significant events were occurring elsewhere which influenced Castorland affairs. Napoleon Bonaparte had assumed power in France and ended the persecution of nobility. In 1802, he pardoned all the French émigrés, promising to restore their confiscated properties if they returned. Many homesick, unhappy exiles were glad to return; the impetus for settling Castorland no longer existed.

Two principals in the Castorland history died in 1803. They were William Constable in America and Pierre Chassanis in Paris. James LeRay's father also died in France that year. Thus family business compelled LeRay to return to France in 1804 and detained him there for four more years.

In Paris wrangling continued and even worsened among the Castorland Commissioners; no clear leadership developed after Chassanis'. The Paris residents wanted a return on their investments, and did not wish to spend any more money on the settlements. LeRay advocated further investment but his advice was rejected.

Few details are known of French life in Castorland during its final decade. Although the Company officially remained in existence until 1814, when its charter expired, there was never a sufficient infusion of people and resources at one time to produce a viable settlement. In all, only about 20 French families resided there at one time or another.

After Coxe took over from Tillier, he established his own headquarters in a non-French community near High Falls, rather than residing in Castorland. He brought along a clerk named Josiah P. Raymond to take over the French store at High Falls.

128

"Coxe...was appointed first county clerk and traded several years on the hill, a little west of Collinsville, where he built a stylish curb-roofed house and store..."[46]

Although William Constable had never set eyes upon the lands he bought and sold in the area, his brother James visited them in September, 1805. He recorded in his diary:

"Passed on to Coxe's at the High Falls, or rather 1½ miles west of them, where he lives and is finishing a house he bought. He is Clerk of the new county of Lewis..."[47]

There is no record of any administrator replacing Coxe for Castorland and it is not clear whether he retained that position simultaneously with his appointment as County Clerk. In any event, he remained in the vicinity until 1816.

Meanwhile in France, LeRay was anticipating a return to America, although still engaged in settling his father's estate. In 1806 he arranged for agents to construct a grand new home for him north of the Black River. They chose a site several miles from the great bend in the river, and the village of LeRaysville grew up nearby. The family arrived to take up residence on their new estate in 1808, and LeRay continued to purchase more land in the area, including some from Gouverneur Morris. Eventually he became proprietor of most of the lands between the Black River and the St. Lawrence.

LeRay's home was a magnificent, European-style mansion, very different from the log cabins and board houses elsewhere in the area. It was damaged by fire around 1821, but rebuilt with additions and still stands today.[48] (It is now used as a guest billet for high-ranking visitors at the Fort Drum Military Reservation.) LeRay imported the finest furniture, artworks, linens and china and established a style of living which was almost regal. He had his own priest and physician and uniformed servants, including liveried postillions on his coach and six.

LeRay entertained lavishly with grand dinners and fine musicals in which family and guests participated. His home was an oasis of culture in the North Country, reputed to be the finest north of Albany.

Singlehandedly, LeRay transported the French manorial system to this region and he became the *seigneur* of the countryside. He established the type of colony which Castorland's proprietors had hoped to create, arranging for large scale emigration of peasants and artisans and their families from France, as well as professional engineers and surveyors. Land was made available on such attractive terms

129

that whole villages emigrated together and re-established themselves on his domains. Although the peasants lacked any capital, loans were granted with generous time allowances for repayment. Breeding stock was also imported, providing the best strains of cattle, sheep and horses.

His favorable land sale terms attracted American settlers as well as Europeans. The large influx of both provided a reservoir of labor sufficient to enable very rapid development of the region. As men were anxious to earn the cash to pay back their loans, they willingly hired themselves out for cutting roads, building bridges and dams, mills, clearing trees and laboring on large, neighboring estates. The LeRays provided well-stocked stores at convenient locations and were also generous with free grants of land for such public needs as schools and churches.

Because business and family affairs required James LeRay to return to France for lengthy periods, the day-to-day management of local development and the LeRay fortunes in America were turned over to his son, Vincent. Vincent was a brilliant young man, a recent graduate of a course in scientific and literary studies at the Ecole de Royal Polytechnic in Paris. He had excelled in both art and engineering, and with experience he quickly developed keen business acumen. Although he did not become the legal proprietor of these estates until 1824, he was intimately involved in their direction from his arrival in 1808.

Vincent often visited Castorland during the latter years of its existence, since its business affairs were so intermixed with those of his family. His father was one of its chief creditors, and Vincent later described his father's frustrations:

> "...M. LeRay de Chaumont [lost] the large advances he had made for interest, etc. He lost besides, many of the best years of his life. He experienced vexation, chagrin, and discouragement — he wore out his strength and his health, to try to remedy the imprudent and ignorant management of the Parisian administration, to which his solemn protest was entered in the books of the Company."[49]

Much of the information extant about the last years of Castorland are derived from the recollections of Vincent LeRay, written in a letter to Dr. Hough in 1859. He reminisced about those settlers he had personally known as a young man, fifty years previously.

Among those he recalled were several retired army officers who apparently lacked common sense, as well as other qualities necessary for survival under frontier conditions. There was one named Devouassoux who, upon his arrival in Castorland, built his cabin

130

Vincent LeRay

James LeRay

(Portraits by courtesy of Charles P. Dunham, Jefferson County Historian)

right upon the banks of the Black River because he liked to fish. LeRay passed by one morning and observed the new settler sitting in front of his doorway in his morning gown and slippers, admiring the view. They engaged in conversation, and LeRay pointed out that the cabin was located within the floodplain of the river and would surely be inundated by the annual spring floods. An account of the conversation is amusing:

> "At these words our Frenchman felt as perhaps he had never felt before the enemy. 'But' resumed Mr. LeRay, after giving him time to compose himself, 'have you not on your lot some higher ground?'
>
> 'Indeed, Sir, I cannot say.'
>
> 'Why, have you not explored your lands before building?'
>
> 'Indeed, no; I thought I could not possibly find a better spot than the banks of this beautiful river. I like fishing. Here I am near my field of operations.'
>
> "Mr. LeRay could not see without apprehension such apathy and levity, for knowing well that Mr. Devouassoux was not an exception among his countrymen, he read in his fate that of many others. He persuaded Mr. Devouassoux to take a little walk upon his lot, and in a few minutes they found a beautiful building spot on a rising ground..."[50]

When the Castorland charter expired in 1814, a public auction was held to liquidate the Company's assets and pay its creditors. James LeRay was one of the chief creditors, since he had held nominal ownership of the lands for so many years and been legally responsible for taxes and debts. There were few interested purchasers, so he became the principal buyer, adding the unsold Castorland properties to his other landholdings.

The majority of Castorland stockholders never set foot in America. Many had bought shares merely for speculation, anticipating a rise in value which never materialized. In later years they failed to pay the land taxes, so their holdings reverted to the State of New York and were resold by the Comptroller. LeRay bought up these properties too; he eventually owned major parts of the four counties of Jefferson, Lewis, St. Lawrence and Franklin.

Therefore, the Castorland story concludes with a brief summary of the LeRay establishments. These flourished for two decades, characterized by vitality and culture — a strong contrast to Castorland's failure. This highlighted the importance of effective management and sufficient resources.

Critical differences between the two were undivided local control, large scale settlements at one time and sufficient funding to facilitate

The LeRay Mansion

(Photo by courtesy of Charles P. Dunham, Jefferson County Historian)

all necessary development. The difference between public and private ownership of land was also significant, as Desjardins had recognized in earlier years, when complaining that hired help had no incentive to work conscientiously.

Historical events in both France and America continued to influence the fortunes of these northern settlements. Waves of immigrants preceded and followed the LeRays to America. As political fortunes revolved in France, followers of the Bonapartes alternated with Royalists as émigrés. After 1815 many of Napoleon's supporters who had taken refuge on LeRay's domains plotted for years to implement some scheme to rescue their emperor. They hoped either to restore him to power once again in France or to bring him to their refuge in America.

Joseph Bonaparte was one of the most prominent purchasers of land from LeRay; he bought a large tract northeast of the Black River, built several imposing houses, and for several summers he visited there, living in royal splender. He finally left behind there a mistress and an illegitimate daughter. However, this and other interesting stories are the subject of many other books and not part of the history of Castorland.

The opening of the Erie Canal caused a change in the LeRay family fortunes. Part of the canal system opened in 1819 and the entire length was completed in 1825. Its unanticipated effect upon the northern part of the State was the diversion of settlers to cheap, fertile western lands which were more easily accessible. Since LeRay's operations depended upon income generated by continuing land sales, he became unable to meet his enormous financial obligations. In 1824, James LeRay went bankrupt, and all his land titles were transferred to his son, Vincent, for benefit of creditors.

Vincent had recently married Cornelia Jumel of New York City, and her dowry probably assisted the LeRay family to regain solvency.[51] In any case Vincent instituted a new era of close fiscal management, and was able to pay all his father's debts and hang on for several additional years. However, land prices continued to remain severely depressed, and their period of major expansion had ended.

The LeRay family all returned to France in 1832 and James died there in 1840. Although Vincent made several return visits to America, he never resided there again. His properties were left in charge of an agent who maintained a land office in Carthage until 1914. From Europe, the LeRays continued to encourage emigration among industrious and ambitious workers; thousands more came from France, Germany and Switzerland to settle on LeRay's lands. They were all of the peasant class, however; the days of noblemen with grandiose plans were never resurrected.

134

CHAPTER SEVEN

The Castorland Region Today —
Touring by Car and Kayak

For those interested in Castorland history, it is disappointing that a visit to the region today yields no view of any remains of the original French settlements.

There is a small village named Castorland, but it commemorates the colony only by name, not location. It is situated across the Black River from the former French lands, opposite its junction with the Beaver. The community developed around a station which was built and named in 1870 by the Utica and Black River Railroad. The weathered old depot still remains, but is in poor condition.

The Black River region today is still sparsely populated. Much of the landscape is dominated by dairy farms, but there are some mills along the river which chiefly produce pulp and paper.

Active communities now occupy most of the places first settled by the French. Watertown, the biggest city in the area (population: 27,861)[1] straddles the Great Falls. Carthage (population: 3,643)[2] is a smaller town, lying along the eastern bank on the site of the Long Falls. The tiny, unincorporated village of Beaver Falls (population 400)[3] lies along the Beaver River just above the site of Castorville. Some bramble-covered ditches along the northern bank of the river contain a few large stones — all that is left of the sluiceways connected with the former French mills.[4] Other traces have been obliterated by later construction in the same area, and by the passage of time, effects of weather and growth of vegetation.

There is no occupation, however, upon the site of the first French establishment below the High Falls on the Black River. The clearing which the French had made with so much effort still lies just above the floodplain of the river, with a view of the falls. Knee-high weeds and bramble bushes cover the area. It can be reached from a secondary road along the eastern bank, identifiable by a cut through the trees from the road which gives a view of the falls.[5]

The falls are now called Lyons Falls, and a village bearing that name (population: 755)[6] is located on the opposite bank of the river. A pulp and paper mill is built out over the falls, dominating and dwarfing the once-spectacular flow. In the spring, when the melting snow produces a large runoff, the waterfall may still be impressive, but upstream dams have now reduced its normal flow to a relative trickle. The mill is presently operated by the Georgia-Pacific Company; formerly it was the Gould Paper Company.

However, the Black River is still surprisingly wild when seen from the vantage point of infrequent bridge crossings or from a small boat. I was eager to view the river as the French had first experienced it, and planned a two-day paddling trip proceeding north from Lyons Falls. We embarked in July of 1979, with my husband and I ensconced in our Klepper touring kayak and two friends accompanying us in a canoe. After two long days on the water, we had covered only three-quarters of the distance from Lyons Falls to Carthage — a 41 mile journey which the French sometimes made in a single day — and this experience increased our admiration for their hard-driving pace.

Very few roads touch the river and few signs of civilization impinge upon it. Bridges span the water about every ten miles; otherwise the river hardly seems noticed as it winds through the valley. In the 31 miles we covered, we passed only five or six other boaters, all fishermen, and saw less than a dozen houses, mostly at the northern end of the trip.

We started at a boat-launching site on the eastern shore, just a little below the site of the French establishment. A picnic ground and ramp for boat launching are operated by the Thousand Islands State Park and Recreation Commission. The falls were visible just upstream, but soon our attention was centered upon the extraordinary beauty and wildness of the first stretch of the river, heading downstream. In the nearly 200 intervening years, the views from the river below Lyons Falls can not have changed very much! For long stretches the river is submerged between high, muddy banks, and is hardly visible from nearby fields. Large, old trees enclose the stream: magnificent willows, sycamores, elms, hickories, maples, birches and aspens.

The river was alive with birds as we started early in the morning — singing, calling, darting, dipping all around us. In addition to such common species as jays, crows and robins, there were colorful killdeer and cedar waxwings and some very active water birds, kingfishers and sandpipers, fishing for their breakfasts. Swooping around us were several varieties of swallows and chimney sweeps, acting as if they were trying to repel such unaccustomed intruders. The most exotic species we saw were green and blue herons and three golden eagles.

Current view of the site of the First Castorland Establishment. The flow of water over the falls in the background has been greatly curtailed by construction of many mills and dams on the Black River and its tributaries. The original French log cabins stood in the clearing shown in the foreground.

We saw many other kinds of wildlife along the river: turtles sunning on rocks and logs, and many species of fish later identified by local fishermen as bass, walleye, pickerel, perch, carp and bull-head. We were intrigued by row upon row of holes — clearly of animal origin — which pierced the high clay banks, and we surmised that they had been made by bank swallows, muskrats or possibly turtles. Mudslides testified to the presence of otters and muskrats.

The unusually dark color of the water may explain why the river is so lightly used for recreation. It is unpleasantly murky, oddly different from the clear Adirondack streams which feed it. Its condition can not be blamed upon recent pollution; in their *Journal* the French had commented upon its dark color and bitter taste. The coloration is caused by deep deposits of iron and manganese embedded in the underlying rock strata and also by tannic acid produced by decaying trees and hemlock bark.[7] It has not been possible to determine who first gave the river its name, but it clearly was a descriptive appellation! Anyway, the water is unpalatable for drinking and unpleasant for swimming, but the birds and fish seem to thrive upon it.

As we paddled along, sufficient variety in the landscape kept the trip from becoming monotonous. Two small stretches of rapids produced some mild excitement, and one unexpected obstacle was a major problem. It developed from the remains of channel markers from the Old Black River Canal, built more than 100 years ago.[8] Large wooden pilings with projecting iron spikes stick up from the river bed in some sections of the channel; in times of low water they protrude and can easily be avoided; when hidden by high water they can be hazardous.

We were vulnerable to sharp objects in our rubber-bottomed boat, and we suffered a series of small punctures from a loose piling. It was lodged underwater, among accumulated debris at a rapid near the entrance of Otter Creek. We attempted to run the rapid, steering between large boulders, but the rush of water swept us into a position where we became stuck upon invisible obstacles. Only by climbing out of the boat were we able to free it. We had to drag it, while wading, over the obstacles, and shortly afterward discovered several small holes in our hull. Fortunately a nearby sand bar presented a convenient stopping place, and a handy patch kit enabled us to make repairs in about 20 minutes.

Our trip occurred during a severe drought, so we encountered unusually low water upon the river and its tributaries. We were disappointed by the view of the Independence River, whose beauty

Author's boating trip on the Black River: the launching site is shown above, just downstream from Lyons Falls. We paddled for two days.

had so impressed Pharoux. It was a narrow, unimpressive flow when we passed it. However, the high rock bluff above the junction of the two streams was still as scenic as when described by Pharoux in 1795, when he had chosen it as a site for his intended home. It is now occupied by someone else's house.

The high muddy banks offer few convenient stopping places for boaters. We had difficulty in locating a suitable place to camp overnight, but finally pitched our tents in a farmer's field, just beyond the fringe of trees atop the river bank. The next morning we came upon several docks on the eastern side of the river at Watson, where a road crosses on a bridge. A general store there offered the opportunity to refill water bottles, purchase additional supplies and get some cold drinks. It could be a suitable stopping place for a one-day trip.

Later on, a road converges with the river on the western side at Dadville, north of Lowville, where there is an office of the Department of Environmental Conservation. We were able to identify its location from the river by a visible line of telephone poles and the unaccustomed sound of automobile traffic. We made a short stop here, despite the difficulty in finding a place to beach the boats and a slippery scramble up the steep bank. When we emerged upon the roadway, we found that the border of trees along its side totally obscured all view of the stream below. Few passersby were aware of the beautiful and historic river which flowed ony a few feet away!

As we resumed our paddle northwards after lunch, on this second day of our trip, the character of the river began to change, broadening slightly and becoming more domesticated. Cow pastures now became visible along the banks; we passed a few people and houses and could see a church steeple in the distance — civilization had finally made an impact upon the landscape. By this time the heat had become oppressive, as the temperature was in the nineties, and we were relieved to reach our destination.

We ended our trip at a fishing access site at the Castorland Bridge, where Route 410 crosses the river, just below the entrance of the Beaver River. We regretted not having time to complete the last ten miles to Carthage, but felt we had covered the most interesting part of the journey.

The Castorland Bridge overlooks the junction of the two rivers, presenting a lovely scenic view which highlights the beauty of the Beaver, upon which Castorville had been located. The village had been four miles upstream upon a flat field partially enclosed by a bend in the river, not visible from present day roads but easily seen from the water.

This bridge over the Black River (Route 410) leads to the present village of Castorland.

View from the bridge shows the scenic junction of the Beaver and the Black Rivers.

Place names north of the Black River reflect the one enduring mark left upon the countryside by French settlers. Many of them are family names connected with the LeRays, such as the villages of LeRayville (now swallowed up by Fort Drum) and Chaumont. James LeRay's three children are commemorated by Cape Vincent, Alexandria Bay and Theresa. DeFeriet, near Great Bend, takes its name from a friend (perhaps mistress) of James LeRay; she had erected a grandiose mansion there upon the riverbank.[9]

The area contains a few old buildings which have peripheral interest to Castorland history. In addition to the LeRay mansion at Fort Drum, described in the previous chapter, there are two other LeRay family homes still standing at Chaumont and at Cape Vincent. Both are now private residences.

At Brownville, a stone mansion built by Jacob Brown is now undergoing repairs and restoration. Local sources indicate that this 22 room house was started in 1811. The local historical society is maintaining it as a museum, displaying some interesting personal and military memorabilia.

A replica of Baron Steuben's log cabin is located at the Steuben Memorial in Remsen, 15 miles north of Utica, just off Route 12. Reconstructed and maintained by the New York State Park Commission as an "Historic Site," it is located just a few hundred feet away from its original site, near a grove of trees which contains his grave and a monument. The cabin contains two rooms, with attic and leanto; although the furnishings are sparse and uncomfortable by any modern standards, they were luxurious in that time and place. During the summer guide services are provided.

Close by, a segment of the first overland route to Castorland is named "French Road." At its crossing with Steuben Road, a small French Road Chapel and graveyard have been maintained by descendents of the early Welsh settlers.

Through interest in all items relating to Baron Steuben, historians[10] in the Remsen-Steuben area became interested several years ago in the *Castorland Journal*. After many fruitless efforts, they were finally able to obtain, in 1977, a copy of Hough's handwritten translation. Under sponsorship of the Remsen Historical Society, they undertook to produce a typewritten copy, carefully reproducing Hough's peculiarities of spelling and punctuation, and properly placing his hundreds of unnumbered foot notes. Completion of this task took over three years.

The magnitude of that job can best be appreciated by anyone else who has struggled, as I did, to decipher Hough's scrawl. (Whether on paper or microfilm, it strains both eyes and temper! My own research

142

Castorville was once located at this bend in the Beaver River, a few miles upstream from its junction with the Black. (Courtesy of Lewis S. Van Arnam)

This bridge at the present village of Beaver Falls now occupies the site of the first French sawmill. (Courtesy of Lewis S. Van Arnam)

Struck in Paris for the 'Land of the Beaver'

There are less than one dozen of these half-ecu coins still in existence.

coin made for the Land of the Beaver (or Castorland), in upper New York State, was a feature of the recent Breen III auction put on by the Pine Tree Auction Galleries at LaGuardia Airport in June. Castorland was a French colony near Carthage, not far from the present Watertown, N.Y. It was in existence in 1796 when France was still in a ferment.

The coin, a silver half-ecu, or half-crown, shows a beaver recumbent in the exergue of the reverse. (Castor is the French word for beaver.) The colony was situated on 630,000 acres of land owned by the "Compagnie de New-York" in the Beaver River area. (A Castorland still exists, complete with zip code — 13620).

•

Rudolph Tillier, one of the chief stockholders in the Compagnie, had these half-ecu pieces struck in Paris to serve as circulating currency in the New World. There are believed to be fewer than a dozen of the original strikings still in existence. The example of this historic rarity at the Breen III sale was in very fine condition and was a bargain at $1,550.

The veiled head, facing left, has a laurel wreath and a coronet topped by a symbol representing a fort in the vicinity of the settlement. The inscription reads "FRANCO-AMERICANA COLONIA." There is a tiny "DUV," standing for the sculptor, du Vivier. Then under the baseline is the word "Castorland" and the date, 1796.

Above the sleeping beaver on the reverse is seen a figure of Ceres beside a maple tree from which sap is flowing into an urn. Ceres holds a cornucopia in one hand and in the other what seems to be part of the tool used to tap the tree. Around this tableau are the words SALVE MAGNA PARENS FRUGUM — "Hail, thou great mother of harvests."

The Red Book lists this coin in section VII — "Private Tokens After Confederation," along with the North American Token, the Bar Cent, the Auctori Plebs, the Mott, the Albany Church Penny, the New York Theatre Token and others of that ilk. The Castorland dies came in for considerable after-use; many restrikes exist, so it is well that this coin has the certification of the bearded numismatist Walter Breen.

Text of Numismatics Column from *The New York Times,* August 6, 1978, Section D, page 29.

144

on the same manuscript was underway during this period, but neither of us were aware of the other's project.) After their typewritten manuscript was completed, some 18 or 20 copies were reproduced. Some were bought by interested individuals; copies are now available for public use at college and public libraries and historical societies in Utica, Oneonta, Rome, Cooperstown, Lyons Falls and Watertown.

Another tangible relic of the Castorland era comes to public notice occasionally. It is a coin mistakenly known as "the Castorland half-dollar." In June, 1978, one of these sold for $1,550 at a numismatic auction in New York City. The sale was reported in *The New York Times* with an illustration, and a comment: "Less than one dozen of these half-ecu coins are still in existence."[11] The article included a brief summary of Castorland's history, incorrectly stating:

> "Rudolphe Tillier, one of the chief stockholders in the Compagnie, had these half-ecu pieces struck in Paris to serve as circulating currency in the New World..."[12]

Actually, the coins were keepsakes, and were never used for currency. Each was called a "jetton de presence"; they were given to members of the Castorland Company in Paris when they attended shareholder meetings. Hough indicated that presentation of such tokens was common practice during that period in Europe and America.[13] The pieces were not rarities in Hough's days; he had seen impressions in gold, silver, white metal and bronze.[14] (See page 181.)

The coin was engraved by the Duvier brothers in Paris, one of whom was a Castorland shareholder. It drew upon classical mythology, rather than any practical knowledge. One side depicts the head of the goddess Cybele, personifying the cultivated earth; the reverse side shows Ceres tapping a maple tree, inserting a faucet for drawing off sap. Since the sap season is generally restricted to March, Hough noted disdainfully:

> "The grain, flowers and foliage appear strangely brought into the sugar season."[15]

A Latin inscription on the coin is a quotation from Virgil. In translation it says:

> "Hail Saturnian Land, Great Parent of Fruits, Great Parent of Heroes."[16]

Thus the coin is an embodiment of all the unrealistic hopes and dreams of the founders of Castorland.

The pathos of Castorland's brief history is captured in a narrative poem written by Caleb Lyon[17] during the last century. Its romantic style is so appropriate to both the conception and the demise of the little colony, that it makes a fitting conclusion for this book:

The Steuben Memorial in Remsen, New York contains a log cabin
built in 1936 as a representation of the original. Its furnishings are
authentic. Front and back views are shown above. This Historic Site
is maintained by the New York State Parks Department.

LEWIS COUNTY IN THE OLDEN TIME

In the lands of vines and olives, over three score years ago,
Where the Bourbon Rulers perished in unutterable woe,
Plans matured for emigration sanctioned were with revel gay,
In saloons of *la belle Paris,* by the friends of Chassanais.

On an hundred thousand acres, never trod by feet of men,
He had mapped out farms and vineyards, roads o'er precipice
    and glen,
And, like scenes of an enchanter, rose a city wondrous fair,
With its colleges, its churches, and its castles in the air.

There was struck a classic medal by this visionary band:
Cybele was on the silver, and beneath was Castorland;
The reverse a tree of maple, yielding forth its precious store,
Salve magna parens frugum was the legend that it bore.

O'er the Atlantic, up the Hudson, up the Mohawk's dreary wild,
With his flock came Bishop Joulin, ever gentle as a child;
Kind words of his dispelled their sorrows and their trials by the way,
As the darkness of the morning fades before the god of day.

By *la Riviere de la Famine,* ocean-tired and travel-sore,
They up-reared a rustic altar, tapestried with mosses o'er;
Crucifix they set upon it where the oak trees' shadows fell
Lightly o'er the lighted tapers, 'mid the sweet *Te Deum's* swell.

Never *Dominus Vobiscum,* falling upon human ears,
Made so many heart-strings quiver, filled so many eyes with tears.
The good shepherd gave his blessing — even red men gathered there,
Felt the sacrifice of Jesus in his first thanksgiving prayer.

After toils and many troubles, self-exile for many years,
Long delays and sad misfortunes, men's regrets and women's tears,
Unfulfill'd the brilliant outset, broken as a chain of sand,
Were the golden expectations by *Grande Rapides'* promised land.

Few among this generation little care how lived or died
Those who fled from Revolution, spirits true and spirits tried;
Or of loves and lives all ended, orbs of hope forever set—
These the poet and historian can not let the world forget.[18]

This picturesque French Road Chapel was built by early Welsh settlers on the Steuben Estates. As indicated by the roadsign, it is located on a still existing segment of the old French road.

CHAPTER EIGHT

Sifting Discrepancies: A Survey of Writings about Castorland

So many errors have been published in reputable sources about Castorland that it seems useful to survey such writings in order to identify those details which may continue to mislead readers. This is not intended to cast aspersions upon other authors, but rather to ease the frustration of readers who have not read the *Journal* itself, and therefore lack sufficient information to discriminate between conflicting accounts.

As indicated in the Introduction to this book, Dr. Franklin B. Hough was the first major historian of Lewis and Jefferson Counties. He is considered "the dean of history of northern New York"[1] and his books are looked upon as original sources in themselves. When he wrote his first histories of these two counties, he searched meticulously among all written records then available and also interviewed elderly residents of the area who had some first hand knowledge about past events. However, his information about Castorland was faulty because both books were written prior to the discovery of the *Journal*. Because some of his mistakes have been repeated by so many later writers, it seems useful to identify them here in order to help avoid future confusion.

Such a task is undertaken with the confidence that, if Dr. Hough were alive today, he would be happy to see such corrections published and to see a complete history of Castorland in print. His attitude is indicated clearly in a preface to one of his histories, in which he requests readers to call his attention to any errors detected "for the benefit of those who may hereafter seek more exact information in our local history."[2]

There are four often-quoted errors in Hough's *History of Jefferson County*, published in 1854:

1. When discussing the reduction of the size of the tract purchased from Constable from 630,000 to 210,000 acres, he stated that the original agreement was cancelled, and "the tract reconveyed...in consequence of the amount falling short, upon survey, far beyond the expectation of all parties."[3] In fact, the *real* reason for the acreage reduction was that Chassanis was unable to sell enough shares to finance the larger purchase; the survey did not even commence until a year after the second agreement was signed.

2. Pharoux's relationship to Brodhead was mistaken. Rather than being an "assistant,"[4] he was actually Brodhead's employer.

3. At the time of his writing, Hough was also unaware of Desjardins' position of leadership; he was merely listed as one of the major land-holders in Castorland.[5]

4. Tillier was assumed to be one of the original settlers at High Falls, and Hough mistakenly credited him with the work accomplished by Pharoux and Desjardins.[6]

By the time Hough published the *History of Lewis County* in 1860, he had become aware of the above errors, although the *Journal* was still unknown. Inexplicably, however, he did not specifically acknowledge or correct the above mistakes; he merely wrote an expanded account of the colony which included mention of the official positions Pharoux and Desjardins held as American Commissioners of the Company. He still had no knowledge of the quality of leadership they provided. In this second book, four additional mistakes are persistently repeated by later writers:

1. The first is a disparaging description of Desjardins as "an enterprising but visionary adventurer."[7] Unfortunately, this derogatory characterization has been so frequently cited that Desjardins has been maligned throughout history.

2. Marc Brunel's relationship to the Castorland group is incorrectly described. Hough states that they first met in Albany[8] when Pharoux and Desjardins were planning their 1793 exploration, and that they recruited Brunel to become captain of their expedition. Actually, he had been a fellow passenger on their trans-Atlantic voyage, and had become a trusted friend. Their meeting was not by happenstance; he had sought them out purposely and was warmly welcomed as a companion. His naval experience enabled him to "captain" the batteau when sailing through a storm on Lake Ontario, but they were always in charge of the expedition.

3. Hough surmised that the route of the first journey to Castorland in 1793 went "from the Mohawk across to the Moose River, and down that stream to the High Falls."[9] This assumption was based upon the unearthing of an old silver spoon, which bore Brunel's initials, along the banks of the Moose River. Their true route, via Lake Ontario, is now known from the *Journal*; they never reached High Falls in 1793, and Brunel did not ever visit Castorland again.

4. Hough stated "they mistook the High Falls for the Long Falls" in establishing their first settlement "remote from the great body of their lands."[10] Such a "mistake" was impossible, because they did not even know the Long Falls existed, when they first arrived. They selected the site for their first settlement deliberately as the closest to sources of supply.

Question must also be raised about the origin of a colorful description of some of the Castorland settlers:

"...It may be questioned whether any number of tradesmen, jewelers and barbers from Paris could form a flourishing establishment in this wild wooded country, without a long previous course of misspent labor and fruitless expense; for of what avail is industry when applied, as it was here, from dawn til twilight, in clearing land with a *pruning hook?*"[11]

No source is given for this description, and it disagrees with all the information available about the background of those émigrés who did reside in Castorland. As far as is known, there were no tradesmen, jewelers or barbers. Attacking a forest with a pruning hook is a vivid, Don Quixote-like image which captures the imagination, but is figurative rather than authentic.

It was several years after the preceding book was published that Hough found out about the *Journal of Castorland* and was able to obtain his copy. His personal diaries reflect his interest and excitement, as well as accounts of talks he delivered at the Albany Institute in 1866 and in a series of later lectures at Lowville, New York. Unfortunately the texts of these talks were not published, although some summaries appeared in local newspapers and were reprinted by W. Hudson Stephens.[12] The talks were delivered while he was still in the process of translating the *Journal,* but they reflect his revised opinions of the two main founders of Castorland. In describing their *Journal,* he commended the "purity and elegance of their style."[13] With admiration, he described Desjardins as:

"...a gentleman of culture and learning [who] possessed a keen sense of the ludicrous, a habit of close observation, and much scientific merit..."[14]

Pharoux was lauded as:

"an architect and engineer...especially noted for his scientific attainments."[15]

Dr. Hough was a man of scholarly habits and he attempted to correct and amplify his mistaken accounts of Castorland. Whenever

151

he came across additional information pertinent to any of his writings, he would scrawl a footnote upon any piece of paper he happened to have handy. Some of the footnotes inserted in his translation of the *Journal* illustrate this habit. Also among his papers in the New York State Library is an annotated manuscript of his *History of Jefferson County* with handwritten revisions and updated materials. Because it includes references to the *Castorland Journal*, it was obviously written after he had completed its translation. However, it was never published and its existence seems practically unknown.

In 1883, Hough did publish the revised and updated edition of the *History of Lewis County*, as noted in the Introduction to this book. In its main text, he deleted erroneous information about Castorland, and an inconspicuous footnote on the same page promises a new chapter on the subject. However, instead of a full chapter, which would have drawn attention to a corrected version of the Castorland story, there is merely an Appendix about Castorland, largely limited to the full text of the letter he had received from Vincent LeRay in 1859. Only four pages are devoted to a disappointingly brief summary of Castorland's history — disappointing to a reader and disappointing to Dr. Hough, as well. In his Preface, he had alluded to running out of space towards the end of his task, and in the Appendix he explains his intention to publish an entirely separate volume containing his full translation of the *Journal*. Since he died two years later with this hope still unrealized, this very brief summary in the Appendix is the *only* corrected version by Hough which actually appears in print. However, since he failed to direct attention to changes from the 1860 edition, the errors can be detected only by a careful comparison, paragraph by paragraph, of both editions. (One new error appeared in the 1883 history: Hough referred to the Crèvecoeur visitor to Castorland in 1794 as a brother, rather than son, of the noted author.)[16]

Therefore, the major problem with Hough's corrected version of Castorland's history is its low visibility. Readers are very apt to miss both the Preface and the Appendix, since the main text lacks specific references to them. The inconspicuousness of his corrected version is heightened by the fact that the 1883 edition is hardly known or used. Both early histories of Lewis and Jefferson Counties were reissued in 1976,[17] but the presence of a later edition was not mentioned in either of them! Most libraries carry only the earlier editions; the 1883 edition is seldom available or consulted.

Nathaniel Sylvester, writing in the 1870s, was a friend of Hough and was given access to the *Journal* and all the latest information about it. His *Historical Sketches of Northern New York and the Adirondack Wilderness* is an informal book, written in a popular romantic style, and not intended to be a comprehensive history. Two of its chapters are devoted to Castorland, and include a dramatic description of a meeting in Paris between Constable and Chassanis in which he stated:

> "During the negotiations between Constable and Chassanis for the tract, the Revolution burst forth in all its savage fury, and the streets of Paris were slippery with human gore. Constable locked the door of the apartment in which they met with the remark that 'If they parted before the purchase was completed, they might never meet again.'"[18]

The description has been quoted by many later writers who could not resist a good story, but my extensive searching has failed to reveal the source for this incident. If it did occur, it would have related to the preliminary agreement for 630,000 acres, in August of 1792, rather than the actual sale in 1793, since Constable was in London during most of their negotiations. Colonel Ward acted for him in Paris in subsequent business matters affecting Castorland.[19]

Three other authors wrote major histories of Jefferson County during the latter part of the 19th century. The first and most carefully done was by Durant and Pierce, also entitled *History of Jefferson County*. These authors were also personally acquainted with Dr. Hough, as well as with one of his sons, and they acknowledge both men as major sources of information. They obviously read at least parts of the *Journal* since they included a long quotation from it. However, Hough's early books were some of their major sources, and they repeated some of his errors:

1. Pharoux is identified as one of Brodhead's surveyors.[20]

2. They stated that Brodhead was employed by Tillier.[21]

3. They repeated that the initial meeting between Brunel and the Castorland party occurred in Albany.[22]

Curiously, Brodhead's name is correctly spelled in their text, but repeatedly misspelled as "Broadhead"[23] in their quotations from the *Journal*.

In 1895 John Haddock published *Growth of a Century as Illustrated in the History of Jefferson County from 1793-1894*. It appears that he did not consult either edition of Hough's Lewis County histories, but relied extensively upon Hough's first book on Jefferson County, repeating those earliest errors. He quoted directly from Hough: his page 140 is taken directly from Hough's pages 50 and 51 — without specific acknowledgment of the source.

Haddock is also careless elsewhere. He called Pierre Chassanis "Louis Chassanis,"[24] and stated that the land purchased included 800,000 acres.[25] However, he included several items of interest not cited elsewhere: details of the marriage which occurred in Castorland in 1801;[26] personal recollections of Baptiste's later life in Carthage;[27] and an intimate view of James LeRay, obtained from an interview with a former servant:

> "He was an exemplary family man. He always kissed his children when he departed from his home and when he returned..."[28]

In 1898 Edgar C. Emerson published a history entitled *Our County and Its People — A Descriptive Work On Jefferson County, New York*.[29] He included two gross errors about Castorland, in addition to several minor ones:

> 1. "The company made the settlements as contemplated by the Articles of Association, one of the hamlets being on the lakeshore..."[30]

> 2. Speaking of Tillier's administration: "...in 1799, the energetic agent caused to be made a more accurate and detailed survey of the purchase."[31]

It is impossible to imagine what sources he could have used for either of the above flights of imagination!

> 3. Spelling mistakes include Brodhead as "Broadhead"[32] again, and G. Morris is referred to as "Governor"[33] (an office he never held) instead of "Gouverneur," his given name.

Alfred L. Donaldson was the author of a major two-volume work entitled *A History of the Adirondacks*, first printed in 1921 and recently reprinted.[34] In summarizing the history of Castorland, he relied mainly upon Hough and Sylvester. After describing the background of the colony, he disposed of the essence of the story in a single paragraph:

> "So the two commissaries and their new-found friend started for Castorland, about which they knew nothing except that it lay between the Black River and latitude 44 degrees North. They soon learned more by going through a series of surprises, disappointments, and hardships which can readily be imagined. The sequel was correspondence, controversies, recriminations, and compromises, voluminous and manifold."[35]

The description may be admired for its humorous brevity, but is marred by the common mistake about Brunel being a new-found friend, and also by the inference that Pharoux and Desjardins were incompetent.

The North Country[36] by Harry F. Landon is a comprehensive history of five upstate counties, published in 1932. Its coverage of Castorland is a bit melodramatic:

"In the heart of the great woods, they proposed to build a little Paris, the home of happy mechanics and of French aristocrats, snatched from the blade of the guillotin..."[37]

Landon repeated Sylvester's story about the locked door meeting in Paris, and Hough's early error about Brunel fortuitously meeting the other Frenchmen in Albany. The major defect in his account is an inflated view of Brunel's role in the 1793 expedition:

"Neither Pharoux nor Desjardins were the type of men to lead an expedition into unknown lands. Brunel took charge."[38]

Landon included some interesting quotations from the *Journal*, but it is evident that he read only parts of it, and even so he reports inaccurately. In his account of Pharoux's fatal accident, he stated that seven companions also perished.[39] (Although the raft did contain seven passengers, four survived the accident.)

The most extensive history of Castorland published until now is included in *Émigrés in the Wilderness*,[40] published by T. Wood Clarke in 1941. His descriptions of background and contemporary events provide more perspective upon French settlers of that period than any other source. He devoted three chapters to Castorland, relating its history to other French settlers and settlements which were contemporary or subsequent. In addition, he dealt extensively with the LeRay family and various flamboyant personalities associated with them, including Joseph Bonaparte who bought an extensive estate from them for summertime usage. Also included is the story of Eleazar Williams who claimed to have been the lost dauphin, rescued from the prison in Paris during the Reign of Terror.

Clarke's coverage of Castorland is extensive and well done, since he derived much of his information directly from the *Journal*. Unfortunately, however, several minor errors flaw his account:

1. Pierre Chassanis' first name is Anglicized to "Paul" rather than "Peter."[41]

2. Clarke described Desjardins as "a visionary adventurer"[42] without crediting Hough's origin of that phrase or exercising his own independent judgment.

155

3. He stated that Pharoux knew no surveying[43] although the *Journal* gives clear evidence of Pharoux's competence and experience in this field.

4. He reported that Geoffrey Desjardins was not present at Castorland until 1795;[44] actually he worked there throughout the 1794 season.

5. Brodhead is mistakenly called "Broadbent."[45]

6. Clarke refers to James Constable's visit to High Falls in 1804,[46] whereas Constable's diary indicates it was 1805. Also, Clarke assumed that the colony at High Falls had disintegrated by then, because it was not specifically mentioned by Constable. Such an assumption seems unwarranted since Constable did mention a visit with Richard Coxe.

It is regrettable that so many small errors were included in Clarke's book because it, like Hough's, has served as a major reference for many writers since its publication.

The preceding books constitute the major works which have dealt with Castorland, but other sources have also touched upon it.

There is excellent background information in Frances Childs' *French Refugee Life in the United States, 1790-1800*,[47] published in 1940. She dealt mainly with urban immigrants, but did include several brief references to Castorland and to Simon Desjardins. She mistakenly called the *Journal* "Desjardins' Diary,"[48] apparently unaware that Pharoux and Geoffrey Desjardins were co-authors. Combing the manuscript for every adverse comment that was written by the French about Americans, she concluded that Desjardins was a thoroughly negative character with a jaundiced view of mankind! When describing the size of French colonies in various cities, she reported that there were three French families living in Albany in 1794, one of whom was Santo Domingan and one "very common."[49] The third was not described or named, but it must have been the Desjardins.

William Chapman White's *Adirondack Country*[50] contains a very brief summary of Castorland's history. His account is accurate with refreshing injections of humor:

> The Castorland sale was Constable's "most dramatic feat of salesmanship...*The Prospectus* described a portion of heaven rather than of earth...Maps were drawn by men unhampered by any accurate knowledge..."[51]

White clarified the amount of money involved in the land speculation by translating pounds and livres into dollars.

The Proceedings of the New York Historical Association contain three short articles which refer to Castorland, all written more than fifty years ago. Those by William Moore[52] and Alta M. Ralph[53] were both based upon Hough's early books and repeated many of his errors. The former also confused the location of High Falls with Carthage. The third author, J. I. Wyer, Jr.,[54] is much more accurate. He was Director of the New York State Library at the time his paper was published in 1916. He had studied the original manuscripts in both Boston and Albany, as well as various published sources of information.

Several regional writers have written books about this area of New York which include references to Castorland. One is Howard Thomas, author of *Black River in the North Country*,[55] who devoted a chapter to it. He erred in stating that Cockburn's surveyors were on the job in 1792;[56] they did not start working until 1794. He was also mistaken in saying that Pharoux and Desjardins "engaged a small sailboat" at Oswego in 1793.[57] In fact they used the same batteau which had been rowed and poled all the way from Schenectady. Although such boats were primarily designed for river travel, some were equipped with masts and sails.

Hilda Doyle Merriam wrote a slim volume entitled *North of the Mohawk*,[58] published in 1950. Most of her information about Castorland seems to have been derived from Childs and Clarke, as she repeated some of their minor errors. Her imagination was captured by the latter's chapters on the mystery of the lost dauphin, and she has woven a fanciful web of circumstantial evidence about his probable escape to America through a scheme which involved both James LeRay and Simon Desjardins.[59] One of her "clues" is a mention of the presence of a French boy of the right age in the home of the Desjardins in Albany; she leapt to the conclusion that this must have been the dauphin, although the Desjardins' son was that age! This leaves her conclusion open to question, but her source of information is of interest. It is a letter written by a Mrs. Dudley,[60] a member of Governor Seymour's family, who described a visit to the Desjardins' home in Albany in 1795. This is the source from which we learned that Madame Desjardins had been a maid-of-honor to Marie Antoinette.

Castorland Through the Years[61] by Marion Hubbard Johnson is a small privately published book, written in 1976 for use by local elementary students. Its main concern is the present village of Castorland, which is unrelated to the French settlements. However, it does include a brief summary of the colony's history which contains two minor errors. In referring to the law passed in 1798 which forbade land ownership by aliens, she stated it was a New York State law,[62] whereas it was a federal act. She was mistaken also in asserting that Castorville was "a ghost town by 1800."[63]

Two other small books written by local historians touch upon Castorland. Clarence L. and M. Rachel Fisher wrote *A History of Lyons Falls*[64] which summarized the establishment of the colony in two paragraphs. Hazel C. Drew published a volume entitled *Tales from Little Lewis*[65] which devoted two pages to the settlement. It quotes brief excerpts from the *Journal*, including a printing mistake in the recipe for spruce beer: it calls for 12 spruce boughs instead of 12 *pounds* of spruce boughs.[66]

A recent book containing more information about Castorland is Thomas Powell's *Penet's Square*.[67] Although it deals mainly with that small plot of land north of the French colony, its proximity to Castorland and the LeRay holdings resulted in some interaction. As mentioned in an earlier chapter of this book, Desjardins had accepted a commission from Olive to represent him in some transactions in that area.

Powell evidently read parts of the *Journal of Castorland*, but he confuses some of the people and the sequence of various dates and events:

1. His description of the Company's organization states that it was governed by four Commissioners: LeRay and Chassanis in Paris, and Desjardins and Pharoux in America.[68] Actually, Chassanis was the Director and there were *four* Paris Commissioners. LeRay did not become one of them until 1798.

2. Powell stated that Brodhead was employed during the 1793 journey to Castorland, and incorrectly described him as a foreman,[69] rather than a surveyor. Brodhead did not begin work in the region until 1794, and was first employed by Constable's group, then later by Pharoux.

3. His account of Pharoux's death[70] is incorrect in regard to the year, the series of events leading up to it, the people accompanying him and their relationships. Powell seemed unaware that there were two Desjardins, confusing their functions, actions and locations.

4. Two minor common errors are repeated here: Chassanis' first name is given as "Paul,"[71] and the statement is included again that Brunel first met the Company in Albany.[72] His sources for these latter errors are probably Clarke and Hough.

158

5. Powell included an account of the camping trip on which Morris and LeRay visited Castorland in 1803, and after leaving there had to round Cape Vincent in the dark. There is a dramatic description of delays caused by Morris' inclination to fish and serve a fine dinner along the way, topped off with an account of their tent catching fire that night and Morris losing his wooden leg in the conflagration.[73] His footnote reference for this episode is Clarke's *Émigrés in the Wilderness*, but it does not appear in that book. Morris' own diary gives a very different account of that incident, as described herein in Chapter 6.

Despite the foregoing errors, Powell's account is very interesting reading for those interested in Castorland history. He is informative about conditions on the frontier in that time and region, including common health problems and care. He corroborates several *Journal* comments that the American custom of drinking rum as a treatment for dysentery was not beneficial.[74] Other related topics include more information on the LeRay family and their accomplishments, and a detailed description of potash as a cash crop,[75] pertinent since the Castorland founders had hoped to make a fortune from its production.

The most recent regional book is Lewis S. Van Arnam's *Beaver Falls Cavalcade*,[76] printed in 1979. He and his family have been longtime residents of this little village, built near some of the former millsites of Castorville. The bulk of his book is devoted to later residents and local industries, but his earliest chapters summarize the history of Castorland and the LeRay settlements. One minor contradiction is noted in the year Castorland ended.[77]

This extensive survey of writings about Castorand is intended to be helpful to readers who, like myself, have become interested in its fascinating history. I wish to stress that it is not my intention to denigrate anyone else's work — errors of omission or commission slip in terribly easily during research from many sources and revisions of many drafts. I am indebted to all of the writers mentioned for information which has enabled me to piece together this history, and separate out the maze of misinformation which has surrounded the subject.

If readers detect mistakes in this book, I would greatly appreciate having my attention drawn to them for correction. In addition, I hope that other records will be discovered — particularly personal papers and diaries — which will yield additional information about Castorland, especially its later years, after the conclusion of the *Journal.*

APPENDIX I

PLAN OF ASSOCIATION AND
FIRST PROGRAM OF SETTLEMENT

[Reprinted from Hough's *History of Jefferson County*]

46   *The New York or Chassanis Company.*

"ASSOCIATION *for the purchase and settlement of* 600,000 *acres of land, granted by the State of New York, and situated within that state between the* 43d *deg. and* 44th *deg. of latitude, upon Lake Ontario, and* 35 *leagues from the city and port of Albany, where vessels land from Europe.*

Many details suggested by the consideration of the internal and external advantages of this vast and rich domain, of which we have direct knowledge, has led to a plan of developing its resources, and of presenting the speculation to Europeans. It is to be noticed that this tract presents in its fertility, all the wealth of agriculture; by the fine distribution of its waters, the facilities for an extended commerce; by its location in the immediate vicinity of a dense population, security to its inhabitants; and by the laws of a people independent and rich with their own capital, all the benefits of liberty without its drawbacks. These incontestible facts, developed without art, and declared in a public notice, may be easily proved by simple inspection of the geography, and a general acqaintance of the state of New York. Believing that the value of this vast domain would be enhanced by the activity of cultivation and settlement, the proprietors have united in attempting the formation of a family, in some way united by common interests and common wants; and to promote the success of this measure, they here offer an account of the origin, and plan of their association. To maintain this essential unity of interests, the projectors have devised a plan that renders each member directly interested in the property, and require that a division shall be made by lot, that shall give at once a title to fifty acres individually, and to fifty in a portion that shall remain common and undivided until a fixed period; and that these subdivisions may operate in a ready and economical manner, they have adopted a form of certificate [*forme d' Action*], to the bearer, as best combining the desired features, and advantages of being evidences of the first title of purchase, and the undivided portion, and of partaking of the nature of an authentic title. In consequence, they have purchased this estate, and agreed that it should be done in the name of Sieur Chassanis, in whom they have united their confidence, and whom they have authorized to sign the certificates. He is to receive the funds to be credited to each, as titles of property, and furnish declarations to those who desired. Subsequent to the purchase, the parties interested have established the following rules, which shall be the common law of the holders of certificates, as inseparable from the title resulting. These rules are divided into two sections, the one including the articles essential to title, and the unalterable law of the proprietors, the other embracing the provisional rules and regulations of the common interest.

SECTION I. *Article* 1. The 600,000 acres of land which Peter Chassanis has purchased of Wm. Constable (in which are reserved five acres in each 100), shall be subdivided into 6000 portions, including the fractional portions.

Art. 2. A direct title shall be given upon application by the holders of certificates, in their own name.

Art. 3. These certificates shall be of the following form:

Title of the associaton of the New York company, in the purchase of 600,000 *acres of land in Montgomery county, State of New York:*

"The bearer of this certificate has paid the sum of *eight hundred livres* "which renders him the owner of a hundred acres in six hundred thou-"sand acres which have been sold to us as representatives of the com-"pany of Proprietors [*Companie des Actionnaires*], according to the pre-"sent contract, which requires us to pass the necessary titles of this por-"tion of the estate, in favor of the holder of this certificate, whenever he "may wish to receive it in his own name. The present certificate is for

160

"an integral part, and a fraction of the purchase above mentioned, by
"virtue of which, the bearer is entitled to all the rights of this association,
"of which the articles and rules are fixed by the terms of agreement
"annexed to this common title.

"This certificate bears the number ——. In evidence of which it
"has been signed by myself, countersigned by the commissaries of the
"company, and inspected by M. Lambot, notary."

Paris, this——of—— "

These shall remain deposited in the hands of M. Lambot, Notary at
Paris, who shall make the distribution after the inspection and signature,
of which we shall speak hereafter. The price of a certificate, shall remain
fixed at 800 livres, which shall be paid into the hands of M. Lambot. Of
this sum one tenth part shall be placed at the disposal of the trustees, to
defray the expenses of the concern, such as purchasing of tools, materials,
provisions, the opening of roads, necessary fixtures, surveys, and explorations. The nine other tenths, shall belong to the seller, who shall convey,
after the transfer has been duly made by Wm. Constable in America, a title
with all the formalities required by the usages of the country. This remit-
tance shall be made by the depository, directing the sums received to
Messrs. Ransom, Moreland & Hammersley, bankers in London, in drafts
upon that city; which shall be sent as received, without waiting the return
of titles, but till that time that the said Wm. Constable shall not draw
from the hands of the said bankers in London.

Art. 5. The 600,000 acres shall be divided into 12,000 lots of 50 acres
each, of which six thousand shall be divided, and set apart in the beginning, for individual properties, and six other thousand shall belong to the
company, who shall ultimately take measures for increasing its value,
and for a divison after the manner hereinafter mentioned.

Art. 6. Each holder of certificates shall have one separate lot, and one
in common and undivided stock.

Art. 7. The 30,000 acres additional, resulting from the reservations in
the above tract, shall be divided as follows: two thousand acres in the
formation of a city, in the interior of the tract, on the banks of the great
river that traverses the concession,........................... 2000.

Two thousand acres besides, to the founding of a second city, upon
the banks of Lake Ontario, at the mouth of the river upon which the first
city shall be built to serve for a port and entrepôt of commerce... 2000.

Six thousand acres shall be divided among artisans, who shall be distributed in the settlements, such as masons, carpenters, locksmiths, and
joiners, to be charged to them after seven years, by paying a rent of
twelve sous per acre... 6000.

The twenty thousand acres remaining shall be expended in the construction of roads and bridges, or disposed of as the society may
direct... 20,000.

Art. 8. The location of the two cities shall be divided into 14000 lots,
of which 2000 shall be reserved for markets, and edifices, such as
churches, schools, and other public establishments, and for poor artisans,
who shall be desirous of locating there. The 12,000 remaining lots shall
be divided into two classes, the one of separate and the other of undivided
ownership. One lot of each class shall belong to each owner of certificates.

Art. 9. The choice of divided lots, in the country as well as in the
cities, shall belong to the holders of certificates, in the order of the dates
of the presentation of their titles, by themselves or their authorized
agents to the trustees of the company.

Art. 10. The trustees of the company shall make upon the spot, before
the term of seven years, a report of the property remaining in common

and its condition; of the improvements of which it is susceptible, and an estimate of its value. After this report there shall be made a division into 6000 lots, which shall be designated on a plan. The trustees shall advertise three months in advance of drawing, which shall be done in a general assembly, by those only who shall have declared a fortnight before the drawing, that they wished to take part in the same. Those who do not make this declaration, shall be deemed to have chosen the continuation and non-division of the common property.

Art. 11. The holders of certificates, who remain in common, shall regulate in a general assembly their particular interests, as well for the care of lands which remain with them as for selling them, as they may decide.

Art. 12. After the drawing, the society shall no longer exist, except among such as do not take part in it; the certificates shall be furnished to those entitled, containing a title and adjudication of their lots.

Art. 13. The affairs of the company shall be managed by trustees, living in Paris, three in number, and by at least two other trustees, residing upon the tract. These different trustees shall be in regular correspondence, and shall be chosen by an absolute majority of the general assembly. These meetings shall be held in Paris, and every owner may attend and assist by himself or by proxy. Each share shall entitle to one vote, yet no person shall have more than five votes, whatever the number of shares he may possess.

Art. 14. All the articles aforesaid, are essential to the existence of certificates, and can be modified only in a general assembly, convened *ad hoc.* and by a majority of two thirds.

SECTION II.   *Government.   Article* 1. Within one month, there shall be held a meeting of the subscribers, at the rooms of the said Sieur Chassanis, at Paris, No. 20, *Rue de la Jussieune,* for the election of trustees.

Art. 2. The trustees, residing in Paris, shall have the charge of proving the certificates, with the depository, and of personally examining each, to guard against errors; the notary shall also compare them as received, and paid, after which they shall be signed by the said Sieur Chassanis, to be delivered to the shareholders. Consequently no certificate shall be issued until after these inspections and signatures, and the subscribers shall in the mean time only receive a provisional receipt of deposit.

Art. 3. To guard against all errors in distribution, the certificates shall be registered by their numbers, by Sieur Chassanis, upon their presentation by the holders, and the record kept in his office, and without this entry, of which notice shall be written upon the certificate by the said Sieur Chassanis, or by the one whom the trustees shall appoint for the purpose, no holder of certificates shall be admitted to the meetings, nor have right to take his chance in the selection of his location.

Art. 4. The trustees, designated for removal to America, shall be the bearers of the instructions, and of the general powers of the assembly; shall survey the land, decide upon the location of the two cities, and there prepare for the company, within three months from their arrival, a report of their examinations and labors, with a detailed plan of the common property.

Art. 5. trustees shall be chosen from among the holders of certificates.

Art. 6. The trustees shall decide the location of the fifty acres which shall belong originally to each certificate, after which the holders shall have the right of choice.

Art. 7. The locations shall be marked upon two registers, in the hands of the trustees in America, who shall retain one and transmit the other annually to the general assembly in France.

Art. 8. The titles directed to be delivered to the holders of certificates, who make known their wish, shall contain a declaration by Sieur Chassanis, that in his general purchase, there belongs a certain portion to *** as his own, in accordance with a common title, and a social regulation of which he is a party; this declaration shall bear the number of the certificate, which shall remain attached, under pain of forfeiture of the action, even though the certificate had been previously canceled, and this title shall not be complete till after the registration of the trustees to whom it shall be presented.

Art. 9. The trustees in America, shall be clothed with a similar power by Sieur Chassanis, for granting like titles to those who require it. This power shall be granted after a model of the declaration, for the purpose of securing uniformity of registry.

Art. 10. All decisions and acts of the company done in France, as relates to trustees, have no need of public formality when they are legalized by the minister or other public functionary of the United States, residing in France.

Art. 11. There shall be delivered, upon demand, a duplicate of title to the holders of certificates, containing a copy of the original, and in it shall be mentioned that it is a duplicate."

APPENDIX II

PROSPECTUS AND TOPOGRAPHICAL ACCOUNT

Of six hundred thousand acres[1] of land in North America, offered for sale in shares, according to the Plan of Association herein given.

[Printed from Hough's unpublished translation. See the original French cover on page 25.]

The Association of which we are about to offer the Plan, will doubtless attract the Notice of the Fathers of Families, as everything desirable in the way of solidity and advantage will be found united in this Enterprise. Its success cannot be doubted, since it is based upon lands, the cultivation of which it at once offers to the Proprietors of these domains, alike important for their extent and fertility.

It appears to us needless to use a long argument, and it will suffice to describe the location of these lands, and their relations with the surrounding parts, and to give some details upon the varied and useful productions of the soil, which is known to be excellent. We will also give an account of the Population and its progress, which every thing appears to encourage, and of the climate so favorable to vegetation, and so salubrious to the inhabitants, and will give but a rapid view of the government, because its form is generally known; concluding by some remarks upon the advantages which this country offers to Commerce.

This concise and truthful picture will exhibit the means and resources which this Association offers for human industry to acquire, and even to increase by durable riches; and as nothing is exaggerated, it should attract that public confidence which this acquisition deserves.

Location

Thirty five leagues eastward from the Concession, is situated the city and port of Albany,[2] where vessels land from Europe. The passage from Albany to Fort Schuyler or Stanwix, is made through a well settled country, the most fertile yet cultivated in America, and lying along the Mohawk River, which may be ascended by bateaux. Thus with the exception of ten or eleven leagues, we may bring into the interior of these lands everything coming from Europe, but they are now actually at work making canals and sluces (*sic*), by which there will be a communication made entirely by water.

To the West is Lake Ontario, having a length of fifty, and a breadth of twenty five leagues. This beautiful lake offers the finest

164

resources for commerce and fisheries, as it extends ten leagues along our Domain, and on account of its communications with many navigable rivers, as well as with the river Saint Laurence.[3]

On the North, is Canada. The new city of Kingston is there built upon the borders of the lake, and this city in which they have fixed the seat of government of Upper Canada, is not more than five or six leagues from the Concession.

On the South, we find a very well peopled and very fertile region, so productive that it yields most of the grain that they export from the ports of Albany and New York to Europe. Thus in the first years of new settlement upon our lands, we may obtain with the greatest facility and at a moderate cost, every kind of supplies.

It may not be out of place here to observe, that in this happy location, there is no fear of the Indians, who are separated from our tract by Lake Ontario, which is a kind of little sea, and still more, by the English establishments scattered along the North Shores of the lake. The theatre of actual war, is more than two hundred leagues distant.

Independently of the distance and obstacles which afford a shelter from an Indian incursion, the whole county of Montgomery has been purchased by the State of New York from the natives to whom it belonged. This purchase was made by a public treaty, concluded in good faith on both sides, and the Indians never come again upon lands thus ceded.

Such is the favorable location of the lands in Montgomery County, which moreover enjoy the further advantage of a soil fertile and susceptable (sic) of every kind of production.

Productions

Over an extent of about fifteen leagues in length, by eight or ten in breadth, the soil varies considerably, but we may determine its quality by the different kinds of trees that are found, and from the vigor of their growth, which is such, that the surface of the earth is covered with very streight (sic) trees, eighty to a hundred, and two hundred feet high.

These trees are of different species, and quite varied in their kind, such as the Oak,[4] Beech, Elm, Ash, Chestnut, Birch and Silver Fir.[5]

The Wild Cherry tree, very valuable for joinery and cabinet work, is there found very common and, of the finest quality, and may perhaps supply the place of the wood of the mahogany, of which it has many of the qualities.

The Hickory also found there, is the best wood to burn, and its ashes are very suitable for making potash.[6] The nuts which it bears are excellent to eat.

There is also a kind of nut-tree which bears a nut called the butter-nut, on account of its rich quality. This tree is only found in the valleys, and indicates a very rich soil.

Upon the highlands we find Pines of various species, and especially the White Pine, whose majestic appearance strikes the beholder, and whose utility cannot be compared with that of any other tree on the globe. It is much sought for by carpenters, and it also furnishes masts for the largest men-of-war.

In parts less elevated, and on the plains, we observe the Platanus Occidentalis,[7] the wood of which in quality resembles the Beech and the Oak, and we there observe especially the Sugar Maple,[8] so interesting to the cultivator and as Providence seems to have been prodigal in this wood, it appears to merit at our hands a particular notice.

"There are few trees" says Valmont de Boware,[9] "which combine so much that is pleasant and agreeable, which grow more rapidly or more uniformly, or which better adapt themselves to bad exposures or require less care and culture in resisting them. None better withstand the vicissitudes of the seasons, or can be multiplied with greater facility."

It is now only two years since cultivators have learned to derive from this precious tree every advantage which it offers. They knew very well that by extracting a sweet liquor they could reduce it to sugar, but their process was so imperfect that there resulted but a very feeble advantage.

At the beginning of 1790, there was discovered a method of purifying the sugar, which process is so simple, that in Montgomery County, the workman who labors with activity during six weeks in February and March, can make a thousand pounds weight, of as good sugar as that which they send from our islands, and which sells at the same price.[10]

The Maple requires no cultivation. The extraction of the juice requires very little expense, and at a season when the suspended labors of the earth give leisure to cultivators. We should further remark, that this tree does not suffer from the incisions which they then make, and it is certain that in those which have been tapped for fifty years, the liquor flows as well as from those which have never before been cut.

If from trees we pass to plants, we find in this part of America, the same variety and abundance, without speaking of herbs of various kinds which serve to nourish horses and cattle, which they send to pasture in the woods. Among the plants and shrubs, we notice the raspberry and strawberry, which flourish in great abundance.

May-apples,[11] there grow as large as an Orange, of a very good flavor, and they appear to be peculiar to America.

The hop is there indigenous, and its quality is equal to that cultivated in Europe.

The White trefoil[12] as they call the Powel, is so natural to American soil that it grows there without culture, and being found everywhere, is, according to Arthur Young, the most certain proof of an excellent and fertile soil.[13]

Among the roots, we observe everywhere two of infinite value to commerce: the *Salse-pareille*,[14] and the *Gins-eng*, or *Gens-eng*, which are exported with so much profit to China.[15]

We deem it proper to add here what is said of the soil of North America by the learned Savan Ellis, in the Philosophical Transactions of Philadelphia. "We know," says he, "but few plants indigenous in foreign countries, and especially those of the north of China, which cannot be produced successfully in North America."

The details which we have noticed doubtless prove the fertility of the soil which we have purchased,[16] but in order that this proof may be universally recognized as a certainty, we should here add another not less to the point. It is this, that the products of the lands formerly covered with the same kinds of trees that we have mentioned, now cultivated along the Mohawk and Wood Creek, and which border the concession, show a fertility that none in Europe can equal, producing abundantly all kinds of grain, such as Maize or Indian Corn, Wheat, Buckwheat, Barley, Oats and Vetch.

Peas and Beans are there cultivated so successfully that they export considerable quantities to the English and French islands.

Melons, cucumbers and citrons, there grow in the open air without the aid of artificial heat.

Flax and hemp are harvested in very large quantities, and it is an incontestable fact that they export more flax seed from the state of New York, than from all the states of the union together. The exportation has amounted to three hundred thousand bushels.[17]

"Besides these native products," says the American Spectator, "abundantly sufficient for all the wants of life, all the productions of Europe which have been tried in New York, have there succeeded perfectly, and many of them with but little care will there attain a degree of excellence far above that in Europe after a careful and very expensive cultivation."[18]

Clearing

Everyone knows that in America, they do not uproot the trees to clear and cultivate new lands. It is customary to cut them down and then burn whatever is not reserved for building timbers and carpenters work, or for articles of exportation, such as masts, planks and beams etc. From the ashes they make potash,[19] which sells for about enough to pay the cost of clearing. This product is certain lucrative and easy, on account of the markets upon the banks of Lake Ontario, or the navigable river that communicates from it.

It is not in these forests that have never been cut down, as in those of Europe. These ancient groves when once cut do not reappear. The cattle destroy the few shoots that spring up, and their stumps rot away in a few years. We find that on account of the great size of the trees, they are considerably scattered from one another, so that the first year they admit the harrow among the stubble. The harrow alone is sufficient; the harvest is not less abundant, and the man who has cleared the land, will never have occasion during his life to use any fertilizers, or to let it lie fallow, as is the practice in Europe.

Climate

"New York," says the American Spectator, "is in all respects one of the most delightful residences in North America. The salubrity of the climate, and the fertility of the soil are admirable."[20]

They never there experience those excessive heats which in other parts of America follow the spring rains and occasion sickness, and there is no country where fevers are less known than in Montgomery County.[21]

The spring is not of long duration, but the moderate temperature of the summer, renders this season a prolonged spring. Yet its warmth is a little more than that of the spring time in Europe, and is attended with sufficient showers to bring forward to maturity all the productions of the earth.

The autumn which succeeds, is the season most uniformly fine, and the harvest is never interrupted as in Europe, by long rains. It is only by the middle of November that we begin to notice some considerable changes.

The snow then comes to herald the rigors of winter, and this benificent *(sic))*snow, which uniformly covers the ground in this season, protects the grain, fertilizes the earth, and assures to the husbandman abundant harvests.

In the month of April, the spring returns, and the first warm days preceded sometimes by gentle showers gradually melt the snows. When the earth is uncovered, the most beautiful verdure soon embellishes the fields.

The animals peculiar to this climate, and known in New York are Elk, Deer, Bears, Wolves, Red and Gray Foxes, Beavers, Otters, Martins, Badgers, Racoons, Hares, Porcupines, and Squirrels of five or six species, all of which animals offer as much amusement for the chase as resources for the table, besides furnishing supplies of precious peltries for a trade with Europe. None of these make war upon man, and as soon as population appears, they quickly disappear and the wolves and bears soon retire into the distant forests, of which America will long furnish them proper retreats.

Among the birds, we count upon all the varieties of Pheasants, Partridges, Woodcock and Wood Pigeons.[22]

Geese, wild ducks and other aquatic fowls, so multiply there that the rivers and lakes, are, so to speak, covered by them.

Lake Ontario is celebrated for the fine quality and for the quantity and variety of fish, which are there caught. The rivers furnish different kinds which we are acquainted with, such as the Shad, Sturgeon, Salmon, Bass,[23] common and Salmon Trout, Perch, Pike, Eels, etc. These rivers so abound in fish, that a man with a single line, can catch in an afternoon, as many as he can carry, and sometimes more.

Population

It is not surprising that a country so rich in all the gifts of Nature, and so well calculated to satisfy every human want, should attract industry and population, so that each year is marked by a rapid progress. The visible increase of the State of New York, and especially of Montgomery County, will give one an idea of this population, which will ere long animate our lands, and give them a value proportionate to that of the neighboring establishments.

It is believed that the Population of the United States of America doubles every twenty years. But from a census taken by the government we find that the growth of the State of New York has been much more rapid. In fact, the census of 1756, showed ninety six thousand seven and ninety inhabitants, yet notwithstanding eight years of war, the one taken in 1786, amounted to two hundred and thirty eight thousand eight hundred and ninety seven, and that of July 26, 1791, gave the number at three hundred and forty thousand one and twenty souls.[24] According to the details given by order of Congress, the greatest increase of the population has been in the vicinity of the Mohawk River, and Lake Ontario.

Government and Religion

It is not a matter of indifference for a man to know under what form of government he is to live, or own lands. That of the State of New York, much resembles the general government of the United States.

New York is divided into Counties, the Counties into Precincts, and the Precincts into Districts. Each County has a Court of Justice, and each District a Justice of the Peace.

A new settlement leads to the division of a District, as soon as the number of inhabitants becomes too great, and they erect this new establishment into a new District, and so in succession a new County when this becomes necessary on account of numbers, and by the increase of New Districts.

Six months residence in the country and the possession of property worth about five hundred livres Tournois, gives one the right of voting at the elections, and of enjoying the other privileges of Citizens.

Justice is everywhere administered equally. The Laws are founded upon Liberty and Toleration, and the respect which the Americans pay to all Religions is the first pledge of Manners, from whence comes that spirit of gentleness and benevolence which characterizes them.

All religions are equally enjoyed, and the Constitution of the State of New York, "ordains, determines and declares; in the name and by the authority of the good people of this state, that the free exercise and enjoyment of religious profession, and worship, without discrimination or preference shall forever hereafter be allowed within this state, to all mankind: Provided that the liberty of conscience hereby granted shall not be so construed as to excuse acts of licentiousness or to justify practices inconsistent with the peace and safety of this state."[25] Such being the text of the Law, we find twenty different denominations, each one having one or more churches. They have there in America, both Catholic and Protestant Bishops.

The State of New York enjoys an advantage peculiar to itself, in the wealth of its revenues, so that there is no need of imposing any tax upon the Inhabitants as well for the ordinary expenses of government as also for the extraordinary cost of improvements such as new roads and canals. The taxes of the General Government are also levied upon what is imported into the United States. These taxes are very moderate and are only assessed upon objects of luxury. They do not amount year by year, to more than five percent upon the value of merchandises with the exception of tea, coffee, sugar, and spirituous liquors. An increase of import duties is the less to be feared, inasmuch as Congress has enormous territorial resources.

Commerce

In glancing at the geographical location of New York, we may readily conceive that it should enjoy a superiority in commerce over the other states of the Union.

"The whole state of New York," says Morse,[26] "is so cut up and divided by the branches of the Hudson, Delaware, Susquehanna and other rivers, that there are very few places in its whole extent, which are more than five or six leagues from a navigable river."

It is doubtless surprising, that so many natural advantages have been so long neglected in New York,but the activity of her neighbors have drawn off her resources, and have aroused an emulation and rivalry in industry. This State begins to feel that nothing is more easy than to attract to its ports a most flourishing commerce, and to share with the English that of the river Saint Laurence, which presents to it the means.

Located at that end of Lake Ontario nearest to the inhabited parts, and surrounded and divided by several navigable rivers, the Concession made to the New York Company, combines all that is needful to stimulate the industry and activity of its inhabitants.

They have at the beginning, the saving of all the expenses that others are obliged to incur for the transportation of their commodities. They will doubtless at first consume the different kinds of grain that they cultivate, but from the first year, the oaken planks and carpenters' wood may be turned to profit.

Potash,[27] as well as the woods, would be one of the most essential articles, and the *Salse-pareille* and the *gins-eng*,[28] a very considerable subject of exportation.

It is doubtless easy to give an advantageous idea of the tract that has been conceded to us, but we ought also to observe, that all the lands within the limits of the State are sold by the government, and that their value increases in a rapid degree, so that those of the New

171

York Company cannot fail to acquire, even without clearing, a proportionate value.

It already frequently happens, that speculators have bought large tracts of land, and have then again sold them to the benefit of several capitalists, without having made thereon any clearings, but we do not wish to engage in this simple speculation, however profitable it may be, as the end which we propose is to dispose of our lands at such a price, that cultivation and population will bring up their value. Those which we find under cultivation along the route from Fort Schuyler or Stanwix to Albany, sell from five to six Louis per acre, and ours which are only six leagues from Fort Schuyler, should, after our establishment possess at least an equal value.

At that happy period, the Actionaries of the New York Company might therefore sell at from five to ten Louis, that which costs today but eight livres. This benefit is not illusory, and its reality may be readily felt. Another advantage for each Actionary is this, that the expense of clearing and culture is only charged for the half of his shares,[29] and that he enjoys for the whole, the unspeakable advantage of having its possessions united with those of a numerous company so proper to vivify the surrounding countries.

The first establishments are the most difficult to form. They need a road to reach them, and mills for grinding and sawing, because they have first houses to build, and if every thing needed does not exist, an individual would find himself embarrassed, and often perhaps would not venture to undertake to settle. But here the Company is at the expense of opening the road, of building mills, and of establishing one or more Manufactories of Potash, and while it is doing good to the new inhabitants, it is working for itself a great advantage. Thus the first steps, of all others the most difficult that occur, are relieved to the new colonists. The plan of the cities is already fixed. These cities will hasten the progress of agriculture and commerce, and facilitate their early reunion.

Quite recently, in the neighborhood of Albany and of our lands, several cities have sprung up: *Hudson* and *Luseng-berg*,[30] on the banks of the Hudson, *Balls-town* in the interior of the country to the north of the Mohawk river, and *Coopers-town* at the source of the Susquehanna. The location of this city and environs, in a circumference of ten miles, was in 1786, all covered with woods.

If Coopers-town, built within this period, and which owes its origin to only one man, (Cooper),[31] is already famous for its commerce and manufactures, what ought we not to expect from the cities founded by a company whose means and interests are much more powerful than those of a private individual?

APPENDIX III

THE CONSTITUTION OF THE COMPAGNIE DE NEW YORK

[AUTHOR'S NOTE: The Constitution was printed in Paris in 1793 in a quarto pamphlet of 32 pages.

Although translated by Dr. Hough, the Introduction to the Constitution, the list of signatories and the report by Chassanis which follows have never previously been published.

In his listing of signatories, Hough is inconsistent in spelling and punctuation. I have made two changes in spelling: "Guisot" to "Guinot" (#7 & #8) and "Guget" to "Guyot" (#13 & #14). Since these names appear printed in the Constitution, I have assumed they are more correct than the hand-written copy.

The balance of the Constitution is reprinted here from Hough's History of Lewis County (1860), pp. 40-50.]

In the year one thousand seven hundred and ninety three, and of the French Republic the second: on the twenty eighth day of June, at five o'clock in the afternoon, assembled at the rooms of Citizen Pierre Chassanis, at Paris, in the Street of La Jussienne, in the Section of Mail;

The undersigned, actual holders of provisional certificates convertible into shares of the company about to be established by this instrument, each one for the number of shares herein after specified, according to a verification to be made by the said Pierre Chassanis and Citizen Lambot, Notary, to whom are delivered the said certificates; both being previously nominated for this purpose according to an agreement made by the said undersigned, owners of the said provisional certificates of which they are the bearers, as well as of those which may result from a Proces-verbal of this fact, upon this subject, signed by the undersigned, and deposited in the archives of the company: Namely:

1. The said Pierre Chassanis for two hundred and four shares   204
2. Jacques Donatien LeRay de Chaumont, Junior, proprietor in North America, a hundred shares.   100
3. Michel St. John de Crèvecoeur, formerly Consul of France at New York, in the said North America for 10 shares.   10
4. Louis Moreau, stipulating for Citizen Couginasse Desjardins, Merchant-commissaire of the Executive Consul of France in the said city of New York for 60 shares.   60

173

5. Renoit Van Prandelles, Merchant at Baltimore in North America for thirteen shares.   13
6. René Lambot, Notary, in Paris, for fifteen shares.   15
7. Michel Pierre Guinot, Merchant, for seventy eight shares.   78
8. Etienne Guinot, French citizen, for one hundred and thirty two shares.   132
9. Auguste Victor Chion De la Chaume, Notary in Paris, for five shares   5
10. Charles-Pierre-Joseph Lotran, stipulating for Citizen Maillot, Merchant in Paris, for seven shares.   7
11. Etienne-Pierre Pharoux, Architect, for twenty five shares.   25
12. Alexander-James Desormeaux, Citizen, for twenty shares.   20
13. Julien-Pierre Guyot, Merchant, for twenty shares.   20
14. Citizenne Guyot, elder daughter, for fifty five shares.   55
15. Jean-Nicolas de Livry, Citizen, for three hundred shares.   300
16. Jean-Baptiste Mesnard, Citizen, for three hundred seventy shares.   370
17. Citizenne Lourdet, wife of Simon Le Febre, Merchant, for sixty four shares.   64
18. Nicolas Olive, Merchant, for ten shares.   10
19. Bénigne-Joseph, Varin, Architect, for two shares.   2
20. Ignace Munier, Citizen, for twelve shares.   12
21. Jean-Nicolas-Antoine Army, Citizen, for four shares.   4
22. Antoine-Pierre-Viel-Lunas, farmer, for sixteen shares.   16
23. Charles Davilliers, for sixty shares   60
24. Jean-Louis-Grives, liquidateur of the National Treasury, for ten shares.   10
25. Joseph-Victor Allons, Citizen, for five shares.   5
26. Claude-Amable De la Tremblaye, for five shares.   5
27. Elizabeth-Beneets Reider, elder daughter, for two shares.   2
28. Angerdresne-Isabelle Beneets Reider, daughter of Citizen Bailly, for three shares.   3
29. Charles-Francois Ame, Citizen, for eight shares.   8
30. Jacques Rouland, formerly banker, for fifteen shares.   15
31. Augustin Chendret, Citizen, for three shares.   3
32. Antoine-Francois Charpentier, Notary in Paris, for one hundred shares.   100
33. Jacques-Francois Crin, Citizen, for one share.   1
34. Pierre-Valeve-Petit de la Pequiere, Citizen, for two shares.   2
35. Joseph-Victor Balenat, Citizen, for two shares.   2
36. Angelique-Francois-Paul-Mathieu Cousin, for two shares.   2
37. Henri-Agathe-Decriene, Citizen, for ten shares.   10

38. Jean-Baptiste-Edmon, Citizen, for three shares.   3
39. Pierre-Thomas Jubault, Citizen, for thirty shares.   30
40. Citizen Deshayes, stipulating for Citizen Sarrasin, agent of
    exchange, for twenty shares.   20
41. Etienne-Louis-Prudent Moreau, Citizen, for five shares.   5

The whole making eighteen hundred and eight shares.   1,808

And furthermore all the undersigned stipulate collectively, as composing the majority of two thirds, and over, required by the prospectus above mentioned, for the entire number of the bearers of provisional certificates convertible into two thousand shares, this being the number of those of which the company is composed, proprietors collectively of one hundred of the shares, which by the present act it is decided shall be reserved subject to its disposal — 100

Making the number of shares for which the undersigned, by this act declare for themselves and those whom they represent, or for the company collectively, nineteen hundred and eight shares ——— 1,908

And further by the terms of the said prospectus the right is reserved to the undersigned of ordering by this act, for themselves and those whom they represent and who are not present, (the majority requisite for two thirds being only thirteen hundred and thirty four shares, while those represented by those present, exceeded this number by five hundred and seventy four shares) the certificates convertible into shares of which they are the bearers, those which are not actually present, comprising ninety two shares. ——————————— 92

Forming in all two thousand shares of which the company is composed by the present act ————————————————— 2,000

The said Assembly being regularly convened by circular notice and advertisement in the public papers, the said undersigned bearers of provisional certificates do hereby declare, that having become proprietors by the payment for the said shares, of two hundred and twenty thousand five hundred acres of land, in the State of New York in North America, they will proceed to lay the foundations of their society, fix its rules, and establish every point, relative to the division, survey, placing in market and disposing of their property in America.

But proceeding to this, the Citizen Chassanis, who has been the representative of the stockholders for the purchase of the said lands, has thought proper to recite the origin of this property, and the manner in which it has been conveyed to the shareholders. He accordingly announced to the assembly as follows:

175

The land sold to the Company of New York, forms a part of the lands purchased by the State of New York of the original Indians who inhabited it.

It is located upon the Black River and near Lake Ontario, beginning on the north bank of the Black River, opposite the Western limits of the William Inman tract, and extends along the bank westward to Lake Ontario, and thence northward along the lake to a certain point, from whence a line drawn south eighty seven degrees east would strike the northwest corner of a tract known as Totten and Crossfield's purchase and from this latter point it extends eastwardly along the said line to the northwest corner of the William Inman Tract, nine miles from the place of beginning, from whence it runs to the first point.

Of the lands bought by the State of New York, nineteen hundred and twenty thousand acres were conveyed by the said State to Alexander Macomb, by Letters Patent, on the 10th of June, 1792.

A. Macomb, conveyed the property to William Constable by an instrument dated on the 6th of June, 1792, and renewed by him and his wife, by another conveyance of the 3rd of October of the same year.

These conveyances are executed in all the formalities prescribed by the American laws, and are further authenticated by the certificate of Messrs. John Coxe and Jared Ingersol under date of November 19th, 1792, and deposited in the office of the French Consulate at Philadelphia.

Mr. Constable, not wishing to retain the whole of his purchase, authorized Citizen Chassanis, to sell for him in France a quantity intended to be six hundred and thirty thousand acres. He has adopted the form of the conveyances for this sale. The number of these shares was designated at six thousand, and he has fixed the price of each share at eight hundred livres per hundred acres. A prospectus was issued in October, 1792, to announce the sale of these shares.

But by December, the period fixed upon when Mr. Constable might depend on a part of the funds which this sale was to produce, no purchaser had appeared. It was then, that fearing the non-success of his operation, he directed Colonel Ward, to withdraw the lands from sale, which he had offered to French Capitalists. Nevertheless, upon the purchase of Citizen Chassanis, Colonel Ward, who was charged with the business of Mr. Constable, agreed to allow two thousand shares to be sold in France, and agreed that two hundred thousand acres taken on the Black River, and extending to Lake Ontario, should be assigned for these two thousand shares.

176

Upon this latter basis the provisional certificates have been delivered to the stockholders. And to fulfill this near engagement, Mr. Constable, by a contract dated April 13th, and passed at London, in all the legal formalities of the country, has transferred to Citizen Chassanis, not only two hundred thousand acres, and the five percent of land additional for roads and public objects, but also ten thousand acres more, in order to facilitate the improvement of the said two hundred thousand acres, the whole to be taken in the purchase made by him from Mr. Macomb, in conformity with the boundaries hereinbefore specified.

In this conveyance of Mr. Constable, he further engages to transfer to the Company the indemnities which are granted him by the State of New York, as to lands covered with water, in by the same instrument, he acknowledges the total payment which the said Citizen Chassanis has made for the said lands.

The facts stated by Citizen Chassanis being found to agree with the titles and documents which he had communicated to the stockholders, and to the provisional Commissaries whom they had appointed to examine them, the assembly after hearing the report of the said provisional Commissaries, and having discussed article by article the project of the Company which they presented, have unanimously adopted deliberated and decreed the following:

CONSTITUTION.

Seal.

TITLE I.—*Declaration of the Rights of the Company.*

Article 1. Citizen Chassanis declares, that all the lands and rights by him definitely acquired of Wm. Constable, by the final contract of the 13th of April last, have been, for the benefit of the purchasers of 2,000 shares of 800 livres each, amounting to the total price of the said purchase, which has been paid to Constable, as appears from the receipt inserted in the said instrument of sale, and repeated by him upon the fold of the said contract. Citizen Chassanis acknowledges, that this payment has been made from funds received from the sale of nearly all of the shares, of which it is well to notice, that one-tenth of the price has been remitted by Constable to the shareholders. Consequently, citizen Chassanis cedes and conveys, so far as need be, to the said shareholders, all the rights of property or otherwise resulting from the said contract, to them collectively, consenting that from this time forth they shall enjoy and dispose of the whole property.

Art. 2. The bearers of receipts controvertable into shares of the said property, who are here present, stipulate, as well for themselves as for those absent, that they accept, as far as need be, and collectively, the property which has been anew declared and ceded by the said citizen Chassanis, with the original conditions annexed to the cession by the state of New York, by letters patent hereinafter mentioned, it being well understood that the said shareholders are not held by these conditions, beyond the proportion of the land which they have purchased under the name of the said citizen Chassanis, by the final contract of April 13th last.

177

Art. 3. Citizen Chassanis has exhibited and placed upon the table, the documents which establish the original and actual property in the lands and rights which he has bought, to wit:

1st. A copy, in legal form, of the letters patent of Jan. 12, 1792.

2d. A copy, also in legal form, of the contract of sale made by Alexander Macomb to Wm. Constable, dated June 6, 1792.

3d. A copy, in legal form, of the renewal of the said contract of sale by Alexander Macomb and Jane his wife, dated Oct. 3, 1792.

4th. Certificate delivered by the Secretary of the Consulate General of France, of the act of deposit of the three above named instruments in the said office.

5th. The originals of two certificates of a Master in Chancery of New York, proving that the lands sold are not encumbered by any debt of Alexander Macomb.

6th. The original contract of sale of Wm. Constable to Pierre Chassanis, of April 12, 1793, in parchment, with the original pledge of possession.

7th. The original bond of the said Wm. Constable in behalf of P. Chassanis, of £50,000 sterling, dated April 12, 1793, to be paid in default of ratification by his wife.

Moreover, a printed copy of the prospectus issued by citizen Chassanis, upon the faith of which the shareholders were led to the purchase of their shares.

Lastly, a printed copy of the provisional receipts delivered to the purchasers of shares, to which is annexed a reduction of title of the sale proposed by the prospectus.

Art. 4. The Assembly deposits all of these papers in the hands of citizen Chassanis, and charges him with providing a place of deposit for the archives of the Company of New York.

TITLE II.—*Title of the Shareholders as a Society, and Name of their Property in America.*

Article 1. In adopting as for this, the arrangement implied in the prospectus above mentioned, the Assembly declares that all the said shareholders, as well present as absent, are, by the act of their purchase, co-proprietors in common and of, the lands and rights declared in the first title, and by these presents are constituted dormant partners under the title of *Company of New York,* for the occupation of the said lands and rights, excepting, however, the exceptions and modifications hereinafter specified.

Art. 2. The lands of the Company of New York shall henceforth be known under the name of *Castor Land.*[1]

TITLE III.—*Specification of the Rights which the Company Enjoys and thos*^e *which it Does Not.*

Art. 1. The ends proposed by the association founded under the preceding title, are: *1st.* To extend more rapidly life and improvement over all the extent of the lands acquired by the company. *2d.* To relieve the greater part of the shareholders who can not consent to a passage beyond seas, from the embarrassment and expense attending the first settlement of a large portion of the lands. *3d.* To aid them with regard to the surplus. *And 4th, and lastly.* To accelerate in that country the population, which will one day become its wealth.

It appears indispensable, that in order to more speedily work these happy results, there should be established over a great part of the purchase that is to remain undivided and in common, a general and capable administration, by the union of the common interests, to give value to that portion, and cause it to realize advantages above what could be derived from the separate exertions of the shareholders through their several agents.

---

1 Castor, signifies *Beaver.*

Art. 2. The portion of the said purchase which shall remain with the company, and be held undivided by the associated shareholders, to be enhanced by a general administration, shall be,

1st. 100,000 acres of land, to be taken from the 200,000 acres forming the principal object of the said purchase.

2d. 20,500 acres, granted as above, to the shareholders by Constable, to wit: 10,000 for roads, canals and public establishments on account of the 5 acres per 100, and 10,000 to be derived from the indemnity. It is observed that in the 220,500 acres mentioned, lands covered by water should not be included, according to the terms of the patent, and the sale of Constable.

3d. The tenth part remitted by Constable as an encouragement to the shareholders, upon the whole of the 2,000 shares, in the 1st Article of Title I, amounts to 160,000 livres. This sum is now in the hands of Mr. Lambot, Notary, subject to the order of the shareholders, and is represented by 80,000 livres in credit paper, and a like sum in 100 shares of 800 livres each, which alone remain of the 2,000 shares above mentioned, and were left by Constable to the shareholders, to complete the tenth which he remitted to them, and of which values the Assembly declares its acceptance on account of the said remission.

Art. 3. That portion of the said purchase to be owned separately by the shareholders immediately, shall be divided as soon as may be, in the manner specified in the Title IX, and is composed—*1st,* Of 100,000 acres of land ; and *2d,* Of the land which 2,000 divided lots shall occupy in the plan of the first city which shall be projected by the Company of Associates.

TITLE IV.—*Form and Duration of the Society.*

Art. 1. The society which has been formed for the possession and enjoyment in common of the objects specified in Art. 1 of the preceding title, shall consist of 2,000 proprietary shares.

Art. 2. The said shares shall be numbered from 1 to 2,000. These shares instead of being in the form announced in the prespectus, shall be divided into two coupons. The one shall be called *coupon divis,* and shall confer the right to 50 acres in the 100,000 acres divided, and to a divided lot in the plan of the first city which shall be projected upon the lands. The other shall be a stamped *coupon indivis,* and shall give an interest in a two-thousandth part of the objects remaining undivided and in company among the shareholders ; and the coupons shall bear the same number as the shares. These coupons shall be drawn in the following form :

Company of New York.

Purchase in the name of Peter Chassanis, of 200,000 acres of land and dependencies known by the name of *Castorland,* and situated in the state of New York, Montgomery co., upon the banks of lake Ontario and of Black river. By deed of April 12, 1793. No.—— Divided coupon. The bearer by full payment of the price of a whole share, of which the present coupon forms a part, is owner by virtue of the said coupon, of divided lot which shall correspond in division with No.—— as well in the plan of the first city which shall be laid out upon the company's land, as in the 2,000 lots of 50 acres each which shall be formed in the division of the divisible property of 100,000 acres making a part of the purchase above named, after the manner determined by the organization of the said company dated June 28, 1793, of which a quadruple remains in the archives of the company and another shall be registered and deposited in the city of New York. Note. This coupon shall be exchanged for a deed upon delivery of the lot.

GUYOT,	CHASSANIS,	GUINOT,
Commissary.	Director.	Commissary.

Inspected according to the act of June 28, 1793.

LAMBOT.

(The second part or undivided coupon is similar, excepting that it gives the holder a final right to one two-thousandth part of the undivided property of the company upon its dissolution.)

Art. 3. Agreeable with the prospectus, the coupons forming each share shall be signed by citizen Chassanis and two commissaries of the company, and inspected by citizen Lambot, notary at Paris.

179

Art. 4. The provisional receipts delivered by the said Lambot, notary, who has been instructed to receive the payment of the said shares, will need to be exchanged for shares in the above form, which shall bear the same numbers as the receipts to which they correspond.

Art. 5. This exchange shall be made at the company's office, and when done, the exchanged receipts shall be canceled and left with the director of the company, to be sent to the said Lambot as they become worthless by exchange, and by the discharge of the said Lambot to Constable, shall operate by the release inserted in the contract of sale aforesaid.

Art. 6. The society, beginning to-day, shall continue twenty-one years from the 1st of July next, with the privilege of dissolving before the expiration of this term, as will be hereafter explained in Title XII.

Art. 7. None shall be regarded as true members, except the bearers of *coupons indivis* of the two thousand shares aforesaid.

Art. 8. The *coupon divis* of each of the said shares, shall never give the privilege of the society, except as an action against it, to compel the delivery to the bearer of the divided lot mentioned in the coupon, in the manner hereinafter explained in title IX.

TITLE V.—*Government of the Society, a Director and four Commissaries living in Paris, their Functions and Powers.*

Art. 1. The interests of the company shall be managed by a director and four commissaries living in Paris, where the government of the society shall remain fixed.

Art. 2. The director and commissaries, shall always be chosen at a general meeting of the shareholders, by an absolute majority of votes and viva voce.

Art. 3. They can only be chosen from the company, and a person to be director or commissary, must be the owner or holder of at least ten entire shares or of twenty *coupons indivis*, of which deposit shall be made into the hands of citizen Lambot, notary, within eight days after their nomination to the said places, and their powers shall cease if they become the owners of a less amount than above named.

Art. 4. The director once chosen, shall hold his office during the existence of the society, without the power of change, unless in a general assembly called for the purpose, and by a majority of two-thirds.

Art. 5. The commissaries in Paris, shall be renewed seven times in the course of the society, namely, the first time in three years from the 1st of July next, and at intervals of three years after, until the complete revolution of 21 years which the society is to last.

Art. 6. The director shall be charged with the correspondence, and the preservation of the titles, registers, papers, and in general with whatever may enter the archives of the company. He shall convene general assemblies of the shareholders and those of the commissaries, shall provide a convenient place for meeting, and preserve the record of general and special meetings. He shall deliver shares to the bearers of receipts of citizen Lambot. He shall have a consultive voice in the meetings of commissaries, and a casting vote when they are equally divided. He shall hold the funds of the society, and pay and receive money, but he shall make no payment but upon an order signed by two commissaries. He shall keep or cause to be kept for the company, the necessary registers, namely :

1st. A stock-register, for the verification of shares and their coupons.

2d. A record of correspondence.

3d. A record of deliberations.

4th. A register of accounts.

5th. A register which shall show the numbers of *coupons indivis*, and the names of the proprietors who might wish to make this known.

Lastly. He shall, conjointly with the commissaries at Paris, pass to the credit of the shareholders, all titles of property that may fall due, for all of which acts the company confers upon him the necessary powers.

Art. 8. The commissaries at Paris are charged with deliberating and deciding among themselves upon all the affairs and interests of the company, with following and regulating all the operations in which it may be interested ; with carrying into effect the decisions of the general assemblies of the company, and with giving, in the name of the company, to the director and the commissaries in America, the instructions and orders that may be necessary; with directing the employment of the funds of the society, and watching the recovery of sums due to it; with ordering payments; with making purchases to send to America; with passing conjointly with the director all declarations of property to the name of the proprietor of shares or coupons when they fall due; with signing the coupons of shares, to deliver to the shareholders, and with watching the operations of the director and commissaries in America. They shall audit annually the accounts of the director, and lastly, submit to the general assemblies all projects they may deem useful, and for these services the company confers upon them all needed powers.

Art. 9. The commissaries in Paris shall receive no salary, but in recognition of the care which they may bestow upon the common concerns, there shall be given them an attendance fee (*droit de presence*) for each special or general assembly where they may meet on the affairs of the company. This fee is fixed at two Jettons of silver, of the weight of 4 to 5 *gros*. They shall be made at the expense of the company, under the direction of the commissaries, who shall decide upon their form and design.[1]

Art. 10. The commissaries in Paris, shall meet at least once a month; their deliberations shall be held before the director, and shall be determined by a plurality of individual votes.

Art. 11. All decisions thus made, and signed by three commissaries, or by two of them and the director in case he shall have had a deliberative voice, shall have as full and entire force as if they had emanated directly from the majority of the society, and hence the engagements and decisions which result, shall be binding upon the company.

Art. 12. Nevertheless, the commissaries shall neither make nor authorize any loan in the name of the company, without having received a special order at a general assembly of the associates.

Art. 13. The assembly confirms anew the nomination which the shareholders made in their deliberations of the 19th and 20th of the present June, of citizens Guyot, Maillot, Guinot and la Chaume, as commissaries of the company at Paris.

Obverse.

1. These pieces occur in coin cabinets, and have been erroneously called "Castorland half dollars." A *Jetton* is a piece of metal struck with a device, and distributed to be kept in commemoration of some event, or to be used as a counter in games of chance. The one here noticed was termed a *Jetton de presence*, or piece "given in certain societies or companies to each of the members present at a session or meeting." (*Dic de l'Acad. Francaise.*)

This custom has its analogy in the existing practice of certain stock companies in New York, in which a half eagle or a quarter eagle is given to each director present at each meeting held on the business of the company. The piece above figured was doubtless designed to be given to emigrants and others as a keepsake, and was not a *coin*, as it wanted the sanction of law, nor a *token*, as it was not to be redeemed. It was engraved by one of the Duvivier brothers, eminent coin and medal artists of Paris,

who became a shareholder in this company, and drew 500 acres of land. This family was celebrated in this particular art. Joannes Duvivier, the father, died in 1761. The design represents on the obverse the head of *Cybele*, as indicated by the turreted mural crown. In Classic Mythology, this goddess personified the earth as *inhabited and cultivated*, while Titæa or Tellus, represented the earth taken in a general sense, Ceres, the fertility of the soil, and Vesta, the earth as warmed by internal heat. The laurel wreath is an emblem of victory, and represents Cybele as conquering the wildness of nature and bringing the earth under the dominion of man. The design is arranged with classic elegance, but shows a palpable ignorance of the country. Ceres has just tapped a maple tree, and inserted a *faucet* for drawing off the sap at will, and the grain, flowers and foliage appear strangely brought into the sugar season The Latin legend reads on the obverse—"French American Colony," and on the

Reverse.

reverse it presents a quotation from Virgil, which, with its context, reads as follows:

"*Salve magna parens frugum, Saturnia tellus,*
Magna virum: *   *   *   "   GEOR., ii. 173.

"Hail Saturnian Land, great Parent of Fruits, great Parent of Heroes!" The apostrophe thus addressed to Italy, was intended to apply to Castorland, a country situated in nearly the same latitude, and for aught these Parisians knew to the contrary, equally adapted to the vine and the olive.

A *gros* was 59.02 grains, the actual weight of the piece was 206.25 grains, its fineness about nine-tenths, and its intrinsic value 50 cents. Dealers value it at about $3, and Riddel, in his Monograph of the Silver Dollar, states that he knows of but a single copy. Its history was entirely blank until noticed in Hickcox's American Coinage, where a fine steel engraving is given. The figure here inserted, was engraved from a fresh copy, received from Mr. V. Leray, through the favor of P. S. Stewart, Esq., of Carthage.

TITLE VI.—*The Commissaries in America, their Functions and Powers.*

Art. 1. Two commissaries shall regulate the affairs of the company in America; this number shall be increased if there be occasion.

Art. 2. The said commissaries shall necessarily be chosen from among the shareholders: the nomination shall be made in a general assembly of the company, by an absolute majority and viva voce.

Art. 3. The commissaries in America, shall be required within eight days after their election, in case of acceptance on their part, to execute a bond of 40,000 livres, in which shall be included at least ten entire shares of the company of New York, or at most twenty at their original value. These shares shall be deposited with citizen Lambot, notary, who shall give his private receipt. The company leaves it to the commissaries at Paris to judge of the validity of the securities tendered for these bonds.

Art. 4. The mission of the commissaries in America shall be: to verify and mark the exterior boundaries of the whole tract sold to the shareholders by the said Constable; to direct the surveys, divisions and subdivisions of the said lands; to see to the formation of the divided lots mentioned in title IX, that their value may be nearly equal; to put the divided lots herein mentioned, in possession of their proprietors in the manner to be specified, and to give value to that portion of the lands remaining in the society; and for this end,

1st. To cause the erection of all mills, shops, stores and cottages that may be needed.

2d. To cause all cutting and burning of wood, as well as grubbing out and culture.

3d. To purchase all implements, tools, provisions and animals, necessary and of indispensable utility.

4th. To sell at a moderate profit to new colonists, who may settle upon the lands of the society, portions of the tools and provisions which may belong to the society.

5th. To make all treaties, arrangements, estimates and bargains with surveyors, artizans, workmen and day laborers which should be employed for the labor of the lands and woods.

6th. To arrange all rents and sales, in the advantageous manner for the society, but only upon the lands which overrun the 100,000 acres remaining undivided.

7. To fix the conditions and price of leases of farms upon the whole of the undivided lands. These leases shall nevertheless in no cases exceed the time of the duration of the society, and shall be drawn according to the usages of the country, having regard to the progressive increase of the territorial revenue.

8th. To solicit of the government of New York the opening and maintenance, at its expense, of great routes and canals of communication.

9th. To project and cause to be made, special roads from one district or canton to another. Their mission shall also be to receive the price of sales, rents and hirings, and to give receipts, and to make, on account of the company, all shipments to France of the commodities harvested on the lands of the company. In short, they shall carry and administer, with zeal, economy and intelligence, all the interests of the society in America

Art. 5. These commissaries shall be under the surveillance of those at Paris, and shall be held to conform to the mandates and instructions which shall be given them by the commissaries in Paris, for the exercise of the mission confided to them by the preceding article.

Art. 6. The company authorizes the commissaries in Paris, to confer upon those in America the said powers and all others generally, whatever they may deem necessary for managing, usefully, the property and affairs of the company in America.

Art. 7. The said commissaries shall remove directly to New York, and from thence upon the lands of the company, to reside there and execute the operations which the company or the commissaries of Paris may indicate. The expense of their passage to America, and of their removal to the said lands, shall be borne by the company to the extent of 1,000 livres tournois.

Art. 8. The company, besides the advantages hereafter mentioned in title IX, will allow to the commissaries in America, an annual allowance of $600, to indemnify for their expense of travelling to the place, and of building a house and an office.

Art. 9. Independently of this allowance, the company reserves the privilege of granting to the commissaries, if satisfied with their labors, a commission upon the benefits which they may confer upon it.

Art. 10. The commissaries in America, shall keep a journal of all their operations, and shall transmit annually to the director of the company a duplicate copy of this journal. They shall send at least once in three months to the director, the state of the labors done during the three months preceding, and they shall maintain a frequent correspondence with him.

Art. 11. The said commissaries shall employ upon the spot, a clerk to keep their writings, and aid in their operations, who shall be allowed a salary half as great as that of a commissary.

Art. 12. The functions of the commissaries in America, shall continue until their recall and the revocation of their powers by the commissaries in Paris, authorized to that effect in a general assembly by a majority of the associates present.

Art. 13. In case the commissaries in America can not agree in opinion, relative to the objects of their administration, they shall then take upon the spot an arbitrator to decide between them. He shall be chosen by preference among the shareholders who may be found in the country.

Art. 14. The assembly confirms anew the nomination which was made in the session of June 19 the present month — of citizens [Simon] Desjardins and [Peter] Pharoux, as commissaries in America, the first as honorary only, and the second with the emolument heretofore fixed.

TITLE VII.—*Of General and Special Assemblies.*

Art. 1. Annually on the 11th day of January, May and September, or in case of a holiday on the morrow, there shall be held a general assembly of the associated shareholders, at which the commissaries in Paris shall render an account of all that has been done since the last assembly, and the news which shall have been received from the commissaries in America concerning the affairs of the company. General assemblies shall also be convened whenever the commissaries in Paris may deem necessary.

Art. 2. General Assemblies shall be held in Paris at the house of the director of the company, at the day and hour appointed, and shall be presided over by one of the commissaries.

Art. 3. There shall be no business done in a general Assembly, unless the shareholders present are collectively holders of at least 1000 *coupons indivis*, of entire shares, or of 500 only if they are to the number of ten persons, besides the commissaries, and the shares shall be deposited before the assembly in the hands of the director, who is to hold the deposit.

Art. 4. To have admission and a voice in the deliberation of the general assembly, one must be the owner or bearer of five *coupons indivis* of whole shares.

Art. 5. The number of votes in the deliberation shall be in the following proportion to the number of shares : Five shares give one vote, and after that each ten shares shall give one vote up to 45 only, but all shares found in the hands of the same person above 45 shall not be counted, to the end that no shareholder shall ever have more than five votes.

TITLE VIII.—*Of the Survey and Division of the Lands.*

Art. 1. The survey of the exterior of the domain belonging to the shareholders, shall be made at the expense and under the care of Constable, who has stipulated this. This survey shall be verified if there be occasion by the commissaries in America or their agent.

Art. 2. They shall cause an interior survey of the lands after the plan of instructions which may be given them by the commissaries in Paris.

Art. 3. A duplicate of the results of the survey, shall be sent to Paris, to the director of the company.

Art. 4. The general survey of the land being finished, the subdivisions which may be useful and necessary shall be made.

The first shall be the laying out of the public roads ; the second, that of the 100,000 acres to be divided among the bearers of *coupons divis* of whole shares, and their subdivision into 2,000 lots ; the third that of a city in the most convenient part of the land remaining in common, and the arrangement of the divided lots in this city ; the fourth and last, shall be the marking out of lands to be conceded to American families at a moderate price. The subdivisions shall be made in the above order, unless some great interest of the company requires otherwise. The other subdivisions shall be made afterwards, after the order shall have been given by the company or its commissaries in Paris.

TITLE IX.—*Subdivision of the* 100,000 *acres belonging to the bearers of* coupons divis, *into* 2000 *lots, and the arrangements which are designed in the first city projected by the society.*

MANNER OF CHOOSING THE LOTS.

Art. 1. The 100,000 acres designed to be owned separately by the bearers of *coupons divis* of whole shares, shall only be chosen from [the good and medium lands, without including any land of no value, that is to say, which is not susceptible of any cultivation.

Art. 2. The said 100,000 acres shall be divided into several strips, intermixed as much as possible with the lands which are to remain in common.

Art. 3. As soon as the several portions of land which are to form the said 100,000 divided acres be determined, there shall be laid out 2,000 lots of 50 acres each, and of very equal value, and these lots shall be numbered from 1 up to 2,000.

Art. 4. The lots on Black river, lake Ontario or other navigable waters, shall not have more nor a tenth nor less than a twentieth of water front, and there shall be reserved for the undivided portion one-half of the lands upon Black river and lake Ontario.

Art. 5. The bearers of *coupons divis* shall have a right to one-half of the lands which shall be appropriated by the society to a city, deduction being made for the parts occupied by streets and public establishments.

Art. 6. This right shall only be exercised in the location of the first city which shall be marked out by the society, at whatever period this city may be determined upon.

Art. 7. The divided shareholders shall not have the choice of the portion of land which shall be reserved in the location of the said city, but shall be bound to accept whatever portion may be assigned them by the society.

Art. 8. This portion of land shall be divided into 2,000 separate lots, which shall be scattered through the whole extent of the location of the city, and adjoining the property that is to remain with the society.

Art. 9. To facilitate the division of the lots above mentioned in Articles 3 and 8, among those having rights, these lots shall be designated in a statement by boundaries, according to the nature of the ground, and there shall be prepared two maps at the expense of the company. One of the two originals, duly signed and legalized, shall be sent in the month they are finished, to the director of the company, at Paris, to be deposited in its archives, and the duplicate shall remain in the hands of the commissaries of the society in America.

Art. 10. The division of the lots mentioned in Articles 3 and 8, shall be made as follows, according to the prospectus : The choice shall be made in the order of the numbers of the *coupons divis* of the shares, that is to say, that preference of choice shall pertain to priority of numbers.

Art. 11. The choice of divided lots will need to be made within three months after the deposit of the description and plan of division in the archives of the society, and the shareholders shall be advertised to this effect, as well in the public papers as by letters. Each divided shareholder shall be held, within these three months to notify the director of the company of the choice he has made, and note upon the description his signature, the number of his *coupon divis*, and the precise lot which he has chosen, in default of which the choice shall be void.

Art. 12. To facilitate this operation, at the end of the second month, the commissaries shall cause to be prepared a table of the numbers of the *coupons divis*, of which the bearers have not made choice of lots, and in the course of the third and last month they shall indicate the week in which a determinate series of shareholders must make choice, or in default lose the opportunity of selection and be left eventually to the division by lot hereafter mentioned

Art. 13. Those who have not made choice before the end of three months, or who have not given notice in the manner indicated, shall have no further privilege of choice, and the remaining lots shall then be distributed by lot to the numbers of the coupons which have not selected lots.

Art. 14. The drawing of the remaining lots shall be done in a general assembly of the holders of *coupons divis*, convened for this purpose, and in the manner that shall be arranged by the commissaries in Paris.

Art. 15. The bearers of *coupons divis* who share in this drawing shall be bound to accept the lots drawn, without the power of refusal, and shall note their signatures and the number of their *coupons* into several strips, intermixed as much as possible with the lands which are to remain in common.

Art. 16. In derogation of Article 6, and those following as above given, since it is the interest of the society to hasten the population of the tract, to this end it is deemed proper to offer advantages to the shareholders who may remove upon the lands to reside and begin improvement. It is agreed that every bearer or proprietor of *coupons divis*, upon removal to the tract, may choose from time to time as the survey progresses, without waiting its completion and the turn of his number, provided that he shall not have more than ten coupons. The privilege of choosing before his turn shall be restricted to ten lots, and he shall not have more than 2,000 feet of land along the Black river, lake Ontario or other navigable waters.

Art. 17. The choice by virtue of the privilege implied in article 16 above stated, shall be made in the presence of the commissaries in America or their agent, for this purpose, and on condition that the shareholder, before making choice, shall engage in writing to inhabit or cause to be inhabited a house upon the whole of the lots which he may select, and this in the course of the year following his choice, under pain of an indemnity to the company equal to the value of one tenth part of the lot chosen.

Art. 18. The commissaries sent to America, shall have the privilege of choice expressed in the 12th (16th?) article above named, to the same limit of ten lots, but shall cause to be inhabited at least two houses upon the lands they may have chosen, under pain of the indemnity named in the preceding article.

Art. 19. The choice mentioned in the three preceding articles shall not be made, except in accordance with the plan of division of the 2,000 divided lots, and a distinction shall be made of the lots chosen upon the map.

Art. 20. The commissaries in America, shall keep statements of the selections made by virtue of articles 16 and 18 above named, and shall pass a duplicate to France to the director of the company.

Art. 21. Each shareholder who may make choice either in France or America, and comply with the formalities heretofore prescribed, shall remit or cause to be remitted to the commissaries in America or in France, the coupons representative of the lots of which he may make choice, and the said commissaries shall pass a declaration of property of the said lots by virtue of which declaration he shall enjoy, hold and dispose of all the property in the said divided lots.

Art. 22. The same shall be observed by those who have submitted to the drawing by lot, and to them shall be passed by the commissaries the same declaration of property to the lots which may fall to them.

Art. 23. The coupons surrendered shall be canceled and deposited in the archives of the company, and notice of this shall be made in the title above mentioned.

Art. 24. The declarations of property shall be passed in the form required in the state of New York.

TITLE X.—*Of the Application of the* 160,000 *Livres, Derived from the Remission made by Constable to the Shareholders.*

Art. 1. The company entrusts to the commissaries in Paris, the care and disposal of the funds composing the 160,000 livres in shares and credit-paper resulting from the remission granted to the society by Constable, and allows them to sell as many as the wants of the society might require, of the 100 shares forming a part of these funds, at the best price they can obtain, provided it be not less than 1,200 livres per share.

Art. 2. The product of the said shares, with the surplus of the said funds existing in credit-paper, shall be employed by the said commissaries to the best advantage they may be able, as well in the purchase of utensils, provisions and other expenses necessary for the success of the first labors to be done upon the estate of the company in the purchase of convertible values in goods and credit in the funds of the bank of New York, and the wants of the commissaries in America shall measure these expenses necessary to the putting in value and the survey of the lands of the company.

Art. 3. The employment and destination above indicated shall be governed by circumstances, under the care and orders of the commissaries in Paris.

TITLE XI.—*Of the End of the Society, and the Division or Disposition of the Property and Rights which shall then belong to it.*

Art. 1. The duration of the society has been fixed as above stated, at 21 years from July 1, 1793, although it may be dissolved before, in the manner now to be indicated.

Art. 2. Nine months before the end of the seven or fourteen first years of the term fixed for the life of the society, the commissaries in America shall send to the administration in Paris, a report of the property and rights then remaining to the society and the nature of the improvements of which it is yet susceptible, and in short, their estimate from the best of their knowledge, calling to their aid, if necessary, the opinion of experts near them.

Art. 3. In the month following the receipt of the report mentioned in the preceding article, there shall be convoked a general assembly of the associated shareholders, and they shall deliberate upon the dissolution of the society, both at the end of the first seven and of the fourteen years. If the dissolution is not decided by a majority of the holders of two shares, the society shall continue seven years longer, yielding to effect this, the mode of voting established by article 2 of title VII.

Art. 4. Six months before the period when the society shall cease, it shall deliberate in a general assembly, in the manner indicated in Title VII, what measures shall be taken to liquidate and divide the property and rights which shall then be found to compose the substance of the society.

TITLE XII.—*On the Form of the Shares and on the Execution of the Clauses of the Present Treaty.*

Art. 1. It is observed that the present act of the society, as well as the shares and all other instruments of the society in France, need no further care for their execution but the public formality of their legalization, which will be done by the minister or other public functionary of the United States in France, in the terms of article 10 of the second part of the prospectus heretofore published, and the assembly repeats, as far as need be, this arrangement, upon the faith of the execution of which the shareholders acquired their shares and established their society.

Art. 2. All the conditions embraced in the present treaty are essential to the constitution of the society, and no part of them shall be derogated during its existence unless by virtue of a deliberation of the general assembly, and by a majority of two-thirds of the *coupons indivis*, yielding in this to the mode of voting mentioned in title VII.

Art. 3. In consequence of the present act, the prospectus under which the shareholders purchased their shares, shall henceforth be regarded as a simple record, and as such a copy shall be placed in the archives of the company.

Art. 4. The record of general and special deliberations of the company, and its commissaries, shall be signed by at least two of the commissaries in Paris, and by the director of the company in his character as common manager; provided, with these three signatures, the said documents shall have as much force as if all the deliberators had signed them.

Art. 5. Collated copies or transcripts of the said records, and of the titles relative to the said property of the shareholders in America, shall be made out by at least two commissaries in Paris, and by the director as a further guaranty. The seal of the society shall also be affixed.

Art. 6. There shall consequently be engraved a special seal for the Company of New York, and the design of the seal shall be determined by the commissaries in Paris.

Art. 7. All the titles of the property of the company which are not already registered in New York, shall be registered there under the direction of the commissaries in America, and if need be, in the name of Peter Chassanis.

Art. 8. The present treaty shall be signed in quadruple; one shall remain in the archives of the society, another shall be placed in charge of Citizen Lambot, Notary, another shall be given to the commissaries who are to go to America, to be registered and deposited in New York with a public officer, and the last shall remain in the hands of the commissaries in America.

Done and executed at Paris, at the dwelling of Peter Chassanis above said, the year 1793, *the said 28th day of June.* [1]

187

TRANSLATION

OF A

MEMORIAL

OF

RODOLPHE TILLIER's

JUSTIFICATION

OF THE

ADMINISTRATION

OF

CASTORLAND,

County of ONEIDA, State of NEW-YORK.

ROME:

PRINTED BY THOMAS WALKER.

OCTOBER—1800.

MEMORIAL
OF
RODOLPHE TILLIER.

IT is incumbent on a person who has been charged with the interests of a company to justify his conduct in the administration which has been confided to him: And although deprived of his powers by the directors which that company have chosen, he considers it, nevertheless, as an obligation on his part to warn the persons interested, of the danger which threatens them, if they continue to follow the measures which that director has hitherto adopted. Such are the two objects that R. TILLIER proposes in his Memorial.

Those interested in the property of the land called *Castorland*, in *America*, will, without doubt, recollect that on the 28th June, 1793, 41 sharers, holding 1808 shares, all bearers of receipts convertible to shares in the company of *New-York* assembled at *Paris*, and there deliberated upon and settled the constitution of said company.

By the 1st article of the 1st chapter, PIERRE CHASSANIS declares that all the lands and rights by him purchased from Mr. WILLIAM CONSTABLE, by a deed of the 13th April, 1793, were for the profit of the purchasers of 2000 shares of 800 livres each, forming together the total price of the said purchase, and that the payment had been made of the funds arising from the sale of nearly the whole of the said shares.

In consequence the said PIERRE CHASSANIS cedes and conveys, as required, to the said holders of shares, all the rights of property and others, resulting from the said contract, that the whole might belong to them collectively.

The 1st article of the 6th chapter prescribes, that two commissaries shall manage the lands and concerns of the company in *America*—and the 12th article of the 6th chapter decides that the functions of the commissaries in *America* shall be in force until repealed; and their powers are revoked by the commissaries of *Paris*, authorised for that purpose in a general assembly, by the majority of the company present at the assembly.

After this constitution of the company, R. TILLIER was named, in 1796, to manage the lands designated under the denomination of *Castorland*, he succeeded in quality of agent to Mr. PHAROUX, who had perished in traversing the Black River; his powers were given him according to the constitutional rules of the company of *New-York*; his instructions shew (art. 3d) that he should regulate himself upon the constitutional act, upon the deliberation which named him upon the resolutions of the commissaries and directors at *Paris*, and co. His conduct has been guided by the spirit of the constitution of the company and his particular instructions.

R. TILLIER immediately after his arrival in the *United States* set about procuring for his constituents, sufficient title deeds for the property; the negligence of his predecessors having subjected the interests of the company, in delaying the most necessary precautions. Annexed is the copy of a Memorial made and written by the hand of M. DESJARDINS, in 1795, which proves the uncertainty of the titles. Had any accident happened in the intermediate time to Mr. or Mrs. CONSTABLE, it would have thrown the company into a labyrinth of difficulties, whereby they would have been infallibly the sufferers. As soon as he had caused his powers to be registered, he chose for his counsel, General HAMILTON, a lawyer distinguished by his genius and virtues.—In the examination which he made of the papers and first deed given by CONSTABLE to CHASSANIS, he discovered some errors in the limits, which rendered that deed invalid—besides some legal form, which were wanting. R. TILLIER dispatched the finishing of a new survey, for the purpose of rectifying in another the irregularities of the former one :—He exerted all his zeal to follow the advice of Gen. HAM-ILTON, and finally the company obtained a regular title, an exact survey, and soon after a typographical map of all the lands of the company.—R. TILLIER afterwards directed all his attention to the buildings, only rough hewed, upon the lands of *Castorland*, not finding any of those which had been announced to him—no ground being cleared, no cultivator established in the ideal town of *Castor*, no practicable road, no established communications, only one or two barracks honored with the name of houses, a yard sowed rather than a garden, in a word, nothing which evinced the former settlement of the pretended establishments, still less the expences which had been made thereon. What afflicted him most at first was the repugnance strongly impressed on the *Americans* of the neighboring places to establish themselves upon the lands of the company where they perceived nothing enticing.

R. TILLIER struggled sometime against those obstacles, but by conciliatory conduct and fair dealing (his situation not permitting him any liberality in such cases so necessary) he was able to procure some workmen, who all seemed desirous to purchase some lands, which he sold them in small portions, in hopes of very soon selling a greater quantity, and to unite a certain number of cultivators, which would have given a permanent footing to the new colony. This was the object of his ambition : He felt the consequence of a progressive increase to the holders of shares in the company of *New-York*.— R. TILLIER was unanimously elected and named a Justice of Peace for the county of *Oneida*, which marked confidence and esteem from the inhabitants, fortified his hopes of reaping the fruits of all his cares and jus-

tifying the truſt which the company had given him;
he rendered an exact ſtatement of all that related to his
management; his correſpondence, journal and accounts
prove his conſtant attention to conform himſelf to the
act of the conſtitution. Theſe different papers ſhew
his exertions, and how he was employed, and the manner in which the ſums have been expended under his
adminiſtration ; and it cannot be doubted that the company were ſenſible of his zeal and care, as he then received, as well as at different other times, acknowledge-
ments of their ſatisfaction.

The affairs were in this condition when the company ſent new French ſettlers to eſtabliſh themſelves upon the lands of *Caſtorland.* Their preſence only occa-
ſioned conſiderable expences, without being of any u-
tility, and they occeſioned a great expence upon the
land—conſuming the proviſions—introducing the ſpi-
rit of diſcord and diſcontent, and finally they went a-
way, threatning to make known their complaints in
France, and to impeach thoſe who had deceived them
at *Paris,* by ſending them into a' deſert. Much mild-
neſs and moderation were neceſſary to diſperſe them ;
but on going from *Caſtorland,* they made bitter complaints againſt the place and perſons, by which means
they left traces very diſadvantageous to *Caſtorland,* and
thoſe intereſted in the ſaid company. That theſe cir-
cumſtances, which took place at a time when war appeared inevitable between *France* and the *United States,*
and the greateſt prejudices exiſting againſt the French,
have alſo tended to deſtroy thoſe riſing ſettlements, and
to injure the concerns of the company very much.

At the ſame time Mr. BLAKE arrived calling himſelf the ſon-in-law of Mr. LAMBOT, one of the company, and particularly charged with his intereſts ' Coming into the *United States* without any reſource, R.
TILLIER received him with kindneſs, and in ſuch an
hoſpitable manner that any other perſon would have

thought he merited some acknowledgement. Mr. BLAKE on the contrary became his calumniator, as well in the *United States* as in *Europe*; but it appears the company were not deceived by his calumnies;—they did justice to TILLIER, and they wrote to him through their director CHASSANIS, that they were satisfied with his services.——In the mean time one PIERRE JOULAIN also arrived at *New-York*, appeared to be secretly charged with the interests of the company; it is at least presumable and what we are authorised to believe from the mystery which has enveloped his conduct. This man did all he could to conceal it without shewing his powers.—He insinuated to TILLIER, that he desired to see his accounts, who answered him with the frankness that characterises him, that he had sent to *Paris* a faithful copy of all his accounts—that those of the current expences were at *Castorland*, kept by a secretary who made his residence there, according to the intention expressed in the act of the constitution—that he was besides ready to render them all, having no reason to delay a settlement.

R. TILLIER foresaw that Mr. JOULAIN did not treat with him with the same good faith and candour that he used towards the said JOULAIN. He obtained information, indirectly, that he was bound by close and secret ties with M. BLAKE, and he was convinced of it by some letters which were sent him from *Castorland*.—Finally, he no longer doubted their employing deceit, to divest him of his administration, in the capacity of agent to the company, without his, however, receiving any direct or indirect advice, either from that company or M. CHASSANIS, his agent or director at *Paris*.

The indignation of an honest man in such a case must be great, and TILLIER cannot refrain from expressing his feelings. It is without doubt right to dispossess an agent when he is not faithful; but before such a step is taken some proofs should be obtained of

his bad conduct, and they ought to take suitable meafures that he is reimburfed all the expences he has been
at for the concern, and that he fhould be difcharged
from all the engagements which he has made, by virtue of his powers, towards the different perfons employed for fupplies, wages and work. To act as they
have done towards an honeft citizen, who is invefted
with a public function, who has held in his country a
place at the council of Berne, is being deficient of all
refpect and good manners.—But, finally, if they admit
that he is irreproachable in his conduct—that he has
managed the affairs of the company ably and with hon-
or, and that there is nothing but calumny againft him,
they then muft admit that he has been treated with
great injuftice without reafon. Their conduct, never-
thelefs, muft appear very contemptible to a reflecting
and difcerning nation; whofe confidence it was the in-
tereft of the company to have cultivated.

Finally, the plot, of which thefe gentlemen were
the agents, is unveiled. GOUVERNEUR MORRIS, late
ambaffador of the *United States* in *France*, has appeared
to be the only bearer of the powers for the company of
New-York, or rather of P, CHASSANIS. He has filed,
in the name of Chaffanis, a bill againft TILLIER, in
the Court of Chancery of this State, and claims as his
property the 220,500 acres of land, when by the con-
ftituion of the company, he has conveyed them in the
moft formal manner, to the holders of fhares.—He
moreover pretends to annul all the choice made of the
divided lots—all the fales to divers fettlers, by R, TIL-
LIER, who has acted only in conformity to, and in
virtue of fufficient powers, and agreeably to the in-
ftructions given him; and this fuit having been very
generally promulgated it has refulted therfrom, that in
the public opinion there are doubts, as well of the validity of the original title, as the partial fales of the powers and rights of CHASSANIS and of the old and new

agents. These scandalous reports have given rise to every kind of mistrust and suspicion on the minds of the Americans—disgusted the new settlers, and occasioned the lands of the company to be absolutely deserted.—Thus the imprudence of the director CHASSANIS, has produced the unfortunate effect of ruining the holders of shares; who are the true proprietors, of depreciating the land and the titles, has caused the new settlements to be abandoned, which will of course go to ruin, and all the expences to this time will be useless and lost. It is difficult to conceive how the company of New-York has been induced to adopt such a conduct, so contrary to its interests.—If from all these measures, there was only one that had any appearance of utility, it might, perhaps, be some palliation for the others ;— but they are all equally contrary and destructive to the prosperity and success of the undertaking.

The object of R. TILLIER in addressing the present observations to the holders of shares is, 1st—To justify himself in their opinions and prove that his administration has been faithful and free from reproach. 2d— To exhibit to the holders of the shares, the folly and injustice of all the operations of the company, or of the director CHASSANIS, and to call their attention to the dangers which threaten them ; if, after having done what he thinks his duty concerning it, the holders of shares remain indolent and careless of their interests; they are perfectly their own masters, but, at least they will recollect, when their eyes are opened, the advice which R. TILLIER gave them, and they can then only blame themselves for the losses they may experience.

The best method, and it may be said the only one, to be convinced whether TILLIER's administration has been good and able, is to examine what he has done and the means he had for doing it. When he came to take possession of the lands of Castorland every thing was to be done—the land itself was not ascertained—

B

there was a deficiency in the title to assure the property. When one considers a man in such a situation, in a strange country, at a great distance from any inhabited place, with very small funds to put in order an immense tract of land, the difficulty of success must be evident : But it is very hard to give an adequate idea to a person who has not been a witness to the difficulties of a similar undertaking, of the magnitude and full force of the obstacles to be surmounted, and which R: TILLIER had to encounter with. If the holders of shares will carefully examine, his correspondence, his journal and accounts, they will therein see the use he has made of his time and of his means. If the interest of CHASSANIS has induced him to conceal that knowledge from the holders of shares; it is the interest of TILLIER that those papers should be made public, as they afford unequivocal proofs of his zeal; trouble and attention ; they will there see the pains he took to ascertain the lands, his steps to procure a valid title, his activity in causing an exact survey to be made; and to obtain a typographical map:—They will there see what he has done, what he has attempted; the lands which he has settled, the roads which he has opened; the journeys he has made; the arrangements which he has entered into with different families to establish them upon the lands, and by these means to give them a value :—They will finally see the prospect of success which he might naturally flatter himself with, and which would undoubtedly in time have succeeded, if he had not been obstructed in his proceedings by the wrong measures of the director:

Let them once again ascertain the truth of these facts, and have recourse to the testimony of the neighbors, consider the times and means, examine with attention his correspondence and journal, which shew what he has done, and they will be convinced that his administration has been able, good and regular.

He does not pretend to say that no other person could have acted as well ; perhaps even his administration may not be totally free from faults, for mistakes are almost inevitable in every undertaking which requires so many details, in which the objects are not specifically traced nor the plans fixed, but where, on the contrary, he had in fact, to determine on the first principles of this extensive concern, he can with the utmost truth declare, that no person could have exerted himself with more pains and application than he did ; and he thinks that it would not have been found that he was deficient in the necessary experience and knowledge, to insure the success of the undertaking, if he had been permitted to wait the event of his designs.

His plans were well formed and conceived, and he wanted nothing to accomplish them but to be aided by the necessary funds, which always came to hand too late, and, indeed, were never sufficient at any time.— He was also injured in his plans by the measures of the director of the company at *Paris*, who, far from executing what was necessary for such an establishment, took such steps as were adverse to its success, and who has uniformly, by his actions, opposed the views and measures of the agent at *New-York*.

The main object of the undertaking, was to give a value to the lands of *Casterland*, for which purpose they should have cultivated the confidence of the natives of the country ; in order to entice them to settle upon the places they should have seen on the part of the company, a regular and uniform plan to improve the lands, and to secure and benefit the property of those who were inclined to become purchasers ; but instead of that, How have the company of *New-York* acted ?

Mr. PHAROUX, the first agent sent, was a well informed and honest man, and he gained the esteem of the Americans ; but he was ignorant of their language, and therefore, he could with difficulty, treat with them.

197

—He loſt his life by an exceſs of zeal and temer-
itity.

Mr. DESJARDINS ſucceeded him, but he was alſo
ignorant of the Engliſh Language, which being joined
with a haughty character, drove the inhabitants from
him; although he expended much of the company's
money, he did nothing uſeful for it.

He was replaced by RODOLHE TILLIER, who
thinks he underſtood well the object of the undertaking,
and that he made every effort to accompliſh it; his being choſen a juſtice of peace is a ſufficient proof that
he had gained the confidence of the inhabitants

Sometime after, ſeveral Frenchmen came to ſettle
upon the lands, in purſuance to an arrangement made
with the company at *Paris.* They had ſcarcely arrived,
when diſguſt, miſunderſtanding and hatred took place,
tranquility was deſtroyed & they left the land, abuſing it.

Soon after Mr. BLAKE, a new envoy appeared, whoſe
powers are myſteriouſly concealed, except when he can
promote diſcord and utter calumnies.

After him PIERRE JOULIN, an ancient Prieſt came,
who imitated the example of his predeceſſor and load-
ed TILLIER with injuries and defamation.

At length Mr. GOUVERNEUR MORRIS, the late
American ambaſſador to France, arrived, who, charged
with the powers of PIERRE CHASSANIS, revokes
TILLIER, the only agent who had diſplayed activity,
and the only one whoſe zeal and experience had ex-
tricated the eſtabliſhment from confuſion and diſorder.
And to aggravate all thoſe changes and imprudences, a
ſuit is commenced againſt Tillier, who offered, and ſtill
offers to render his accounts, and ſubmit them to arbitra-
tors; much noiſe and clamor is raiſed, and it is rendered more ſcandalous, as it appears to be deſigned to annul
the titles given by TILLIER, to the purchaſers of lands,
altho' he granted them in virtue of acknowledged and
approved powers; they would thus deſtroy thoſe acts

which are legal, and difpoffefs and ruin the proprietors
—This true ftatement, which faithfully points out the
actual ftate of things, is fufficient to excite and account
for the aftonifhment with which the Americans view
the capricious, irrefolute and ridiculous adminiftration
of the company at *New-York*, which is increafed when
they compare it to the wife, enlightened and uniform
adminiftration of the Dutch company in the vicinity
of *Caftorland*, and to the large concern under Captain
WILLIAMSON's charge, not far from thence, of which
laft an able writer (Mr. LAROCHEFOUCAULT DELL-
ANCOURT) gives fo flattering an account in his travels
through America.

Let the holders of fhares cooly reflect on the confe-
quences refulting from this multitude of imprudent actions, and they will form fome conceptions of the great
injury which they have fuftained in the minds of the
inhabitants of America, by fuch an inconceivable feries
of imprudent, falfe, impolitic and inconfiftent meafures.

Let them then change their plans, let them adopt u-
niform one and purfue them, let them truft their interefts to honeft and well informed men, attached by ties
of confidence and efteem, let them give to their agent in
America very extenfive powers ; it is in vain to imagine a great defign and a large eftablifhment, can be
governed at a diftance without it. The perfon actually on the fpot can only attain juft ideas on the fubject.
—In the execution, his experience will enable him to
rectify, immediately, any miftake that may happen.—
Let them renounce the idea of felling lands in *France*,
becaufe the execution of fuch contracts are always attended with fome difficulties, as to the places and portions of land to be given, which inconvenience cannot
take place when the purchafer fees before he purchafes
the propofed object.—Let them renounce the idea of
felling their lands half divided and half undivided,
becaufe a confufion refults from it, which deranges all

the operations of the purchasers, and that plan, so fine in speculation, is in fact, very bad in the execution.—Let them always provide funds before hand, that the managing commiffary may be able, without delay, to accomplish his plans, and that he may with confidence undertake them under the certainty of having it in his power to difcharge in time, the engagements which he may enter into.—Let them abstain from making any a-greement in *France*, and from engaging people either from *France* or *Switzerland*, as they have done, for the lands of *Castorland* can never be cultivated but by the natives of the country. Thefe even will not fettle on the lands, without they have an eafy accefs to an agree-able abode, and until they are convinced of the authen-ticity of the titles to fecure their poffeffions.

In adopting fuch maxims, the holders of fhares may reafonably hope to reap a profit, and that time will give value and credit to the lands of *Castorland*, and that they may fee the fettlement flourifh and increafe to that degree to which the pofition of the lands juftly entitles them to expect. Without fuch meafures it may be that the defign of the holders of lands will totally fail, and ruin be inevitable.

They alfo run another danger, which R. TILLIER thinks he ought to warn them of, they are expofed to lofe their property, perhaps it is already out of their hands. P. CHASSANIS has given his new powers, not as director and agent of the company, but in his own name.—Mr. GOUVERNEUR MORRIS, who is the bearer of it, has inftituted the fuit againft TILLIER, for the purpofe of proving PIERRE CHASSANIS to be acknowledged as individual proprietor of the 220,500 acres of land, whilft by the conftitution of the compa-ny he has transferred them in the moft formal manner to the bearers of fhares. Does not this manner of act-ing announce on the part of PIERRE CHASSANIS, a defire to difpofe of that property as belonging to himfelf, to the prejudice of the holders of shares ? They will be ready to believe it, when they learn that CHAS-SANIS has already difposed of 130,000 acres of thofe fame lands, in favor of J. LE RAY, either on a deed of fale, bond or mortgage. Thofe acts have by chance paffed under the eyes of R. TILLIER, to whom they certainly had not an intention of fhewing them.

One of thofe contracts of alienation, is

for - - - -	90,000 *acres.*
The fecond of - - -	22,000
The third of - - -	18,000

Which makes, - 130,000 *acres.*

Let them add to that 80,000 acres which have been mortgaged to *Carrare* and Co. of *Laufane*, for what they have lent to the company - - 80,000

It appears then that at this moment there are 210,000 acres fold or engaged 210,000 *acres.*

Here are pofitive facts, which perhaps may give them reafon to believe that it is at length time to look into, and take their concerns into their own hands, and watch to their own interefts, and let them get poffeffion again of their property, if it is not yet too late to do it—For it is clear, that if P. CHASSANIS appears to be the only proprietor of all the lands of *Caftorland*, he will have the right of felling them, and that if thofe fales are once completed in a legal manner, it will be in vain for the holders of the fhares to reclaim any portion whatfoever. This danger has appeared to R. TILLIER, to be of too high importance to the holders of fhares to leave them ignorant of it.

TILLIER ftill owes them the information of a fact, which, in the midft of many others, will give them an idea of the character of P. CHASSANIS and LE RAY DE CHAUMONT, whofe interefts appear to be joined and confounded together. Some time before the arrival

of P. JOULAIN, CHASSANIS sent a bill of exchange to
TILLIER for 3772 dollars, to provide for the expense
of the company. It was drawn by CHAUMONT, on that
same Mr. JOULAIN. Immediately after his arrival,
TILLIER took the first opportunity to present it to him
for acceptance; but he did nothing therein—CHAU-
MONT having precisely ordered him not to pay it.—
What can be said or tho't of such an action; one may
judge of CHASSANIS' administration from this conduct.
R. TILLIER will not extend his reflections further;
his object is not at present to throw the blame on any
particular person; he therefore confines himself to a
statement of facts, and bringing them to the view of
the holders of the lands in order to let them ascertain
them, and that they may thereby convince themselves,
whether their director of *Paris;* is worthy or not of their
confidence—whether his connections in the affairs and
interests with CHAUMONT, are not injurious to the interests of the company. TILLIER's object is fulfilled,
if he has been enabled to persuade them that his administration has been pure, and free from reproach—if he
has convinced them of the causes to which the want of
success in the undertaking ought to be attributed, and
if he has pointed out to them the means of accomplish-
ing their purposes better in future. He does not seek
to maintain himself in their confidence—he is satisfied
in knowing he has always been worthy of it. He wish-
es to render his accounts; and to discharge himself from
a trust which he has executed with fidelity and honor;
but before he does this, it is just that he should be re-
imbursed for his advances, and guaranteed from all the
engagements which he has entered into in the name of
the company. He should not have been forced to sustain a law-suit; if the new agent would have agreed to
this fair proposition, which indeed is only an act of justice, and of universal usage in similar cases.

ROME, *Oct.* 30, 1800.   R. TILLIER.

Clement Biddle & Co.
and
Rodolphe Tillier.

At their Stores in Water-Street, between Arch and Race Streets, are now opening a very large and general Assortment of European and East-India Goods, suitable for the season, which they will sell by the Package.

A Cargo of wines and brandy just landed from on board the brigantine St. Raphael, from Barcelona; London particular Madeira wine by the Pipe, claret and port in hogsheads, bottled Rhenish and Malaga wines, a large quantity of cordage and Sail duck, &c. for cash. Tobacco. The Hon. Mr. Morris's notes, a short credit.

Nov. 18. 1783.

Penn a Packet
14 Nov. 1783
3: 3:

[AUTHOR'S NOTE: The above is scrawled upon the cover of one of the copies of Tillier's *Memorial* at the New York State Library. It is the only indication available that Tillier had business experience in America prior to his Castorland appointment in 1796.]

APPENDIX V

CHASSANIS' REPLY TO TILLIER

[Reprinted from Hough's *History of Lewis County* (1860 ed.)]

To this memorial Chassanis published the following reply:

" Without doubt one who has been charged with the interests of a company, owes it to himself to justify his conduct; for the same reason the Company of New York two years ago, in vain recalled Mr. Tillier. But instead of justifying his conduct, this agent feared to expose himself to the light, he opposed difficulties, and the course he has taken will only postpone the shame of his condemnation. Tillier would wish, in throwing suspicion upon the direction of citizen Chassanis, to gain the interest of the shareholders, and thus cover his own disorders by a hypocritical zeal; but every shareholder knows, that their director has never written or done anything but in accordance with the deliberations of the company. It would be important could Tillier prove the contrary; but citizen Chassanis defies him to produce a single fact to impair this assertion.

" The company finding but very little result coming from so great expenses, and failing to obtain from Tillier any thing but vague information, took a decisive part against this agent himself. It was impossible for the commissaries and director in Paris to learn exactly the state of things in America, to remedy seasonably and effectually the abuses which were introduced, and this led the company to a precautionary measure upon which depended the fate of Castorland. It authorized its director at its session of May 1, 1798, to confer upon Mr. G. Morris, minister plenipotentiary of the United States to the French government, the 'powers necessary to investigate, reform and settle the accounts of Tillier, acting commissary of the company in America; to take cognizance of the details of the administration of Castorland, its actual condition, the ability and conduct of its chief and subordinate agents employed in its service, to suspend or discharge those who might have compromised the interests of the company, or shown themselves incapable of filling the places they occupied; and lastly, power in advance, of removing Tillier in case his functions ought to cease.' This appointment was demanded by circumstances, and although of the highest importance, Tillier terms it *the*

I

recklessness of director Chassanis, and that *by the scandalous scenes which it occasioned, it had ruined the shareholders.* But if it had produced these scandalous scenes, were they not caused by Tillier, who, under the false pretext of serving the shareholders, had rejected the deliberations of the company, and ignored the signature of Pierre Chassanis until now recognized?

"In Tillier's memorial, there is a grave accusation against citizen Chassanis, which appears specious, and must be refuted; for all the rest are only the declamation of a justly suspected servant, who defends himself with words, but has nothing to show in his favor. He distinctly charges Chassanis with having sold or bargained 210,000 acres of land without the consent of the shareholders. The fact, says he, is positive; and he invites them (page 17) *to take their concerns into their own hands and watch to their own interests, and let them get possession again of their property if it is not already too late to do it.* How can Tillier know this fact without knowing the cause? and knowing the cause, how can he dare to utter a calumny so easily refuted? Can he flatter himself that by misconstruing a fact consigned to the record he can prove his end without challenge? However it may be, the abuse of trust with which Tillier reproaches citizen Chassanis, is only an imaginary phantom to tarnish his reputation, and the apprehensions with which he would inspire the shareholders, have not the slightest foundation. They can regain their property, or rather they have never been deprived of it, for in this operation it has been as in all others. It was at a general assembly held May 14, 1798, that the conveyance of 90,000 acres to Le Ray was decreed. The first article of that deliberation read as follows:

" 'Art. 1. The commissaries at Paris and the director, are authorized to transfer to the name of Mr. Le Ray, citizen of the United States of America, all their real and personal estate of the company in the state of New York, in the name of citizen Chassanis its director.'

" This conveyance did not dispossess the company of its property, but it was a measure required by the circumstances, which had 'no other end than to consolidate the rights of the shareholders and their creditors, as evidently appears in the next article.

" 'Art. 2. The assembly charges the commissaries and the director, to take all proper measures to the end that in this conveyance the rights of the company be preserved, and that they may be maintained in the enjoyment and improvement of their actual possessions, according to the mode established by the act of the society of June 28, 1793.'

"As to the 40,000 acres for which the director has given bonds and mortgages, and which completes the 130,000 acres that Tillier pretends to have been alienated, it was not a sale, but simply a security to a loan ordered by the general assembly of March 16, 1798, and which the director was authorized to execute.

" Nor was this all. Tillier thought he still owed the shareholders information of a fact *which will give them an idea of the character of citizen Chassanis.* It is stated in the memorial, that the director sent a bill of exchange to Tillier to serve the wants of the company, and that Mr. Le Ray the drawer of the letter, caused its payment so be suspended. Upon this Tillier exclaims: *What can be said or thought of such an action? One may judge of Chassanis' administration from his conduct!*

" But whom does this transaction compromise? We can see only its very obvious bearing, and it was exceedingly bad taste in Tillier to allude to it. It is natural when an agent is charged with having abused the confidence of a company, that he should remove the pretext of further censure, and to this the director will limit himself. Tillier had provoked this by his conduct, and it saved the company $3,772. It is certain that citizen Chassanis ought to appear blame-worthy in the eyes of Tillier, for being knowing to Le Ray's opposition to the payment of the draft. It is a very bad turn that both have shown him, and and he can scarcely pardon them. Thus we may regard the refusal of payment as one of the sources of trouble which excited Tillier to the calumnies which defile his memorial. Had it not been for this fatal counter-order which deprived Tillier, for the moment, of his salary, it is to be presumed that the director would have appeared as showing better management, and above all, greater justice.

" If Mr. Tillier wished to prove that his administration, as he says, has been pure, and that it was free from reproach, he has failed to show the result. It is from the fruit that we judge the tree. We will render him justice, if, by the establishments formed and his model accounts, he can show a good employment of his time and of the funds which he has received. His obstinate refusal upon these points, forces upon us the suspicion that he can not report an honest administration. It is not by telling us that his affairs have been well administered that he can persuade us of the fact; it is not by addressing a memorial full of absurd and calumnious accusations, founded rather upon ignorance of facts rather than upon facts themselves, that Mr. Tillier can conciliate our esteem. The only means of justifying his administration is to render his accounts in a proper manner, with vouchers of their correctness."

APPENDIX VI
LETTER DESCRIBING CASTORLAND IN 1800

"This northern part of the state of New York, which contains the three great districts, known as Richland, Katarkouy, and Castorland, is bounded on the north by the River St. Lawrence, on the west by the Ontario, on the east by the counties of Washington and Clinton, and Lake Champlain, and on the south by the new cantons of Oswego, Onondaga, and Herkimer, is traversed nearly its entire length by Black River, which has 45 to 50 miles of navigation to its falls, situated a short distance from its mouth, in the bay of Niahouré, on Lake Ontario. This river receives in its course many considerable streams and creeks, abounding in hydraulic privileges. This region is very favorably situated for access. On the one side it communicates with Canada by the St. Lawrence, with the English establishment upon the right bank of the river, as well as those from Kingston, in the bay of Katarokouy, on the other with Lake Ontario, by the bays of Niahouré, and Cat Fish. and lastly with the Mohawk Country, by a route just opened by Richland, Rome, and Castorville. They have surveyed another from the chief place, (Castorville?) the first navigable waters of the Oswègatchée, at the confluence of which with the St. Lawrence, Major Ford has founded a considerable establishment, Long Lake, the waters of which are nearly parallel with the Great River, offers another route to those who wish to go to Ford'sbourg and Lower Canada. With the exception of the mountains, the soil is deep and fertile, as may be judged by the height and variety of the trees that compose the forest. The country, which borders the river from our Katarakouy to the line which separates us from Canada, (the 45th parallel) abounds in oak, a timber the more precious, as it is rare and valuable at Montreal and Quebec. In other sections we see a mixture of elms, button wood, sugar maple, butternut, hickory, beech, water ash, and basswood. We also find hemlock, white pine, and different kinds of spruce, wild cherry, and red¹,and white cedar. From the boughs of the spruce is made that beer so praised by Capt. Cook, and known to be the best of anti scorbutics. The sugar maple is so common in some sections as to form a third of the trees. Not only do we derive from thence all the sugar we need, but vinegar also of an excellent quality. As is the case in all northern countries this is filled with woody marshes and natural meadows, in which pasturage is had in summer, and forage for winter. We find in many places limestone, clay, and ore of iron, very ductile, but we are still too young to think of building a furnace or large forges. It will not be so in ten years; it is probable we shall then be in a condition to furnish to the inhabitants of Upper Canada, who, not having contracts to assure them the possession of their lands, can not think of engaging in such enterprises. We already begin to cultivate corn, wheat flax, and even hemp, since it had been observed to what height it grows on land, formerly flowed by beaver dams; but it being only the fourth year of our settlement, the details of our progress can not be very interesting.

An event, as unfortunate as unexpected, has much hindered the prosperity of this colony. The death of a young man of much talent, whom the Castorland Company had sent from Paris, to render a wild and hitherto unknown country fit to favor the reunion of a new born society, to divide the lands, open roads, begin the first labors, built bridges and mills, and invent machines, where man is so rare. A victim of his zeal, in taking the level of a bend of the river, he perished in trying to cross above the great falls. His comrades, so unfortunate as not to be able to assist him, have collected the details of this disastrous event in a paper, which I have been unable to read without emotions, and which I send.

Our rivers abound in fish, and our brooks in trout. I have seen two men take 72 in a day. Of all the colonies of beavers, which inhabited this country and raised so many dams, only a few scattering families remain. We have destroyed these communities, images of happiness, in whose midst reigned the most perfect order, peace, and wisdom, foresight and industry. Wolves, more cunning and warlike than the former, live at our expense and as yet escape our deadly lead. It is the same with the original elk. It is only seen in this part of the state, for our hunters will soon make it disappear, for, you know, that, wherever man establishes himself, this tyrant must reign alone. Among the birds we have the pheasant, drumming partridge, wild pigeon, different kinds of ducks, geese, and wild turkey, &c. Our chief place, situated on the banks of the pretty Beaver River, and from thence so appropriately named *Castorville,* begins to grow. It is still only, as you may justly think, but a cluster of primitive dwellings, but still it contains several families of mechanics, of which new colonies have so frequent need. Several stores, situated in favorable places, begin to have business. The Canadians, on the right bank of the river, come thither to buy the goods which they need, as well as sugar and rum, which, from the duties being less at our ports than at Quebec, are cheaper with us than with them. The vicinity of these French settlements are very useful to us, in many respects. Cattle are cheaper than with us, as well as manual labor. Such are the causes of communication between the inhabitants of the two sides, that it is impossible for the English government to prevent it.

Our colonists are, like others, a mixture of many nations; we have some families of Scotch and Irish, but the greater number come from the northern states, which, as you know, is the *"officina humani generis"* of this continent. Many of the settlers have already made considerable improvements. One of these families from Philadelphia, besides a hundred acres well enclosed, has begun a manufacture of potash, where the ashes of the neighborhood are leached; another of the Quaker sect has settled on the route to Kingston, where he has already built a saw mill, and a considerable manufactory of maple sugar, where he made last year about 16 quintals. The head of this family is a model of intelligence and industry; the goods which he brought, easily procured him much labor at a good rate. He paid twelve dollars per acre for clearing his lands and half the ashes;* besides this he furnished to the potash makers the great iron chaldrons and hand labor, and retains half of the salts, the value of which, with the first crop of wheat, pays and more all the expenses of clearing, fencing, and harvesting. The average yield per acre, being 24 to 28 bushels, and the price of wheat 6 to 8 shillings, it is easy to see that there is still a margin to cover accidents, and that the second crop is clear profit. Among these families we have some, who, driven from their country, by fear and tyranny, have sought in this an asylum of peace and liberty, rather than wealth, and at least of security and of sweet repose. One of these, established on the banks of Rose Creek, came from St. Domingo, where he owned a considerable plantation, and has evinced a degree of perseverance, worthy of admiration. One of the proprietors† has a daughter, as interesting by her figure as by her industry, who adds at the same time to the economy of the household, the charms or rather the happiness of their life. Another yet is an officer, of cultivated mind, sprightly, and origin; who, born in the burning climate of India, here his health is strengthened. He superintends the

* An acre commonly yields 200 bushels of ashes, which are worth 8 cents the bushel.
† St. Mitchel· His daughter married Marselle, and afterwards De Zotelle.

clearing of a tract of 1200 acres, which two sisters, French ladies, have entrusted to him, and to which he has given the name of *Sister's Grove.* He has already cleared more than 100 acres, erected a durable house, and enclosed a garden, in which he labors with assiduity, truly edifying. He has two Canadians, of whom their ancestors were originally from the same province with himself. Far from his country, the most trifling events become at times a cause of fellow feeling, of which those who have never felt it, can have no idea. As for cattle, those raised that only bring $9 a pair, at the end of the year, are worth $70 when they are four years old. Fat cattle, which commonly weigh 7 to 900 lbs., sell at the rate of $5 per hundred. Swine living almost always in the woods, the settler can have as many as he can fatten in the fall. It should not be omitted to give them from time to time an ear of corn each, to attach them to the clearing, and prevent them from becoming wild, for then there is no mastering their wills, for they pining for their wandering life will not fatten on whatever is given them. Butter is as dear with us as in old settled countries, and sells for a shilling a pound. We have no fear, as some think, that the vicinity of the Canadian establishments will withdraw our settlers. The lands in Canada are all in the hands of Government of the Seigneurs. Both give gratuitously, I admit, but they give no titles,* from whence numerous difficulties arise in selling and transferring. Besides they are burdened with a considerable quit rent, the fees of transfer and removal, of escheats to the domain in default of heirs, of *banalité*,† tithes, or reservations for religion, and reserves of mines, and oak timber, restrictions, unknown in the United States, where the lands are franchises and freeholds. It is therefore probable, that sensible settlers will always prefer to so precarious an advantage, a sure possession which can be transferred without fees or formalities.

This country being bounded by the St Lawrence and the Ontario, its population will increase more rapidly than that where men can spread themselves ad infinitum, as in certain districts of Pennsylvania, upon the Ohio, Wabash, &c. What is here called the American Katarokouy, or I, II, III and IV of Macomb's great purchase, will always be the last stage, the *Ultima Thule*, of this part of the state of New York, and we ourselves, the last but one round of the ladder. On this account, lands, which in 1792 were valued at from $2 to $3 per acre, have now become from $3 to $4.

The banks of our great river are not the only ones where our population tends. Already those of Swan's Creek begin to fill up. Were it not for the death of Mr. P. we should have been much more advanced, for it was necessary to await the arrival of another engineer to complete the great surveys and subdivisions. Our winters are cold, but less than those of New Hampshire, and the snows of this climate are beneficial in preventing the frost from injuring our grass and wheat. It is truly wonderful to see with what rapidity vegetation is developed a few days after the snows are melted. I have placed your habitation not far from the great falls, but far enough distant not to be incommoded by the noise, or rather uproar, which they make in falling three different stages. The picturesque view of the chain of rocks over which the waters plunge their tumultuous commotion, the natural meadows in the vicinity, the noble forests which bound the horizon; the establishments on the opposite bank; the passage of travellers who arrive at the ferry I have formed, all contribute to render the location very interesting, and it will

---

* This applies only to Lower Canada.

† The right of obliging a vassal to bake in one's oven and grind at his mill.

become more so when cultivation, industry, and time, shall have embelished this district, still so rustic and wild, and so far from resembling the groves of Thessalia. The house is solid and commodious, the garden and farm yards well enclosed.

I have placed a French family over the store and am well pleased with them. I think, however, they will return to France where the new government has at length banished injustice, violence and crime, and replaced them by the reign of reason, clemency and law. The fishery of the great lake (Ontario) in which I am concerned, furnishes me an abundance of shad,* salmon, and herring, and more than I want. What more can I say? I want nothing but hands. You who live in a country where there are so many useless hands and whose labors are so little productive there, why don't you send as some hundreds of those men? The void they would occasion would be imperceptible; here they would fill spaces that need to be animated and enlivened by their presence. What conquest would they not achieve in ten years! and what a difference in their lot! Soon they would become freeholders and respectable heads of families. The other day a young Frenchman, my neighbor seven miles distant, and established some years upon the bank of the river, said to me: "If it is happy to enjoy repose, the fruit of one's labors and of ease after having escaped the perils of the revolution, how much more so to have a partner of these enjoyments? I am expecting a friend, a brother; it is one of those blessings which nature alone can bestow. What pleasure shall I not enjoy in pointing out to him the traces of my first labors and in making him count the successive epochs of their progress and the stages of my prosperity! but above all to prove to him that his memory has been ever present to me. The objects which surround me I will tell him are witnesses to the truth of this: this hill upon the right, covered with sombre pines, is designated upon my map under the name of *Hippolites Absence*, the creek which traverses my meadow under that of *Brothers Creek*, the old oak which I have left standing at the forks of the two roads, one of which leads to my house and the other to the river *Union Creek*,† the place of my house *Blooming Slope*. Soon he will arrive from St. Domingo, where Toussant L'Ouverture has allowed him to collect some wreck of our fortune."

* White Fish? F. B. H.
† An apparent omission in the original MSS.   F. B. H.

[The preceding letter, dated September 4, 1800, is reprinted from Hough's *History of Jefferson County*. It was originally included in an Appendix to a book Crèvecoeur had published in Paris in 1801, entitled *Voyage dans la haute Pennsylvanie, et dans l'état de New York, par un membre adoptif de la nation Oneida*. Hough made his own translation; others have since been published.]

APPENDIX VII
LETTER FROM VINCENT LERAY TO DR. HOUGH
[Reprinted from Hough's *History of Lewis County* (1883 ed.)]

PARIS, 16 Nov., 1859. }
Rue St. Florentin, 2. }

" FRANKLIN B. HOUGH :—

Dear Sir—I received yesterday a letter from Mr. Stewart, in which he tells me your wish to have some details about the part of Castorland, which lies in Lewis county. As he says you go to press in December, I hasten to write you by the *return mail*.

" From an act passed 28th June, 1793, before M. Lambot, Notaire a Paris, it results: By letters patent dated 10 January, 1792, the State of New York, conveyed to Alex'r Macomb, 1,920,000 acres. A. Macomb conveyed the same to Wm. Constable, 6 June, 1792, who authorized Mr. Chassanis to sell for him, 630,000 acres, divided into shares. The sale not having been effected, Constable withdrew the authorization and left for sale in France, 200,000 acres, divided in 2,000 shares.

" The 12th April, 1793, Constable conveyed to Peter Chassanis these 200,000 acres, with 5 p. c. for Public Works, and 10,000 acres to facilitate the sale of the 200,000 acres. A company is therefore formed of these 2,000 shares at 800 Livres Tournois each, (which had been paid to Constable); said company to be called The New York Company, and their territory Castorland, (Castor means Beaver.)

" The property of the Company shall consist of two parts, one undivided, including 100,000 acres, and of 2,000 lots for a town, to be founded by the Company. The Company to last 21 years. A *Director*, and four Commissioners residing in Paris, and two Commissioners in America. The first named of these last, is Mr. Pharoux, whose sad fate has been related in the History of Jefferson County. Then come most minute details about the formation and the administration of this Company.

" One disposition among others, will show the manner in which these Parisians at their chimney-corner managed their property. The 100,000 acres to be divided were to be entirely composed of good, and middling good land, *without any part unfit for cultivation*.

" I come now to the History of this ill-fated Company. Castorland was divided in two parts; one above the Great Bend of Black River, called Upper Castorland, and the other below the Bend, Lower Castorland. The latter has been generally known in the office of Mr. LeRay de Chaumont, as Beaver-Land. These tracts were divided in Ranges running East and West, North and South of two Cardinal Lines. The consequence was, that the boundaries being irregular, a series of unequal lots exists along these boundaries—some lots being fractions of acres, and some lots on the Black River particularly having no existence but on the paper.

" The regular lots contain 450 acres. To conform with the provisions of the Notarial act, these lots were divided on the map into nine lots of 50 acres each. These are numbered from 1 to 4,828. Lower Castorland contains 964 lots, and 40,522 acres; Upper Castorland 3,864 lots, and 182,695 acres—together 223,417 acres. Lower Castorland, and a small triangular part of Upper Castorland—part of Wilna, are in Jefferson county. Another small triangle in the east part, lies in Herkimer county, and the rest in Lewis.

" The Parisian administration, ruled by some large shareholders who had unreasonable expectations, managed the concerns of lands which they knew nothing about, as they would have done estates in France. Everything was to be regulated at home, and even roads were laid out on the maps, without any knowledge of the localities—but it is true, in beautiful straight lines. I would hardly dare state such a fact, if a sample of this folly was not known in the country, where the traces of a road once opened, but of course never travelled, were visible a few years ago, in the south part of the tract, which among other obstacles, was to cross an almost impassable precipice; but orders were imperative, and the road was made on both sides, leaving them to be connected when the thing became feasible.

" These gentlemen were so obstinate, that they were deaf to the remonstrances of two persons who had every right to be listened to,—Mr. Gouverneur Morris, Minister to France from the United States, and Mr. LeRay de Chaumont, who owned together 200,000 acres, bounded upon an extent of 60 miles by the lands of the Company. They had the greatest interest in the success of the Company, since the lands of the latter lay between theirs and the old countries. Besides, they had bought a large number of their shares in order to have an influence in their deliberations. For that reason, Mr. LeRay de Chaumont was named one of the four Commissioners, and as such he caused to be adopted in the Committee the sale of 12,000 acres to an American company, in which he was himself interested, and of which he had the direction. This company was to make improvements; build and establish various works, etc.

"In reading the debate on this motion, persons conversant with land concerns will perceive that the New York Company, instead of the ruin that overtook them, would have derived considerable benefits,—but no reasoning would do:— the proposal of the committee was rejected in the General Assembly, and the opposite system was only persisted in. Senseless works were undertaken, and brought the recourse to loans. An additional misfortune was the choice of Mr. Rodolphe Tillier, as commissioner in America. The difficulty of sending the French people to America, turned the views towards Switzerland. Tillier was a Magistrate from Bern, and warmly recommended; but in America, the consequence of violent remedies he was obliged to take, deranged his mind so that he caused great losses to the Company, who had to sustain with him a costly law-suit of several years' duration. He attacked the title of the Company, discouraged those who wanted to settle on their lands, and even to make the projected improvements and establishments. Messrs. Morris and LeRay de Chaumont had the greatest trouble with this unfortunate law-suit, which was finally gained by the Company, when they got once more possession of their property.

"The Company, however, persisted for several years, in its unfortunate system of preferring to make establishments, by means of loans, instead of selling their lands at fair prices, which they could have done then; but they never found these prices high enough. In 1800, after contracting a debt of more than 300,000 livres, all their expenses had produced only one saw-mill, eighteen log-houses, and eighty-two acres of clearing. So few settlers had been obtained, that there were only eleven log-houses, and one hundred and thirty acres cleared, in addition to those of the Company. Several roads had indeed, been made, and at a great expense; but besides being ill made, or injudiciously laid out, the want of population soon rendered them useless.

"At last, in January, 1802, the Company, seeing a debt of 360,000 livres, felt the necessity of diminishing it, and consented to a sale of 17,000 acres in Lower Castorland, at \$2 per acre. They might have paid up the whole of their debt, if they had accepted the offer which was made, of fifty-two cents per acre, for the undivided part of Upper Castorland, but they refused obstinately.

"M. LeRay de Chaumont had a great interest at stake in bringing the Company to sell; he had, with Mr. Morris, a large amount of shares, and he was creditor of the company. Besides, he had been obliged, with the other three commissioners, to become personally responsible in Switzerland, for the loans. The other commissioners had cleared themselves of the responsibility, by means which were particular to them.

The first of July, 1814, ended the twenty-one years which had been fixed for the duration of the Company. A public sale was resolved, to pay the enormous sum of 561,766 livres, and the Swiss creditors were obliged to bid the land in, as no accepted offer was made. The Company lost all their undivided property remaining, and M. LeRay de Chaumont, the large advances he had made for interest, etc. He lost besides, many of the best years of his life. He experienced vexation, chagrin, and discouragement—he wore out his strength and his health, to try to remedy the imprudent and ignorant management of the Parisian administration, to which his solemn protest was entered in the books of the Company.

"Of the undivided property, the greatest part of the owners remained perfectly passive; at first, probably, from the idea that the expected success of the undivided part, and of their neighbors, would raise the value of their property; and afterward from discouragement, which became so great that they for the most part left their taxes unpaid, in consequence of which their lands were sold by the Comptroller. A few came and settled on their land, remained a few years, and almost to a man left the country. I will mention a few of them, among whom naturally, particularly those who remained."

Mr. Devouassoux was a retired officer, who owned a good lot on the river, and had built a log house a few feet from the water, on a beautiful flat piece of ground, which he hoped before long to see changed to a smooth verdant lawn. One day, as he was sitting by the door in his morning gown and slippers, Mr. Le Ray came along, on his way down the river, to visit his lands. After the usual salutations and a little general conversation, the visitor asked Mr. Devouassoux whether he was not afraid the water would reach his house in the spring. This was a new idea to the old soldier, and he was asked to explain. "Well," said Mr. Le Ray, "this river does not, by any means, cause such ravages as most rivers do in snowy countries, but it does overflow its banks in very low grounds, I think I even saw some marks left by it on some trees near your house, and according to them, you would have been about two feet under water in your house next spring."

At these words our Frenchman felt as perhaps he had never felt before the enemy. "But," resumed Mr. Le Ray, after giving him time to compose himself, "have you not on your lot some higher ground?" "Indeed, sir, I cannot say." "Why, have you not explored your lands before building?" "Indeed, no; I thought I could not possibly find a better spot than the banks of this beautiful river. I like fishing. Here I am near my field of operations." Mr. Le Ray could not see without apprehension such apathy and levity, for knowing well that Mr. Devouassoux, was not an exception among his countrymen, he read in his fate that of many others. He persuaded Mr. Devouassoux to take a little walk upon his lot, and in a few minutes they found a beautiful building spot on a rising ground.

"A little below, M. de Saint Michel had settled on a lot belonging to the three sisters, daughters of Mr. Notary Lambot. The spot was, therefore, called "Sistersfield." He tarried there several years, and settled for the rest of his days on the left bank of the river.

"Still below, we find a name familiar to all travellers to Ogdensburgh, or having occasion to cross the Black river at the Long Falls. John B. Bossuot had settled there under Mr. Sauvage, who owned the land, and had a large clearing made. The second man remaining after the first had gone. He kept the ferry, a tavern, hunted, etc. With more order or system, he could easily, in such a position, have realized an independent fortune. The making of the bridge, the settling of Carthage, improved much Bossuot's property, if indeed we may call so, a possession founded upon an alleged promise of Mr. Sauvage, of an acre of land, but not a scrap of paper— no limits had ever been agreed upon— and with the value the property had acquired, it was very lucky for Bossuot that he fell in no worse hands. But 'Othello's occupation had gone,' Bossuot, who had lived alone (with his family) for a considerable distance, saw the population covering the meagre field of his slothful farming. No more ferry and no more tavern, for others came to rival and dethrone him. He had reached a good old age, and he left a world that was getting along without him!

"A few miles from the last, on the north bounds of Castorland, lived a man whose name is familiar to the visitors of Mont Blanc, as that of a family of the best guides to that mountain—Balmot. Whether he died on his farm or retired with his sons to St. Lawrence county, I do not remember.

"A neighbor of his, Mr. Carret, was a man of good education. If he had been brought up a farmer he would probably have fared better on his large farm. His eldest son was a very interesting man, possessor of several languages, and of good general education. He was still obliged to seek in manual labor, in the concerns of others, a help for himself and family. His good luck caused him to manage the ferry boat at Long Falls once, that Mr. LeRay de Chaumont was crossing. This gentleman, who neglected no opportunity of knowing and studying those whom he met, and of being useful to them if possible, soon perceived that young Carret was not in his place. He took him to his office, and in 1810 to France with him as his secretary.

"Before relating the second great step in Mr. James Carret's fortune, it may be interesting to relate the incident which led to it. Mr. LeRay de Chaumont was at his estate in Tourraine, in 1815, when he heard of Joseph Bonaparte's arrival at Blois. He had known this prince before his great elevation, and was his guest at Mortefontaine, when the treaty between the United States and France, of September 30, 1800, was signed there, but he ceased seeing him afterwards. Seeing however, misfortune had assailed the prince, he remembered the man, and hastened to Blois. The prince having invited Mr. L. to dinner, said suddenly to him 'well, I remember you spoke to me formerly, of your great possessions in the United States. If you have them still I should like very much to have some in exchange of a part of that silver I have there in those wagons, and which may be pillaged any moment. Take four or five hundred thousand francs and give me the equivalent in land.' Mr. L. objected that it was impossible to make a bargain, where one party alone knew what he was about. 'Oh,' said the prince, 'I know you well, and I rely more on your word than on my judgment.' Still Mr. L. would not be satisfied by this flattering assurance, and a long discussion followed, which was terminated by the following proposition, immediately assented to by the prince: Mr. L. would receive four hundred thousand francs, and would give the prince a letter for Mr. L.'s son, then on the lands, instructing him to convey a certain designated tract, if after having visited the country (whither he was then going) the prince confirmed the transaction—otherwise the money was to be returned. (The prince did confirm.)

"Mr. Carret had been called upon to do some of the preliminary writings, and the Prince struck with his capabilities, begged Mr. L. to permit that he should propose to Mr. C. to come with him as Secretary, urging his total helplessness in his new situation, in a country whose language was entirely unknown to him. Mr. L. was extremely reluctant to part from so valuable a man, but listening only to the goodness of his heart, he not only consented to the Prince's request, but argued with Mr. C. to overcome the objections he had on his side, to separate himself from Mr. L. The arrangement was at length concluded, and Mr. C. went with the Prince; became afterwards his general Land Agent, but was forced after a few years

to return to France, by the state of his eyes, and retired near Lyons.

"The last three persons we have named, were in Jefferson county, but on the verge of Lewis county. I will mention only one more, who was not a settler, but an owner, to give a sample of the spirit which moved that class of men in Castorland. He owned half the peninsula opposite Sackett's Harbor. The most flourishing town in that part of the State, was, according to Mr. Desjardins' calculation, to rise at the isthmus which was to be cut, and the best harbor on Lake Ontario to be made. He had formed such ideas of the rise of the land in consequence, that he never would sell an inch. The emigrants persuaded that there could be no owner where there was no settler, poured upon the tract, which was good land, and took up every part of it. Mr. Desjardins getting old, gave up, it seems, the idea of seeing the northern city rise, since squatters had taken up possession of it, as of a common farm land. He sold the tract, and died a few years ago in Versailles, the survivor of all the persons whom we have mentioned, as settlers in Castorland.

"These good people would be amazed if they returned in this world and saw this immense wilderness, of which they had such poor opinions, now covered with a large population, flourishing establishments, etc., cut up in all directions by good roads, for it is amazing, and instructive too, to recollect the reputation which this tract had not many years ago. This cannot be better represented than in the picturesque words of a hunter, who had searched every corner of it north of Beaver river:—'It is *one swamp*, in which you see now and then *an island of dry land.*' And this is not only the saying of an ignorant deer-killer. A judicious surveyor sent about 1815, to explore a road from Carthage to the lowest falls of Beaver river, reported that he could find no feasible road; that it would be a continuous causeway, etc. Now, more than one good road joins these two points, and along them are to be seen some of the best settlements in the county.

"In short, all the remaining lands in Castorland, are for sale to settlers in the Carthage Land Office of Mr. LeRay de Chaumont. After many years' labor and great expenses, a large population has been brought on them. Of late years it has been furnished by all the countries of Europe, from Sweden to Piedmont, and from Ireland to Bavaria. About five hundred families of these emigrants, have been added to the Americans, and from a valuable population.

*   *   *   *   *

"I have thus given you *currente calamo*, a sketch of what may be interesting to you. It is of course very imperfect as to composition, but I wrote without a previous thought, since of course I meant to give you only some notes from which you will draw what you please. Wishing you all success in your undertaking,

"I am respectfully Sir, yours,

V. LeRay de Chaumont.

To Franklin B. Hough."

FOOTNOTES — INTRODUCTION

1. Franklin B. Hough, *History of Jefferson County* (Albany: Munsell; also Watertown, N.Y.: Sterling and Ridell, 1854).

   Franklin B. Hough, *History of Lewis County* (Albany: Munsell and Rowland, 1860).

2. The date is deduced from a Memoir of William S. Appleton by Charles C. Smith in the *Proceedings of the Massachusetts Historical Society, Vol. 37* (Boston: 1903), pp. 516-531. The memoir does not mention the *Journal*, but describes his trip. The flyleaf of the *Journal* contains an inscription:

   "Given to the Massachusetts Historical Society by William Appleton, Esquire. September 10, 1863."

3. W. Hudson Stephens, "Notes on the Voyage in '93, Towards Castorland." Summaries of Hough Lectures reprinted from *Lewis County Democrat* and *Journal and Republican* (Lowville, N.Y., Dec., 1868), p. 6.

4. *Proceedings of the Massachusetts Historical Society, Vol. 7* (Oct. 12, 1864), p. 463.

5. Memoir of Dr. John Appleton by Charles Deane, *Proceedings of the Massachusetts Historical Society, Vol. 15* (1876), pp. 365-367.

6. *Proceedings of the Albany Institute, Vol. 1* (May 15, 1866), p. 37, and Stephens.

7. Hough, *History of Lewis County* (Syracuse: D. Mason & Co., 1883).

8. *Ibid.*, p. 600.

9. *Ibid.*, p. 599.

FOOTNOTES — CHAPTER ONE

FORMATION OF THE NEW YORK COMPANY

1. Michel G. St. Jean de Crèvecoeur, *Letters from an American Farmer*. (London: Thomas Davies and Lockyer Davis), 1782. The book was originally printed in English and then reprinted in 1783. Then French editions were published in Paris in 1784 and 1787. It was republished in London and Toronto (Everyman Edition, 1912). "What is an American" has been widely reprinted in anthologies. We used *Selected American Writings*, ed. by O.E. Winslow (New York and London: Harper and Bros., 1927), pp. 34-44.

2. *Ibid.*, pp. 41-44.

3. William Chapman White, *Adirondack Country* (New York: Alfred A. Knopf, 1967), p. 76.

4. Among the prefaces to the Hough translation of the *Journal of Castorland* are "The First Program of the Settlement of Castorland" (pages 1-11) and "The Prospectus" (pages 12-30). Then the page numbering restarts with "The Constitution" (1-8). The Chronology of the *Journal* starts on page 9. The citation in this reference is his first page 4.

5. The Introduction is on the first page 13 (Prospectus).

6. *Ibid.*, p. 14.

7. *Ibid.*, pp. 16-21.

8. *Ibid.*, p. 22.

9. *Ibid.*, p. 23.

10. *Ibid.*, p. 25.

11. *Ibid.*, p. 27.

12. *Ibid.*, p. 29.

13. *Ibid.*, pp. 1, 2.

14. *Ibid.*, p. 2.

FOOTNOTES — CHAPTER TWO

1793: VOYAGE TO AMERICA AND FIRST EXPLORATIONS

1. Hilda Doyle Merriam, *North of the Mohawk* (Chicago: Chicago University Press, 1950), p. 93.

2. *Journal of Castorland*. Hough's English translation, pp. 13, 14.

3. *Ibid.*, p. 21.

4. *Ibid.*, Footnote to p. 22.

5. *Ibid.*, p. 23.

6. La Marquise de La Tour du Pin, *Recollections of the Revolution and the Empire* (Edited and translated by Walter Geer, New York: Brentano's, 1920), p. 211.

7. *Journal*, p. 24.

8. *Ibid.*, pp. 25, 26, 30.

9. *Ibid.*, pp. 32, 33.

10. *Ibid.*, p. 35.

11. *Ibid.*, Foonote to p. 34.

12. *Ibid.*, p. 32.

13. *Ibid.*, pp. 37-39.

14. *Ibid.*, pp. 54, 55.

15. *Ibid.*, p. 57.

16. *Ibid.*, p. 62.

17. *Ibid.*, p. 64.

18. *Ibid.*, p. 94.

19. *Ibid.*, p. 119.

20. *Ibid.*

21. *Ibid.*, Footnote to page 118.

22. *Ibid.*

23. *Ibid.*, p. 121.

24. *Ibid.*, p. 132.

25. *Ibid.*

26. *Ibid.*, p. 134.

27. During this discussion, they called the waterfall "the Great Falls." It clearly refers to what is now Lyons Falls. However it may cause confusion because of inconsistency; in every other reference to this site, they called it "High Falls," and used "Great Falls" to refer to those at Watertown.

28. *Journal.* pp. 140, 141.

29. *Ibid.*, p. 143.

30. The letter is quoted in full by Frances S. Childs, *French Refugee Life in the United States, 1790-1800* (Baltimore: Johns Hopkins Press, 1940), p. 82.

31. *Journal*, p. 144.

32. *Ibid.*, pp. 144, 145.

33. Brunel later gained recognition as an architectural and engineering genius, and was winner of various awards and competitions in the U.S.

and in England, to which he emigrated in 1799. His specialty became canal workings and improvements for river navigation; his most famous construction project was the first tunnel under the Thames River, built to his own design. An award of British knighthood was in recognition of his technical innovations.

I visited southern France in 1982, and came across a village named "Brunel" near Lac Ferreol, source of water for the Canal du Midi, which links the Atlantic Ocean and the Mediterranean Sea. The village was named after the Director of Forests and Waters, who purchased the job and title in the early 18th century. Marc Brunel was a native of Brittany, but I can not help speculating whether he was related to this official whose responsibility included a complicated series of dykes and flumes which fed the entire canal system. This ingenious canal contained 66 locks which were built prior to 1700, and was a major transportation artery in France. It is probable that well-educated engineers such as Pharoux and Brunel were intimately acquainted with its design and construction.

FOOTNOTES — CHAPTER THREE

1794: FOUNDING OF THE SETTLEMENT

1. *Journal.* (Hough's English translation), p. 164.

2. *Ibid.*, p. 168.

3. *Ibid.*, p. 179.

4. *Ibid.* , p. 182.

5. *Ibid.*, p. 190.

6. *Ibid.*, p. 193.

7. *Journal of Castorland.* French copy prepared for F. B. Hough. Hand-written, unpublished manuscript at the New York State Library in Albany, p. 197.

8. *Ibid.*, p. 201.

9. *Journal.* (Hough's English translation), p. 210.

10. *Ibid.*, p. 244.

11. Julia Post Mitchell wrote a biography of Louis' father: *St. Jean de Crèvecoeur* (New York: Columbia University Press, 1916), in which she refers to Louis' journey to America and his arrival in New Jersey, but does not mention his trip to Castorland.

12. The diary of La Marquise La Tour du Pin is cited frequently by historians of the period.

13. *Journal*. (Hough's English translation), p. 253.

14. *Ibid.*, p. 260.

15. *Ibid.*, pp. 282, 283.

FOOTNOTES — CHAPTER FOUR

1795: CONSOLIDATION AND DISASTER

1. Although the issue of a public road through Castorland remained alive in the legislature for several years, it was never granted. Instead, as more prosperous settlements developed on the opposite side of the Black River, a public road was constructed on the western side.

2. Seven handwritten pages containing the text of this letter were inserted by Hough between pp. 300 and 301 in his translation of the *Journal*.

3. *Ibid.*, pp. 3, 7.

4. *Journal* (Hough's English translation), p. 312.

5. *Ibid.*, p. 326.

6. *Ibid.*

7. *Ibid.*, p. 316.

8. *Ibid.*, p. 368.

9. *Ibid.*, p. 315.

10. *Ibid.*, p. 328.

11. *Ibid.,* p. 329.

12. *Ibid.*, p. 321.

13. *Ibid.*, p. 330.

14. Penet Square was a tract of land north of Castorland. It also has an interesting history, but is not part of this story. It is mentioned here because Desjardins acted as a middleman, in assisting Nicolas Olive with a land purchase there; this transaction was separate from his administration in Castorland.

15. *Journal* (Hough's English translation), pp. 351-354.

16. Hough, *History of Jefferson County*, pp. 50, 51.

17. T. Wood Clarke, *Émigrés in the Wilderness* (New York: The MacMillan Co., 1941), p. 46.

Howard Thomas, *Black River in the North Country* (Prospect, N.Y.: Prospect Books, 1978), p. 24.

Several other writers, mentioned in Chapter 8, also based their accounts on Clarke's version.

18. *Journal* (Hough's English translation), p. 356.

19. *Ibid.*, p. 361.

20. *Ibid.*, p. 362.

21. *Ibid.*, p. 385.

22. *Ibid.* Spruce tea was a common drink in the Adirondacks during the 19th century and was believed to help prevent scurvey. Spruce beer may have served the same purpose.

23. *Journal* (Hough's English translation), p. 387.

FOOTNOTES — CHAPTER FIVE

1796 AND 1797: DESJARDINS' DOWNFALL

1. *Journal*, p. 395.

2. *Ibid.*, p. 396.

3. *Ibid.*, p. 412.

4. *Ibid.*, pp. 422, 423.

5. *Ibid., p. 425.*

6. *Ibid.*, pp. 426, 427.

7. *Ibid.*, p. 441.

8. On one of the printed copies of Tiller's *Memorial and Justification* in the New York State Library, a handwritten note is included which seems to be a copy of an advertisement from the *Pennsylvania Packet*. It is dated November 14, 1783, and lists high quality imported merchandise for sale at stores in Philadelphia operated by Clement Biddle and Co. and by Rudophe Tillier.

9. *Ibid.*, p. 463.

10. *Ibid.*

11. *Ibid.*, p. 473.

12. *Ibid.*, p. 476.

13. *Ibid.*, pp. 491, 492.

14. *Ibid.*, p. 487.

15. F.B. Hough, unpublished manuscript, handwritten revision intended to update the *History of Jefferson County*. A footnote for insertion on page 51 states: "I am of the opinion that it must have been written by Rudolphe Tillier, but Mrs. Skinner, sister of General Brown, who was personally acquainted with many of the parties concerned in that settlement, thinks it must have been James LeRay."

16. *Journal*, p. 488.

17. *Ibid.*, p. 491.

18. *Ibid.*, p. 495.

19. *Ibid.*

20. *Ibid.*, p. 505.

21. *Ibid.*

22. *Ibid.*, note inserted before page 246.

23. *Ibid.*

24. *Jefferson County — 1976.* (By the Jefferson County Bicentennial Committee, Watertown, N.Y., 1976).

25. Vincent LeRay, Letter to Dr. Hough, printed in *History of Lewis County* (1883), pp. 602-606 and pp. 163, 164.

FOOTNOTES — CHAPTER SIX

SUBSEQUENT HISTORY OF CASTORLAND

1. Hough, *Lewis County* (1860), p. 55.

2. *Journal, p. 504.*

3. *Ibid.*, pp. 49, 50.

4. Samuel W. Durant and Henry B. Pierce, *History of Jefferson County, New York* (Philadelphia: L.H. Everts and Co., 1878), p. 332.

5. Hough, *Lewis County* (1860), p. 140.

6. *Ibid.*, p. 75.

7. From letter to Hough by Vincent LeRay.

8. Nathaniel Sylvester, *Historical Sketches of Northern New York and the Adirondack Wilderness* (Troy, N.Y.: William H. Young, 1877. Reprinted Harrison, N.Y.: Harbor Hill Books, 1973), pp. 168, 169.

9. Letter from Vincent LeRay.

10. Alfred L. Donaldson, *A History of the Adirondacks, 2 Vol.* (New York: Century Printing Co., 1921. Reprinted in Harrison, N.Y.: Harbor Hill Books, 1977), Vol. 1, p. 85.

11. John A. Haddock, *Growth of a Century as Illustrated in the History of Jefferson County, New York from 1793-1894* (Albany: Weed Parsons Printing Company, 1895), p. 464.

12. Durant, *Jefferson County*, p. 295.

13. *Ibid.*

14. *Ibid.*

15. Hough, *Jefferson County*, p. 98.

16. Hough, *Lewis County* (1860), p. 56.

17. Rudolphe Tillier, *Memorial* [English edition: Rome, N.Y.: Thomas Walker, 1800. Partially reprinted in Hough, *Lewis County* (1860)], pp. 57-65.

18. Vincent LeRay's letter.

19. Tillier, *Memorial*.

20. Hough, *Lewis County* (1860), pp. 65-67.

21. Vincent LeRay's letter.

22. The letter is contained in an Appendix to St. Jean de Crèvecoeur's *Voyage dans la haute Pennsylvanie et dans l'état de New York par un Membre Adoptif de la Nation Oneida* (Paris: 1801). It was translated and reprinted by Hough, *Jefferson County*, pp. 52-55, and is reprinted here in Appendix VI, pp. 207-210.
duced in Appendix VI of this book.

23. *Ibid.*

24. *Ibid.*

25. Hough, *Jefferson County*, p. 51.

26. Haddock, *Growth of a Century*, p. 332.

27. *Ibid.*, p. 767.

28. Durant, *Jefferson County*, pp. 522, 523, quoting from Vol. 4 of Washington Irving's *Life and Letters*.

29. *Ibid.*

30. *Ibid.*

31. Haddock, *Growth of a Century*, p. 768.

32. Durant, *Jefferson County*, p. 523.

33. Vincent LeRay's letter.

34. Durant, *Jefferson County*, p. 524.

35. Haddock, *Growth of a Century*, p. 464.

36. *Ibid.*

37. Gouverneur Morris, *Diary and Letters, 2 Vol.* Edited by Anne C. Morris. (New York: Charles Scribner's Sons, 1888), Vol. 2, p. 376.

38. *Ibid.*, p. 406.

39. Letter by Gouverneur Morris to John Parish from Washington, D.C., Jan. 20, 1801. Printed by Jared Sparks,*Life of Gouverneur Morris, 3 Vol.* (Boston: Gray and Bowen, 1832), Vol. 3, p. 138.

40. *Diary* of Gouverneur Morris, Vol. 9. (Microfilm by Library of Congress) Entry on August 19, 1800.

41. *Ibid.*

42. *Ibid.*, Sept. 3, 1803.

43. *Ibid.*, Sept. 22, 1803.

44. *Ibid.*, Sept. 25, 1803.

45. *Ibid.*, Sept. 26, 1803.

46. Hough, *Lewis County* (1883), p. 559.

47. *Ibid.*, p. 562.

48. Some controversy exists as to whether the original building was partially or completely destroyed by fire. When I toured the mansion in July, 1981, my guide pointed out the charred beams in the attic which date from the house's earliest construction. This seems to be proof that the present building did survive the fire.

49. Letter from Vincent LeRay.

50. *Ibid.*

51. Glenn Hawkins, *The Historical LeRay Mansion* (Fort Drum: U.S. Army Publication, Undated), p. 7.

FOOTNOTES — CHAPTER SEVEN

CASTORLAND REGION TODAY

1. 1980 Census.

2. *Ibid.*

3. *Ibid.*

4. Lewis S. Van Arnam of Beaver Falls graciously interrupted his own work to personally show us these remains when we visited Beaver Falls.

5. Information from Mary Teal, Village Historian of Lyons Falls.

6. 1980 Census.

7. Information from personnel of the N.Y. State Health Department (Bureau of Public Water Supply) and the N.Y. State Department of Environmental Conservation (Division of Pure Waters).

8. Described in detail by Howard Thomas, *Black River*, pp. 65-73.

9. Clarke, *Émigrés*, p. 159.

10. The local historians who produced a typewritten copy of Hough's English translation are:
    Myron Senchyna, Steuben Town Historian and project initiator;
    Margaret P. Davis (deceased), former Village of Remsen Historian;
    Augustus L. Richards (deceased), local authority on Baron Steuben;
    Hazel Black of Remsen, who began typing the manuscript;
    Alex Senchyna of Montreal, who completed its typing, working with and also translating from a French microfilm copy, as well as a xerox copy of the English manuscript;

Sandra Senchyna of Boston, Joseph Senchyna of Albany and Marcia Smith (deceased), former librarian of the Adirondack Museum at Blue Mountain Lake, who all assisted in locating and procuring copies of both manuscripts;

Lorena Jersen, President of the Remsen Historical Society, helped market and distribute the typewritten copies.

11. Russ Mackendrick, "Struck in Paris for the Land of the Beaver," *New York Times* (Numismatics, Section 2, August 6, 1978), p. D 29.

12. *Ibid.*

13. Hough, *Lewis County* (1860), p. 44.

14. Hough, *Lewis County* (1883), p. 599.

15. Hough, *Lewis County* (1860), p. 44.

16. *Ibid.*

17. Caleb Lyon was born in 1821 and was a prominent citizen of his time: essayist, poet, lecturer, traveler and politician.

18. Reprinted from Hough, *Lewis County* (1860), p. 107. Taken from *Evening Post*, date unrecorded.

FOOTNOTES — CHAPTER EIGHT

SIFTING DISCREPANCIES:

A SURVEY OF WRITINGS ABOUT CASTORLAND

1. Arthur Einhorn, "Introduction" to the reissue of Hough's *History of Lewis County* (1860); (Merrick, N.Y.: Richwood Publishing Co., 1976).

2. Hough, *Lewis County* (1883), Preface.

3. Hough, *Jefferson County*, p. 49.

4. *Ibid.*, p. 50.

5. *Ibid.*, p. 51.

6. *Ibid.*

7. Hough, *Lewis County* (1860), p. 51.

8. *Ibid.*, p. 50, 51.

9. *Ibid.*, Footnote to p. 51.

10. *Ibid.*, p. 53.

11. *Ibid.*, p. 104.

12. Stephens, "Notes..."

13. *Ibid.*, p. 7.

14. *Proceedings of the Albany Institute, Vol. 1.* (1873), p. 37. Reference to meeting of May 15, 1866 in which Dr. Hough read a paper on the *Journal of Castorland.*

15. Stephens, "Notes...," p. 6.

16. Hough, *Lewis County* (1883), p. 426.

17. Hough, *Lewis County* (1860 reprint) and *Jefferson County* (Reprint edition: Ovid, N.Y.: W.E. Morrison & Co., 1976).

18. Sylvester, *Historical Sketches,* p. 154.

19. Hough's handwritten translation of the Constitution, pp. 7, 8.

20. Durant, *History of Jefferson County,* p. 47.

21. *Ibid.*, p. 48.

22. *Ibid.*, pp. 55, 56.

23. *Ibid.*, pp. 56-64.

24. Haddock, *Jefferson County,* pp. 329, 330.

25. *Ibid.*

26. *Ibid.*, p. 333.

27. *Ibid.*, p. 768.

28. *Ibid.*, p. 336.

29. Edgar C. Emerson, *Our County and Its People — A Descriptive Work on Jefferson County, New York* (Boston: Boston History Company, 1898).

30. *Ibid.*, p. 47.

31. *Ibid.*

32. *Ibid.*, p. 48.

33. *Ibid.*

34. Donaldson, *History of the Adirondacks.*

35. *Ibid.*, p. 85.

36. Harry F. Landon, *The North Country,* 3 *Vol.* (Indianapolis: Historical Publishing Company, 1932).

37. *Ibid.*, pp. 96, 97.

38. *Ibid.*, p.p. 97. 98.

39. *Ibid.*, p. 99.

40. Clarke, *Émigrés in the Wilderness.*

41. *Ibid.*, p. 28.

42. *Ibid.*, p. 32.

43. *Ibid.*, p. 34.

44. *Ibid.*, p. 46.

45. *Ibid.*, pp. 46, 47.

46. *Ibid.*, p. 49.

47. Childs, *French Refugee Life in the United States, 1790-1800.* (Baltimore: Johns Hopkins Press, 1940).

48. *Ibid.*, p. 48.

49. *Ibid.*, p. 67.

50. William Chapman White, *Adirondack Country* (New York: Alfred A. Knopf, 1977).

51. *Ibid.*, pp. 76, 77.

52. William Moore, "Some French Influences in the Early Settlements of the Black River Valley," *Proceedings of the New York Historical Society,* *Vol.* 14. (1915), pp. 122-131.

53. Alta M. Ralph, "The Chassanis or Castorland Settlement," *Proceedings of the New York Historical Society, Vol.* 27 (1929), pp. 333-345.

54. J.I. Wyer, Jr., "Later French Settlements in New York State: 1783-1800," *Proceedings of the New York Historical Society, Vol.* 15 (1916), pp. 176-189.

55. Thomas, *Black River*.

56. *Ibid.*, p. 22.

57. *Ibid.*

58. Merriam, *North of the Mohawk*.

59. Ibid., pp. 93, 94.

60. *Ibid.*

61. Marion Hubbard Johnson, *Castorland Through the Years* (Carthage, N.Y.: Carthage Printing and Publishing Co., 1976).

62. *Ibid.*, p. 2.

63. *Ibid.*

64. Clarence L. and M. Rachel Fisher, *History of Lyons Falls* (Boonville, N.Y.: Willard Press, 1918).

65. Hazel C. Drew, *Tales from Little Lewis*(Lyons Falls, N.Y.: By author, 1961).

66. *Ibid.*, p. 4.

67. Powell, *Penet's Square* (Lakemont, N.Y.: North Country Books, 1976).

68. *Ibid.*, p. 120.

69. *Ibid.*, pp. 122, 128.

70. *Ibid.*, pp. 128, 129.

71. *Ibid.*, p. 120.

72. *Ibid.*, pp. 121, 122.

73. *Ibid.*, p. 140.

74. *Ibid.*, p. 130.

75. *Ibid.*, p. 149.

76. Lewis S. Van Arnam, *Beaver Falls Cavalcade* (Beaver Falls, N.Y.: 1979).

77. *Ibid.* On pages 12 and 15, the date is misstated as 1801, but on page 13 it is correctly given as 1814. The confusion probably results from the nominal transfer of the land titles to LeRay's name after the federal law was passed which forbade land ownership by aliens.

FOOTNOTES FOR APPENDIX II

1. The acre is a land-measure containing about an arpent and a half. *Note in Original.* The topographical account here given was printed in Paris in 1792. A copy is bound in with the Castorland Journal in the library of the Massachusetts Historical Society.
2. This fine little city built by the Hollanders on one of the finest rivers in the world, is surrounded by a rich and extensive country and has attracted by the advantages that it offers, a great number of speculators. It is the *entrepôt* of the commerce carried on with Canada, and they there speak as many different languages as in the other large cities of the United States. Its harbor, its proximity to the sea, and its communication with the lakes, ought to render it one of the most flourishing and populous cities on the continent. *Note in Original.*
3. By this river which has a course of three hundred leagues, we may go down to Montreal, which is only seventy leagues from the Concession. Montreal is upon an island formed by the river Saint Laurence. *Note in Original.*
4. There occurs there the black, white, red and water oak, and the chestnut oak. *Note in Original.*
5. Argente. *Note in Original.*
6. Potash is an alkaline fixed salt, derived from the ashes produced by the combustion of various plants, and is used in glass making, in dying *(sic)*, and in bleaching cloths. *Note in Original.*
7. Sycamore or Button-wood. *Note by Hough.*
8. This kind of Maple is peculiar to the climate and soil of North America. In 1762, we saw several of these plants in the gardens of M. de Buffon, at Montbard, which although ten years old had not yet borne any flowers or seeds. *Note in Original.*
9. *Dict. d' Hist. Nat.* article. *Erable. Note by Hough.*
10. Judge Cooper has actually formed near Otsego Lake, an establishment for refining Maple Sugar, in which several Philadelphia merchants are interested. *National American Gazette.* Feb. 21, 1792. *Note in Original.*
11. Fruit of the *podophyllum peltatum*, or mandrake, now seldom regarded as worth notice. *Note by Hough.*
12. *Trifolium repens*, or white clover. *Note by Hough.*
13. This plant, adds the same writer, demonstrates that the American soil is particularly suited for meadows, which should form the highest object of ambition with the true cultivator. *Annals of Agriculture XVII, 207. Note in Original.*
14. The *Aralia nudicaulis*, or false sarsaparilla, grows abundantly in the Castorland Tracts but has never been sent to market, or indeed much used as a domestic remedy. It is a gentle stimulent and diaphoretic, but loses much of its properties upon drying. *Note by Hough.*
15. The *Panax quinquefolium*, or ginseng, had become an article of exportation to China before the revolution, and in 1770, the quantity sent from the North American Colonies was 74.604 pounds, which at 4d. amounted to £1.243.8.s. During the first twenty seven years of our nation's existence, the quantity exported annually was as follows:

Years	Pounds	Years	Pounds	Years	Pounds	Years	Pounds
1791	29.208	1798	59.165	1805	370.932	1812	33.129
1792	42.310	1799	147.192	1806	448.394	1813	----
1793	90.350	1800	268.371	1807	368.207	1814	58.710
1794	23.232	1801	286.458	1808	----	1815	16.863
1795	20.460	1802	201.410	1809	271.693	1816	75
1796	10.813	1803	384.971	1810	279.246	1817	253.840
1797	4.004	1804	301.499	1811	314.131	Total	4.285.081

The exportation continues to the present day, but with considerable variation in amount. The greatest value in one year, down to 1844, had been $437.245 in 1841. The Chinese entertain the most extravagant ideas of its medicinal properties, use it for all diseases, and trust to its miraculous powers in preserving health, invigorating the system, and prolonging life. It has never been exported in any quantities from northern New York, a few pounds being sometimes bought up by druggists, for the foreign markets. *Note by Hough.*

16. In speaking of this very soil Mr. Morse says: "The best lands in the State of New York, are situated along the Mohawk River to the west of the Allegany Mountains. They are still in a state of nature but they have begun to form some establishments there." *American Geography* P. 247. *Note in Original.*

17. The Bushel is a measure which when filled with wheat weights about 54 pounds Marc. *Note in Original.*

18. *American Spectator,* P. 256. *Note in Original.*

19. Five or six hundred English bushels will furnish one ton of Potash. The ton ways *(sic)* 2.200 pounds, and sells now at Albany at from thirty five to forty Louis. *Note in Original.*

20. *American Spectator,* P. 256. *Note in Original.*

21. The County of Montgomery had been divided by the formation of Herkimer Co., Feb. 16, 1791. The Castorland Tract, was included in the latter, until the formation of Oneida Co., March 15, 1798. *Note by Hough.*

22. These pigeons occur in great numbers near Fort Schuyler, five leagues from the Concession, where they sell at six sous the dozen. They are caught in nets in the spring and autumn. *Note in Original.*

23. The Bass which we call the Oswego Bass, and which appears to be peculiar to Lake Ontario, is taken weighing from three to four pounds. *Note in Original.*

24. National Census of 1790. *Note by Hough.*

25. Constitution of the Thirteen United States of America, page 162. *Note in Original.* Only the latter portion of the section of the Constitution of New York, of 1777, relating to religious liberty is quoted. The first part was as follows. "XXXVIII. And whereas we are required, by the benevolent principles of rational liberty, not only to expel civil tyranny, but also to guard against that spiritual oppression and intolerance, wherewith the bigotry and ambition of weak and wicked priests and princes have scourged mankind: this Convention doth further, in the name and by the authority of the good people of this State, ordain, determine, and declare," etc. *Note by Hough.*

26. *American Geography,* P. 246. *Note in Original.*

27. In 1791 the State of New York alone exported about three thousand tons. *Note in Original.*
28. The city of Hudson, which is twelve leagues below Albany, exported in 1789, an entire cargo to the Cape of Good Hope. *Note by Hough.*
29. Not only are all the expenses paid by the remission of the tenth part granted upon the price, but the company furthermore may without new aid, form establishments which will yield an annual revenue. *Note in Original.*
30. Lansingburg. *Note by Hough.*
31. Judge William Cooper, father of the late Fennimore Cooper. *Note by Hough.*

[*AUTHOR'S NOTE: Approximately half of the preceding footnotes were printed in the original Prospectus. Hough added the balance in his translation to clarify or extend information.*]

BIBLIOGRAPHY

Original Sources

Hough, Franklin B. Undated and unpublished manuscript containing revisions for updating the *History of Jefferson County*. New York State Library, Albany.

Journal of Castorland (1793-1797). Original handwritten manuscript in French. Massachusetts Historical Society, Boston, Mass.

Journal of Castorland. Handwritten copy of above, prepared for Dr. Franklin B. Hough (1864-65); New York State Library, Albany.

Journal of Castorland. English translation (handwritten) by Dr. Hough. New York State Library, Albany.

Morris, Gouverneur. *Diary, Vol. 9.* (Microfilm by Library of Congress, Reel 2).

Prospectus: Description Topographique. Paris: Le Bureau de la Compagnie de New York, 1792. New York State Library, Albany.

Tillier, Rudolphe. *Memorial: Justification of the Administration of Castorland*. Rome, N.Y.: Thomas Walker, 1800. New York State Library, Albany.

Secondary Sources

A Maritime History of New York. Compiled by Workers of the Writers Program of the New York Work Projects Administration. Garden City, N.Y.: Doubleday, Doran and Co., Inc., 1941.

Babcock, Francis G., *et al.*Commissioners.*Annual Report of the New York State Forest Commission for 1893*. Albany, 1894.

Bagg, M.M. *The Pioneers of Utica*. Utica, N.Y.: Curtiss & Childs, 1877.

Beamish, Richard. *Memoir of the Life of Sir Marc Isambard Brunel*. London: Longman, Green, Longman and Roberts, 1862.

Best, T.G. *Boonville and its Neighbors*. Boonville, N.Y.: Herald-Willard Press, 1961.

Campbell, Patrick. "A Journey Through the Genesee Country, Finger Lakes Region and Mohawk Valley" from *Travel in the Interior Inhabited Parts of North America, 1791 and 1792.* reprint ed., Rochester: Friends of the Rochester Libraries, 1978.

Chalmers, Harvey. *Tales of the Mohawk.* Port Washington, N.Y.: Ira J. Friedman, Inc., 1968.

Childs, Frances S. *French Refugee Life in the United States, 1790-1800.* Baltimore: Johns Hopkins Press, 1940.

Churchill, John C. *Landmarks of Oswego County.* Syracuse: D. Mason & Co., 1895.

Clarke, T. Wood. *Émigrés in the Wilderness.* New York: Macmillan Co., 1941.

Cole, Glyndon, ed. *Northern New York Historical Materials.* Canton, N.Y.: North Country Reference and Research Resources Council, 1976.

Crèvecoeur, Michel Guilliame St. Jean. "What is an American?" from *Letters From an American Farmer.* London: 1782. Republished in *Selected Early American Writings*, p.p. 34-44. Edited by O.E. Winslow. New York and London: Harper and Bros., 1927.

——————————. *Journey into Northern Pennsylvania and the State of New York.* Translated by Clarissa Spencer Bostelmann. Ann Arbor: University of Michigan Press, 1964.

Dill, Marshall, Jr. *Paris in Time.* New York: G.P. Putnam's Sons, 1975.

Donaldson, Alfred L. *A History of the Adirondacks,* 2 Vol. New York: Century Co., 1921; reprint ed., Harrison, N.Y.: Harbor Hill Books, 1977.

Drew, Hazel C. *Tales from Little Lewis.* Lyons Falls, N.Y.: By the Author, 1961.

Durant, Samuel W. *History of Oneida County.* Philadelphia: Everts and Farris, 1878.

Durant, Samuel W. and Pierce, Henry B. *History of Jefferson County, New York.* Philadelphia: L.H. Everts and Co., 1878.

Ellis, David M. *Landlords and Farmers in the Hudson-Mohawk Region, 1790-1850.* Ithaca, N.Y.: Cornell University Press, 1946.

——————————. *The Upper Mohawk Country: An Illustrated History of Greater Utica.* Woodland Hills, Ca.: Windsor Publications, 1982.

Emerson, Edgar C. *Our County and its People — A Descriptive Work on Jefferson County.* Boston: Boston History Co., 1898.

Faust, Ralph M. *The Story of Oswego.* Oswego, N.Y.: Palladium-Times Press, 1934.

Fisher, Clarence L. and M. Rachel. *History of Lyons Falls.* Boonville, N.Y.: The Willard Press, 1918.

Greene, Nelson. *The Old Mohawk Turnpike Book.* Fort Plain, N.Y.: By the Author, 1924.

Haddock, John A. *Growth of a Century, as Illustrated in the History of Jefferson County, N.Y. from 1793-1894.* Philadelphia: Sherman & Co., 1894. 2nd ed., Albany: Weed-Parsons Printing Co., 1895.

Halsey, Francis W. *The Old New York Frontier.* New York: Charles Scribner's Sons, 1901.

Hart, Larry. *Tales of Old Schenectady.* Scotia, N.Y.: Old Dorp Books, 1975.

Hawkins, Glenn. *The Historical LeRay Mansion.* Fort Drum: U.S. Army Publication. Undated.

Hislop, Codman. *The Mohawk.* Rivers of America Series. New York: Rinehart & Co., Inc., 1948.

History of Oswego County. Philadelphia: L.H. Everts & Co., 1877.

Hough, Franklin B. *History of Jefferson County.* Albany: J. Munsell, 1854. reprint ed., Ovid, N.Y.: W.E. Morrison and Co., 1976.

——————. *History of Lewis County.* Albany: Munsell and Rowland, 1860. reprint ed., Merrick, N.Y.: Richwood Publishing Co., 1976.

——————. *History of Lewis County.* Syracuse: D. Mason and Co., 1883.

Howell and Munsell. *History of the County of Schenectady, New York from 1662 to 1886.* New York: W. W. Munsell & Co., 1886.

Jefferson County — 1976. By the Jefferson County Bicentennial Committee, Watertown, N.Y., 1976.

Jenkins, David and Hugh. *Isambard Kingdom Brunel: Engineer Extraordinary.* Hove, East Sussex, England: Wayland Publishers, Ltd., 1977.

Johnson, Marion Hubbard. *Castorland Through the Years.* Carthage, N.Y.: Carthage Printing and Publishing Co., 1976.

Komroff, Manuel. *The Hudson.* New York: McGraw-Hill Book Co., 1969.

236

Landon, Harry F. *The North Country: A History Embracing Jefferson, St. Lawrence, Oswego, Lewis and Franklin Counties, New York.* 3 Vol. Indianapolis: Historical Publishing Co., 1932.

—————————. *150 Years of Watertown.* Watertown, N.Y.: The Watertown Daily Times, 1950.

La Tour Du Pin, Henriette Lucie, Marquise de. *Recollections of the Revolution and the Empire.* Edited and translated from *Journal d'une Femme de Cinquante Ans* by Walter Geer. New York: Brentano's, 1920.

Loomis, Stanley. *Paris in the Terror.* Philadelphia and New York: J. B. Lippincott and Co., 1964.

Mackendrick, Russ. "Struck in Paris for the Land of the Beaver," *The New York Times.* Numismatics, Sec. 2, p. D29, August 6, 1978.

Mayer, William G. "The History of Transportation in the Mohawk Valley," *Proceedings of the New York State Historical Society,* Vol XIV, 1915. pp. 214-230.

Merriam, Hilda Doyle. *North of the Mohawk.* Chicago: Chicago University Press, 1950.

Milbert, J. *Picturesque Itinerary of the Hudson River and the Peripheral Parts of North America.* Translated by C. Sherman from French edition of 1826. Ridgewood, N.J.: The Gregg Press, 1968.

Mintz, Maxim. *Gouverneur Morris and the American Revolution.* Norman, Okla.: University of Oklahoma Press, 1970.

Mitchell, Julia Post. *St. Jean de Crèvecoeur.* New York: Columbia University Press, 1916.

Morris, Gouverneur. *Diary and Letters,* 2 Vol. Edited by Anne Cary Morris. New York: Charles Scribner's Son's, 1888.

Moore, William A. "Some French Influences in the Early Settlement of the Black River Valley." *New York State Historical Association,* Vol. 14, 1915. pp. 122-133.

Muhl, Gerard. "The Castorland Story." *York State Tradition.* Vol. 18, No. 4,1964.

O'Donnell, Thomas C. *The River Rolls On.* Prospect, N.Y.: Prospect Books, 1950.

Plum, Dorothy, ed. *Adirondack Bibliography*. Gabriels, N.Y.: Adirondack Mountain Club, Inc. 1958.

——————————. ed. *Adirondack Bibliography Supplement, 1956-65*. Blue Mountain Lake, N.Y.: The Adirondack Museum, 1973.

Pound, Arthur. *Lake Ontario*. Indianapolis: The Bobbs-Merrill Co., 1945.

Powell, Thomas F. *Penet's Square*. Lakemont, N.Y.: North Country Books, 1976.

Proceedings of the Albany Institute. Vol. 1, 1873: p. 37. Reference to reading by F. B. Hough on *Castorland Journal*, May 15, 1866.

Proceedings of the Massachusetts Historical Society:
Vol. 7, 1863: pp. 326-338. Sketch of *"Journal of Castorland"* by J. Appleton.
Vol. 8, 1864: p. 463. Authorized copy of *Journal* for F. B. Hough.
Vol. 15, 1876: pp. 365-367. Memoir of John Appleton, Asst. Librarian.
Vol. 37, 1903: pp. 516-531. Memoir of William Sumner Appleton.

Ralph, Alta M. "The Chassanis or Castorland Settlement," *New York State Historical Association,* Vol. 10, 1929. pp. 333-345.

Sampson, Harold E. *Tug Hill Country*. Lakemont, N.Y.: North Country Books, 1971.

Sparks, Jared. *Life of Gouverneur Morris*, 3 Vol. Boston: Gray & Bowen, 1832.

Stephens, W. Hudson. "Notes on the Voyage, in '93, Towards Castorland." Summaries from the *Lewis County Democrat* and *Journal and Republican* of lectures by F. B. Hough in Lowville, N.Y. Reprinted, 1868.

Swiggett, Howard. *The Extraordinary Mr. Morris*. Garden City, N.Y.: Doubleday and Co., 1952.

Sylvester, Nathaniel. *Historical Sketches of Northern New York and the Adirondack Wilderness*. Troy, N.Y.: William H. Young, 1877. reprint ed., Harrison, N.Y.: Harbor Hill Books, 1973.

Taylor, John. "Journal of the Rev. John Taylor's Missionary Tour Through the Mohawk and Black River Countries in 1802." *Documentary History of the State of New York: Vol. 3*, pp. 671-696. Albany: Weed, Parsons and Co., 1850.

Thomas, Howard. *Black River in the North Country*. Prospect, N.Y.: Prospect Books, 1978.

——————— . *Tales from the Adirondack Foothills*. Prospect, N.Y.: Prospect Books, 1965.

Thompson, J. M. ed. *English Witnesses to the French Revolution*. Port Washington, N.Y.: Kennikat Press, 1938.

Tuckerman, Bayard. *Life of General Philip Schuyler*. New York: Dodd, Mead & Co., 1903.

Van Arnam, Lewis S. *Beaver Falls Cavalcade*. Beaver Falls, N.Y. By the Author, 1979.

Van der Kemp, Francis Adrien. *An Autobiography*. New York: The Knickerbocker Press, 1903.

Van Zandt, Roland. *Chronicles of the Hudson: Three Centuries of Travellers' Accounts*. New Brunswick, N.J.: Rutgers University Press, 1971.

Webster, Clarence J. "French Émigrés in the Wilderness of the North." Text of a radio address, 1946. Unprinted.

Weise, Arthur J. *The History of the City of Albany*. Albany: E. H. Bender, 1884.

White, William Chapman. *Adirondack Country*. 8th Ed., New York: Alfred A. Knopf, 1977.

Wyer, James I., Jr. "Later French Settlements in New York State, 1783-1800." *New York Historical Association*, Vol. XV, 1916: pp. 176-189.

Index

(Communities are distinguished by
capital letters and book titles
by italics.)

Trees, 22, 26, 27, 64, 165, 166, 207, 231
  Clearing of, 26, 168
  see also Balsam, Potash, Sugar Maple •
TRENTON, 92
Tryon, William (British Major General, Governor of New York Province), 22

U

Union College, 7, 18
UTICA, 18, 42, 96, 142
  see also FORT SCHUYLER
Utica and Black River Railroad, 135

V

Van Arnam, Lewis S. (Writer), 18, 143, 159, 226, 230
Van Prandelles, Renoit (Shareholder), 174
Varin, Bénigne-Joseph (Shareholder), 174
Verplank's Point, 36
VERSAILLES, 106, 214
Visitors to Castorland, *see* HIGH FALLS
Voltaire, 20
Voyage, Trans-Atlantic, 20, 31-34, 218, 219
Voyage dans la haute Pennsylvanie et dans l'etat de New York par un Membre Adoptif de la Nation Oneida, 210, 224

W

Ward, Col. (Constable's Agent), 153, 176
Washington, George, 52
WATSON, 140
Watson and Greenleaf (Neighboring Land Owners), 73
Waterfalls:
  see LITTLE FALLS, HIGH FALLS, LONG FALLS, GREAT FALLS
WATERTOWN, 18, 46, 118, 135, 219
  see also GREAT FALLS
Wedding in Castorland, *see* Marriage
Welsh Settlers, 92, 142, 148
West Canada Creek, 57
"What is an American?" 21, 217
White, William Chapman (Writer), 156, 217, 229
White's, *see* Steuben's
Williams, Eleazar (possibly Lost Dauphin), 155
Williams, Emily, 18
Williamson, Col., 119
WILNA, 211
Wood Creek, 42-44, 48, 49, 92, 167
  Photos of, 43, 45
Work and workmen
  Routine chores, 56, 60, 64, 66, 69, 70, 76, 80, 82, 88, 92, 98, 100, 109, 116
  Difficulties with, 60, 61, 64, 68-70, 78, 79, 92, 95, 134
  see also Boussot, Bowman, Briton, Caish, Colinet, Crocker, Cross, Ferlents, Harrison, Perrot, Robinson
  see also Canadians, Indians, Surveyors
Wright, Benjamin (Surveyor), 55
Wyer, J.I., Jr. (Historian), 157, 229

254

Adirondack Classics

Long Lake.
By *John Todd*. Facsimile of 1845 edition, with introduction by *Warder H. Cadbury*. The earliest book entirely devoted to an Adirondack topic. "Remains to this day one of the most readable books on Adirondack letters..." (from a review by Paul Jamieson). The introduction is in itself a fascinating story of the Adirondacks in the 1840s. The cloth binding is a duplicate of the original 1845 binding.   cloth $12.50

The Adirondack, or, Life in the Woods.
By *Joel T. Headley*. Introduction by *Philip G. Terrie*. This 1849 book offers a number of *firsts:* oldest book about the entire Adirondacks; earliest description of many mountains, lakes and streams; first reference to well-known Adirondack guides; earliest pictures (engravings) of Adirondack scenery, and the first (1872) Colvin map. With 1875 supplement. 512 pages, illus., maps.   cloth $24.95

Wild Northern Scenes
or, Sporting Adventures in the Adirondacks with Rifle and Rod. By *S.H. Hammond*. Reprint of the 1857 ed. — One of the earliest sporting books of the Adirondacks and the first known call for a 'forever wild' status of the forest preserve. The book was an inspiration for William Chapman White who observed (in his *Adirondack Country*) that Hammond's "statement was a remarkable vision of what a group in 1894 .... did write into the state constitution". 341 pages, illus.   cloth $12.50

The Indian Pass (and Mount Marcy).
By *Alfred B. Street*. A narrative of a climb during the 1860s in a region now so familiar to Adirondack hikers but wild and unknown then to all but a few mountain guides. Reprint of rare 1869 edition. 202 pages.   cloth $16.95

Trappers of New York
or, a Biography of Nicholas Stoner and Nathaniel Foster; together with Anecdotes of other celebrated Hunters. By *Jeptha R. Simms*. Reprint of the 1871 ed., with new introduction, and an index. — The chief work on early Adirondack trappers and hunters. 320 pages, illus.   cloth $15.00

A History of the Adirondacks.
By *Alfred L. Donaldson*. Reprint of the 1921 ed. With a new introduction by John J. Duquette, Saranac Lake Village Historian. 2 volumes, 856 pp., 34 illus. and maps.   cloth $45.00

The Birch Bark Books of Henry Abbott.
Sporting Adventures and Nature Observations in the Adirondacks in the early 1900s. Introduction by *Vincent Engels*. — First trade edition of 19 books published for private distribution between 1914 and 1932 and originally printed in less than 100 copies. Henry Abbott spent summers at Deerland, Long Lake, and these are his stories of fishing and hunting, of beavers and bears, of camps and trails, and of rivers, ponds and summits. Reprint in one volume, large format, 288 pages, with 156 illustrations from Abbott's own photo s, 7 maps.   cloth $19.95

Harbor Hill Books, P.O. Box 407, Harrison, N. Y. 10528

Through the Adirondacks in Eighteen Days.
By *Martin V.B. Ives.* Intro.by *Neal S. Burdick.* Reprint of the 1899 ed., a description of a "fact-finding" trip made by a legislative committee in 1898, during the heydeys of Adirondack summer camps. Assigned by the New York State Assembly to study the Adirondacks with a view to determining what lands should be added to the Forest Preserve, the committee traveled via Lake Champlain to Plattsburgh, thence to Ausable Forks, St. Hubert's, Lake Placid, Saranac, Raquette and Blue Mountain Lakes, the Fulton Chain, and ended the trip at Childwold. This reprint of a very scarce book has been expanded not only with a new introduction but with a complete list of illustrations and a map of the itinerary. 128 pages, 57 illus., 1 map. cloth $17.50

History of the Lumber Industry in the State of New York.
By *William F. Fox.* With an appendix: Roll of Pioneer Lumbermen, and a large four-color map: First Settlements in the State of New York. — First edition as a separate book. The story of early lumbering in the Adirondacks and elsewhere in N.Y. State, with chapters on lumber camps, rafting and raftsmen, logdriving, log marks, log railroads, sawmills, tanneries, etc. Large size, reprint of 1901 ed., 120 pages, 22 illus. from old photos. cloth $14.95

Why the Wilderness is called Adirondack.
The Earliest Account of the Founding of the MacIntyre Mine. By *Henry Dornburgh.* — The original eye-witness account of David Henderson's accidental death in the woods of the high-peaks region, of the early mining venture at Tahawus, the deserted village, etc. An entirely new and reset edition of this rare 1885 publication, with added pictures and a new preface. 32 pages. paper $3.95

A Brief History of the Printing Press in Washington, Saratoga, and Warren Counties.
Together with a Check List of their Publications prior to 1825, and a Selection of Books relating to this Vicinity. By *William H. Hill.* Reprinted from the Fort Edward 1930 edition (privately printed). 118 pages. cloth $8.50

The French Occupation of the Champlain Valley, 1609–1759.
By *Guy Omeron Coolidge.* First edition in book form, reprinted from a 1938 issue of *Vermont History.* — The only written account of the 150 years of French dominion over northern New York and Vermont, prior to the English conquest. 175 pages, maps. cloth $9.75

History of Lake Champlain.
By *Peter S. Palmer.* The chief work about the military events during the three wars: the French and Indian War, the War of the Revolution, and the War of 1812. Reprint of rare 1886 edition, expanded with 35 new illus. and maps. 272 pages. cloth $16.95

The Mohawk Valley.
Its Legends and its History, 1609–1780. By *W. Max Reid.* Two centuries of Mohawk Valley history, with special chapters on the Indians and the Palatines, on cities such as Amsterdam, Johnstown, Schenectady, Canajoharie, and on historical figures such as William Johnson, Joseph Brant, Van Curler, the Butler family, and others. 455 pages, 71 illus. cloth $22.50

Harbor Hill Books, P.O. Box 407, Harrison, N. Y. 10528